Military in Pakistan and Afghanistan
A Brief History

Military in Pakistan and Afghanistan

A Brief History

Col. C. P. Shankar (Retd.)

Neha Publishers & Distributors

Published by:
Neha Publishers & Distributors
4832/24, Prahlad Lane, S-207 Ansari Road,
Daryaganj, New Delhi-110002

ISBN: 978-93-80318-85-1

Price: 1250/-

Typesetting: JEE-VEE Graphics

First Edition: 2015

Printed by: Neeta Press

Preface

The military history of Pakistan encompasses an immense panorama of conflicts and struggles extending for more than 2,000 years across areas constituting modern Pakistan, and the greater South Asia. The history of the modern-day military of Pakistan begins from post-1947, after Pakistan achieved its independence as a modern nation-state.

The most critical differences are goals and objectives. America intervened in Afghanistan in 2001 on the side of the Northern Alliance to topple the Taliban Islamic Emirate of Afghanistan only after it had been used as a base for the September 11th 2001 terrorist attacks in America. The American goal, endorsed by the UN and NATO, was self-defence against a government that had allowed its territory to be used for an act of war against another state. From the beginning, America has had no ambition to dominate or subjugate the Afghan people, or to stay in Afghanistan once the threat posed by al-Qaeda had been removed and the Taliban defeated. President Barack Obama said this again in his speech outlining his new policy for Afghanistan and Pakistan on March 27th 2009.

Taliban forces fled from Kabul, the capital city, on 11/12/01, and retreated toward the mountainous border of Afghanistan and Pakistan. With U.S. support, a new government was installed, with Hamid Karzai as President. This work is essentially useful for scholars researchers social activists academics government functionaries and the general reader alike.

—Author

Contents

1

Military History of Pakistan

The military history of Pakistan encompasses an immense panorama of conflicts and struggles extending for more than 2,000 years across areas constituting modern Pakistan, and the greater South Asia. The history of the modern-day military of Pakistan begins from post-1947, after Pakistan achieved its independence as a modern nation-state.

The military holds a significant place in the history of Pakistan, as the Pakistani Armed Forces have played, and still continue to play, a vital role in the Pakistani establishment and shaping of the country since its inception. Although Pakistan was founded as a democracy after its independence from the British Raj, the military has remained one of the country's most powerful institutions and has on occasion overthrown democratically elected civilian governments on the basis self-assessed mismanagement and corruption. Almost none of the four military coups had a justified motive. Successive governments have made sure that the military was consulted before they took key decisions, especially when those decisions related to the Kashmir conflict and foreign policy. Political leaders of Pakistan's developing democracy know that the military has stepped into the political arena before at times of crisis through Coup d'état to establish military dictatorships, and could do so again.

The military was created in 1947 by division of the British Indian Army and was given units who had a long and cherished history during the British India such as the Khyber Rifles, and had seen intensive service in World War I and World War II. Many of the early leaders of the military had fought in both world wars. The military draws on inspiration from the rich combat history that has occurred within the area of modern day Pakistani soil and uses example of sacrifice and perseverance to embolden troops, and has named medals of valor, nickname for combat divisions, and indigenous weapons; Such as the short-range ballistic missiles Ghaznavi, which is named in honour of Mahmud of Ghazna who founded the Ghaznavid Empire, and ruled from 997 to 1030.

Since the time of independence, the military has fought three major wars with India. It has also fought a limited conflict at Kargil with India after acquiring nuclear capabilities. In addition, there have been several minor border skirmishes with neighbouring Afghanistan. After the September 11 attacks, the military is engaged in a protracted low intensity conflict along Pakistan's western border with Afghanistan, with the Taliban and Al-Qaeda militants, as well as those who support or provide shelter to them.

In addition, Pakistani troops have also participated in various foreign conflicts usually acting as United Nations peacekeepers. At present, Pakistan has the largest number of its personnel acting under the United Nations with the number standing at 10,173 as of 31 March 2007.

550 BCE–1857

Ancient Empires

The region of modern day Pakistan (part of India before 1947) formed the most populous and richest satrapy of the Persian Achaemenid Empire for almost two centuries, starting from the reign of Darius the Great (522-485 BCE). The first major conflict erupted when Alexander the Great overthrew the Achaemenid empire in 334 BCE, and marched eastwards. Eventually, after defeating King Porus in the fierce Battle of the Hydaspes (near modern Jhelum), he conquered much of the Punjab region. But, his battle weary troops refused to advance further into India to engage the formidable army of Nanda Dynasty and its vanguard of trampling elephants, new monstorities to the invaders. Therefore, Alexander proceeded southwest along the Indus valley. Along the way, he engaged in several battles with smaller kingdoms before marching his army westward across the Makran desert towards modern Iran. Alexander founded several new Macedonian/Greek settlements in Gandhara and Punjab.

As Alexander the Great's Greek and Persian armies withdrew westwards, the satraps left behind by Alexander were defeated and conquered by Chandragupta Maurya who founded the Maurya Empire, which ruled the region from 321 to 185 BC. The Mauryas Empire was itself conquered by the Sunga Empire, which ruled the region from 185 to 73 BCE.

Other regions such as the Khyber Pass was left unguarded, and a wave of foreign invasion followed. The Greco-Bactrian king, Demetrius, capitalized and he conquered southern Afghanistan and Pakistan around 180 BC, forming the Indo-Greek Kingdom. The Indo-Greek Kingdom ultimately disappeared as a political entity around 10 AD following the invasions of the Central Asian Indo-Scythians. Their empire morphed into the Kushan Empire who ruled until 375 AD. The region was then conquered by the Persian Indo-Sassanid empire who ruled until 565 AD before the entire Sassanid Empire was conquered by the Arabs including the region of modern Pakistan.

Muslim Conquests

In 712 CE, a Syrian Muslim chieftain called Muhammad bin Qasim conquered most of the Indus region (stretching from Sindh to Multan) for the Umayyad empire. In 997 CE, Mahmud of Ghazni conquered the bulk of Khorasan, marched on Peshawar in 1005, and followed it by the conquests of Punjab (1007), Balochistan (1011), Kashmir (1015) and Qanoch (1017). By the end of his reign in 1030, Mahmud's empire extended from Kurdistan in the west to the Yamuna river in the east, and the Ghaznavid dynasty lasted until 1187. In 1160, Muhammad Ghori conquered Ghazni from the Ghaznavids and became its governor in 1173. He marched eastwards into the remaining Ghaznavid territory and Gujarat in the 1180s, but was rebuffed by Gujarat's Solanki rulers. In 1186-7, he conquered Lahore, bringing the last of Ghaznevid territory under his control and ending the Ghaznavid empire. Muhammad Ghori returned to Lahore after 1200 to deal with a revolt of the Rajput Ghakkar tribe in the Punjab. He suppressed the revolt, but was killed during a Ghakkar raid on his camp on the Jhelum River in 1206. Muhammad Ghori's successors established the first Indo-Islamic dynasty, the Delhi Sultanate. The Mamluk Dynasty, (*mamluk means "slave" and referred to the Turkic slave soldiers who became rulers throughout the Islamic world*), seized the throne of the Sultanate in 1211. Several Turko-Afghan dynasties ruled their empires from Delhi: the Mamluk (1211–90), the Khalji (1290–1320), the Tughlaq (1320–1413), the Sayyid (1414–51) and the Lodhi (1451–1526). Although some kingdoms remained independent of Delhi - in Gujarat, Malwa (central India), Bengal and Deccan - almost all of the Indus plain came under the rule of these large Indo-Islamic sultanates. Perhaps the greatest contribution of the sultanate was its temporary success in insulating South Asia from the Mongol invasion from Central Asia in the 13th century; nonetheless the sultans eventually lost Afghanistan and western Pakistan to the Mongols.

Mughal Empire

From the 16th to the 19th century, the formidable Mughal empire covered much of India. In 1739, the Persian emperor Nader Shah invaded India, defeated the Mughal Emperor Muhammed Shah, and occupied most of Balochistan and the Indus plain. After Nadir Shah's death, the kingdom of Afghanistan was established in 1747, by one of his generals, Ahmad Shah Abdali and included Kashmir, Peshawar, Daman, Multan, Sind and Punjab. In the south, a succession of autonomous dynasties (the Daudpotas, Kalhoras and Talpurs) had asserted the independence of Sind, from the end of Aurangzeb's reign. Most of Balochistan came under the influence of the Khan of Kalat, apart from some coastal areas such as Gwadar, which were ruled by the Sultan of Oman. The Sikh Confederacy (1748–1799) was a group of small states in the Punjab that emerged in a political vacuum created by rivalry between the Mughals, Afghans and Persians. The Confederacy drove out the Mughals, repelled several Afghan invasions and in 1764 captured Lahore. However after the retreat of Ahmed Shah Abdali, the Confederacy suffered instability as disputes and rivalries emerged. The Sikh empire (1799–1849) was formed on the foundations of the Confederacy by Ranjit Singh who proclaimed himself "*Sarkar-i-*

Wala", and was referred to as the Maharaja of Lahore. His empire eventually extended as far west as the Khyber Pass and as far south as Multan. Amongst his conquests were Kashmir in 1819 and Peshawar in 1834, although the Afghans made two attempts to recover Peshawar. After the Maharaja's death the empire was weakened by internal divisions and political mismanagement. The British annexed the Sikh empire in 1849 after two Anglo-Sikh wars.

1857–1947

British Raj

The British Raj lasted from 1858 to 1947, the period when India was part of the British Empire. After the mutiny, the British took steps to avoid further rebellions taking place including changing the structure of the Army. They banned Indians from the officer corp and artillery corp to ensure that future rebellions would not be as organized and disciplined and that the ratio of British Soldiers to Indians would be drastically increased. Recruiting percentages changed with an emphasis on Sikhs and Gurkhas whose loyalties and fighting prowess had been proven in the conflict and new caste and religious based regiments were formed.

The World wars

During World War I the British Indian Army fought in Egypt, Palestine, Mesopotamia, Gallipoli, and France and suffered very heavy casualties.

The British Indian Army's strength was about 189,000 in 1939. There were about 3,000 British officers and 1,115 Indian officers. The army was expanded greatly to fight in World War II. By 1945, the strength of the Army had risen to about two and a half million. There were about 34,500 British officers and 15,740 Indian officers. The Army took part in campaigns in France, East Africa, North Africa, Syria, Tunisia, Malaya, Burma, Greece, Sicily and Italy. It suffered 179,935 casualties in the war (including killed (24,338), wounded (64,354), missing (11,762) and POW (79,481) soldiers). Many future military officers and leaders of Pakistan fought in these wars.

Birth of the modern Military

On June 3, 1947, the British Government announced its plan to divide British India between India and Pakistan and the subsequent transfer of power to the two countries resulted in independence of Pakistan. The division of the British Indian Army occurred on June 30, 1947 in which Pakistan received six armored, eight artillery and eight infantry regiments compared to the forty armored, forty artillery and twenty one infantry regiments that went to India. At the Division Council, which was chaired by Rear Admiral Lord Mountbatten of Burma, the Viceroy of India, and was composed of the leaders of the Muslim League and the Indian National Congress, they had agreed that the British Indian Army of 11,800 officers and 500,000 enlisted personnel was to be divided to the ratio of 64% for India and 36% for Pakistan.

Pakistan was forced to accept a smaller share of the armed forces as most of the military assets, such as weapons depots, military bases, etc., were located inside the new Union of India, while those that were in the new Dominion of Pakistan were mostly obsolete. Pakistan also had a dangerously low ammunition reserve of only one week. By August 15, 1947, both India and Pakistan had operational control over their armed forces. General Sir Frank Messervy was appointed as the first Army Commander-in-Chief of the new Pakistan Army. General Messervy was succeeded in this post in February 1948, by General Sir Douglas Gracey, who served until January 1951.

The Pakistani Armed Forces initially numbered around 150,000 men, many scattered around various bases in India and needing to be transferred to Pakistan by train. The independence created large scale communal violence in the India. In total, around 7 million Muslims migrated to Pakistan and 5 million Sikhs and Hindus to India with over a million people dying in the process.

Of the estimated requirement of 4,000 officers for Pakistani Armed Forces, only 2,300 were actually available. The neutral British officers were asked to fill in the gap and nearly 500 volunteered as well as many Polish and Hungarian officers to run the medical corps.

By October 1947, Pakistan had raised four divisions in West Pakistan and one division in East Pakistan with an overall strength of ten infantry brigades and one armored brigade with thirteen tanks. Many brigades and battalions within these divisions were below half strength, but Pakistani personnel continued to arrive from all over India, the Middle East and North Africa and from South East Asia.

Mountbatten and Field Marshal Sir Claude Auchinleck, the last Commander-in-Chief, India, had made it clear to Pakistan that in case of war with India, no other member of the Commonwealth would come to Pakistan's help.

1947–1965

The war of 1947

Pakistan had its first taste of war almost immediately in the First Kashmir War where it sent its forces into Kashmir. Kashmir, had a Muslim majority population, but the choice of which country to join was given to the Maharaja Hari Singh of Kashmir he was not able to decided whether to join India or Pakistan. By late October, the overthrow of the maharaja seemed imminent. He sought military assistance from India, for which he sign an instrument of accession with India. The Army was pushed back by the Indians but not before occupying the northwestern part of Kashmir (roughly 40% of Kashmir), which Pakistan still controls, the rest remaining under Indian control except for the portion ceded by Pakistan to China.

U.S. Aid

With the failure of the United States to persuade India to join an anti-communist pact, it turned towards Pakistan, which in contrast with India was prepared to join such an alliance in return of military and economic aid and also to find a potential ally against India. By 1954, the Americans had decided that Pakistan along with Turkey and Iran would be ideal countries to counter Soviet influence. Therefore Pakistan and USA signed the Mutual Defense Assistance Agreement and American aid began to flow in Pakistan. This was followed by two more agreements. In 1955,

Pakistan joined the South East Asian Treaty Organization (SEATO) and the Baghdad Pact later to be renamed as Central Asian Treaty Organization (CENTO) after Iraq left in 1959.

Pakistan received over a billion dollars in military aid from United States between 1954 and 1965. This aid greatly enhanced Pakistan's defense capability as new equipment and weapons were brought into the armed forces, new military bases were created and existing ones were expanded and upgraded and two new Corps commands were formed. Shahid M Amin, who has previously served in the Pakistani foreign service, writes in his book *Pakistan's foreign policy: A reappraisal,* "It is also a fact, that these pacts did undoubtedly secure very substantial US military and economic assistance for Pakistan in its nascent years and significantly strengthened it in facing India, as seen in the 1965 war."

American and British advisers trained Pakistani personnel and the USA was allowed to set up bases within Pakistan's borders to spy on the Soviet Union. In this period, many future Pakistani presidents and generals went to American and British military academies that lead to the development of the Pakistani army on Western models, especially the British one.

After Dominion status ended in 1956 with the formation of a Constitution and a declaration of Pakistan as an Islamic Republic, the military took control in 1958 and held power for more than 10 years. During this time, Pakistan had developed close military relations with many Middle Eastern countries to whom Pakistan sent military advisers and this relationship continues to the present day.

First Military Rule

Since its independence, the democratic system has been disturbed by the Pakistan Army's generals. In 1951, the Military Intelligence foiled a conspiracy against the government of first Prime minister Liaqat Ali Khan. The M.I. under Major-General Syed Shahid Hamid arrested Major-General Akbar Khan, along with other senior officers. Akbar was subsequently court-martialed was relieved from his service. On October 16, 1951, Liaqat Ali

Khan was assassinated by Afghan national Said Akbar, hired by the United States and Pakistan Army. After his death, the political turmoil further destabilized the country. In 1958, retired Major-General and President Iskander Mirza took over the country and deposed the government of Prime minister Feroz Khan Noon, and declared first martial law on October 7, 1958. President Mirza personally appointed his close associate General Ayub Khan as the Commander-in-Chief of Pakistan Army. However, Khan ousted Mirza shortly when he became highly dissatisfied by Mirza's policies. It was said that, at that time when Khan took over the control, Ayub Khan had slapped Mirza and disrespected him and night to pack Mirza off to exile in England. Now as President and Commander-in-Chief Ayub Khan himself appointed him as 5-star Field Marshal and built up the relationship with the United States and the West. A formal alliance including Pakistan, Iran, Iraq, and Turkey was formed and was called the Baghdad Pact (later known as CENTO), which was to defend the Middle East and Persian Gulf from Soviet communists designs.

Border clashes with Afghanistan

Armed tribal incursions from Afghanistan into Pakistan's border areas began with the transfer of power in 1947 and became a continual irritant. Many Pashtun Afghans regarded the 19th century Anglo-Afghan border (historically called the Durand Line) treaties as void and were trying to re-draw the borders with Pakistan or trying to help create an independent state (Pashtunistan) for the ethnic Pashtun people. The Pakistan Army had to be continually sent to secure the country's western borders. Afghan-Pakistan relations were to reach their nadir in 1955 when diplomatic relations were severed with the ransacking of Pakistan's embassy in Kabul and again in 1961 when the Pakistan Army had to repel a major Afghan incursion in Bajaur region.

Pakistan used American weaponry to fight the Afghan incursions but the weaponry had been sold under the pretext of fighting Communism and the USA was not pleased with this development, as the Soviets at that time became the chief benefactor to Afghanistan. Some sections of the American press blamed Pakistan for driving Afghanistan into the Soviet camp.

In retaliation to continuous Pashtun Afghan claims on Northwestern Pakistan, Pakistan's military provided support for the non-Pashtun populations of Afghanistan to re-unite with their ethnic groups who constitute a majority in neighboring countries of Afghanistan, which gained independence after the fall of the USSR.

All this changed after the rise of the Taliban movement, which mainly consisted of Pakhtuns. Seeing the Taliban as a tool to maintain stability, Pakistan's military then shifted its support to the Pashtun-dominated Taliban; losing the trust of the non-Pashtun majority it traditionally supported right until the Soviet-Afghan war era.

Alliance with China

After India's defeat in the Sino-Indian War of 1962, India began a rapid program of reforming and expanding its military. A series of conferences on Kashmir was held from December 1962 to February 1963 between India and Pakistan. Both nations offered important concessions and a solution to the long-standing dispute seemed imminent. However, after the Sino-Indian war, Pakistan had gained an important new ally in China and Pakistan then signed a bilateral border agreement with China that involved the boundaries of the disputed state, and relations with India again became strained.

Fearing a communist expansion into India, the USA for the first time gave large quantities of weapons to India. The expansion of the Indian armed forces was viewed by most Pakistanis as being directed towards Pakistan rather than China. The US also pumped in large sums of money and military supplies to Pakistan as it saw Pakistan as being a check against Soviet expansionist plans.

1965–1979

The war of 1965

In Pakistan, after the Sino-Indian War in 1962, the military of India was seen as being weakened. This analysis was proven true when a small border skirmish occurred between India and Pakistan in the Rann of Kutch on April 1965 where the Indian Army was caught unprepared. The skirmish occurred between the border police of both countries due to poorly defined borders and later the Armies of both countries responded. The result was a decisive one for the Pakistan Army that was praised back home. Emboldened by this success, Operation Gibraltar, a covert infiltration attempt in Kashmir was launched later in the year. The plan was to start a rebellion among local Kashmiris and attack the rebuilding Indian Army thus capturing Kashmir by force, as the Pakistan Army Command believed that it had a qualitative superiority over their neighbours. However this proved over-ambitious as Indian Kashmiris did not support the intruding Pakistan Army and a full-fledged war across the international border (the Indo-Pakistani War of 1965) broke out between India and Pakistan. Pakistan Air Force and Indian Air Force were indulged massive air warfare in this war. Pakistani Army could not achieve the goal of taking over Indian controlled Kashmir while Indian Army failed to fulfill its aspiration of capturing Lahore and Sialkot, while on the offensive both the armies were occupying some of each other's territory resulting in a stalemate.

US had imposed an arms embargo on both India and Pakistan during the war and Pakistan was affected more by the arms embargo as it had no spare parts for its Air Force, tanks, and other equipment while India's quantitative edge making up for theirs. The war was finally ended in a ceasefire.

Rebuilding the Armed Forces

The United States was disillusioned by a war in which both countries fought each other with equipment, which had been sold for defensive purposes and to stop the spread of communism. Pakistan's claims that an Indian attempt to fully integrate Indian Controlled Kashmir into the union of India had compelled it to act fell on deaf ears in the Johnson Administration and by July 1967, the United States withdrew its military assistance advisory group. In response to these events, Pakistan declined to renew the lease on the Peshawar military facility, which ended in 1969. Eventually, United States-Pakistan relations grew measurably weaker as the United States became more deeply involved in Vietnam and as its broader interest in the security of South Asia waned. The Soviet Union continued the massive build-up of the Indian military and a US arms embargo forced Pakistan to look at other options.

It turned to China, North Korea, Germany, Italy and France for military aid. China in particular gave Pakistan over 900 tanks, Mig-19 Fighters and enough equipment to fully equip 3 Infantry divisions. France supplied some Mirage aircraft, submarines and even the Soviet Union gave Pakistan around 100 T-55 tanks, Mi-8 helicopters but that aid was abruptly stopped under intense Indian pressure. Pakistan in this period was partially able to enhance its military capability.

Involvement in Arab conflicts

Pakistan had sent numerous military advisers to Jordan and Syria to help in their training and military preparations for any potential war with Israel. When the Six Day war started, Pakistan assisted by sending a contingent of its pilots and airmen to Egypt, Jordan and Syria. PAF pilots performed excellently and downed about 10 Israeli planes including Mirages, Mysteres, Vautours without losing a single plane of their own.

Jordan and Iraq decorated Pakistani Flight Lieutenant Saif-ul-Azam. Israelis praised the performance of PAF pilots too. Eizer Weizman, then Chief Of Israeli Air Force wrote in his autobiography about Air Marshal Noor Khan (Commander PAF at that time): "...He is a formidable person and I am glad that he is Pakistani and not Egyptian." No Pakistani ground forces participated in the war.

After the end of the Six-Day War, Pakistani advisors had remained in Jordan and were training the Jordanian Forces. In 1970, King Hussein of Jordan decided to remove the PLO and its forces from Jordan by force after a series of terrorist acts attributed to the PLO, which undermined Jordanian sovereignty. On September 16, King Hussein declared martial law. The next day, Jordanian tanks attacked the headquarters of Palestinian organizations in Amman. The head of Pakistan's training mission to Jordan, Brigadier-General Zia-ul-Haq (later President of Pakistan), took command of the Jordanian Army's 2nd division and helped Jordan during this crisis.

Pakistan again assisted during the Yom Kippur War, sixteen PAF pilots volunteered for service in the Air Forces of Egypt and Syria. The PAF contingent deployed to Inchas Air Base (Egypt) led by Wing Commander Masood Hatif and five other pilots plus two air defence controllers. During this war, the Syrian government decorated Flight Lieutenant Sattar Alvi when he shot down an Israeli Mirage over the Golan Heights. The PAF pilots then became instructors in the Syrian Air Force at Dumayr Air Base and after the war Pakistan continued to send military advisers to Syria and Jordan. Apart from military advisers, no Pakistani ground forces participated in this war.

In 1969, South Yemen, which was under a communist regime and a strong ally of the USSR, attacked and captured Mount Vadiya inside the province of Sharoora in Saudi Arabia. Many PAF officers as well Army personnel who were serving in Khamis Mushayt training the Saudi Air Force (the closest airbase to the battlefield), took active part in this battle in which the enemy was ultimately driven back.

During the Gulf War in 1990, the Pakistani government joined the international community in condemning the Iraqi invasion of Kuwait. Pakistan also joined the Coalition forces to expel Saadam Hussein's forces from Kuwait. However that was not an easy decision as the CoAS of the Pakistani Army was against sending Pakistani soldiers to fight the fellow Muslim nation of Iraq. This caused a rare strain in the relationship between Saudi Arabia and Pakistan. Later on, Pakistan agreed to send forces to assist the coalition forces and most of these forces were deployed along the Saudi border with Yemen, which sided with Iraq during the conflict, and Pakistani forces were also stationed around various religious sites throughout Saudi Arabia. Pakistan suffered no casualties in the conflict and later joined the UN in rebuilding Kuwait's destroyed infrastructure.

The war of 1971

The first democratic elections in Pakistan were held in 1970 with the Awami League winning with a substantial majority. However Yahya Khan banned the Awami League and declared martial law after talks on sharing power failed. Bhutto was famously heard saying "break the legs" if any member of [People's Party] attend the inaugural session at the National Assembly. Fearing on capitalization on West Pakistan, West-Pakistanis fears of East Pakistani separatist, and Bhutto demanded to form a coalition with Mujib. Both Mujib and Bhutto were agreed upon the coalition government, with Bhutto as President and Mujib as Prime minister.

The Military government and General Yahya Khan was kept unaware of such of these developments. Both Bhutto and Mujib continued a political pressure on Khan's military government. Pressured by his own military government, General Yahya Khan postponed the inaugural session, and ordered to arrest Mujib and put Bhutto on house arrest. Military Police subsequently arrested Bhutto and put him on house arrest, and Mujib was sent to military court where his case was headed by Judge Advocate General Branch's Brigadier-General Rahimuddin Khan.

Faced with popular unrest and revolt in East-Pakistan, the Army and Navy clamped down through violence. The Military government of General Yahya Khan ordered Rear-Admiral Mohammad Shariff, Commander of Eastern Naval Command of the Pakistan Navy, and Lieutenant-General Amir Abdullah Khan Nazi, Commander of the Eastern Military Command of Pakistan Army, to curb and liberate East Pakistan from the resistance. The navy and army crackdown and brutalities during the Operation Searchlight and Operation Barisal and the continued killings throughout the later months resulted in further resentment among the East Pakistanis of East Pakistan.

With India assisting and funding the Mukti Bahini, war broke out between the separatist supporters in Bangladesh and Pakistan (Indo-Pakistani War of 1971). During the conflict, the coordination between the armed forces of Pakistan were ineffective and unsupported. On major decision, the army, navy, marines and air force were not taken on confidence. Each forces had led their own independent operations without notifying or taking on confidence the higher command. To release the pressure from East Pakistan the Pakistan Army opened new front at western sector when 2000 strong Pakistan army attacked Indian outpost at Longewala. where merely 120 Indian army of 23 Punjab regiment was protecting the post. The attack was backed by tank regiment but without any air support. The battle was decisively own by the Indian army with the help of Indian Air Force & resulted sutting down of western front. It was a shere example of poor coordination of Army & Airforce.

The result was the Pakistan Armed Forces's surrender to the Indian forces upon which 93,000 Pakistan Armed Forces officials and 93,000 soldiers and officers became POWs, the largest since World War II. The official war between India and Pakistan ended in just a fortnight on December 16, 1971, with Pakistan losing East Pakistan, which became Bangladesh. The official Bangladesh Government claim puts the number of Bengali civilian fatalities at 3 million.

Recovery from the 1971 War

The Military government was collapsed as a result of the war, and the control of the country was handed over to the Zulfikar Ali Bhutto. Bhutto became country's first Chief Martial Law Administrator as well as first Commander-in-Chief of Pakistan Armed Forces.

As becoming the leader of his country in January 1972, Bhutto made his move and started the nuclear deterrence programme under Munir Ahmad Khan and his adviser Abdus Salam. In July 1972, Bhutto proceeded the *Shimla Agreement* with Indira Gandhi of India, and brought back 93,000 Pakistan Armed Forces personnel and recognized East-Pakistan as Bangladesh.

As part of re-organizing the country, Bhutto first disbanded the "Commander-in-Chief" title in the Pakistan Armed Forces. He also decommissioned the Pakistan Marines as a unit of Pakistan Navy. Instead, Chiefs of Staff were appointed in the three branches and Bhutto appointed all 4 star officers as the Chief of Staff in the Pakistan Armed Forces. General Tikka Khan, infamous for his role in Bangladesh Liberation War, become the first Chief of Army Staff of Pakistan Army; Admiral Mohammad Shariff, as first 4-star admiral in the navy and as the first Chief of Naval Staff of Pakistan Navy; and, Air Chief Marshal (General) Zulfiqar Ali Khan, as first 4-star air force general, and the first Chief of Air Staff of Pakistan Air Force. Because the coordination between the armed forces were unsupported and ineffective, in 1976, Bhutto also created the office of Joint Chiefs of Staff Committee for maintaining the coordination between the armed forces. General Muhammad Shariff, a 4-star general, was made its first Chairman of the Joint Chiefs of Staff Committee.

Pakistan's defense spending rose by 200% during the Bhutto's democratic era but the military balance between India-Pakistan, which was at a rough parity during the 1960s was growing decisively in India's favor. Under Bhutto, the education system, foreign policy, and science policy was rapidly changed. Under Bhutto's government, the funding of science was exponentially increased; Pakistan Atomic Energy Commission's and Kahuta Research Laboratories's classified projects were launched under Bhutto. Bhutto also funded the classified military science and engineering projects, entrusted and led by Lieutenant-General Zahid Ali Akbar of the Pakistan Army Corps of Engineers.

The United States once again became a major source for military hardware following the lifting of the arms embargo in 1975 but by then Pakistan had become heavily dependent on China as an arms supplier. Heavy spending on defense re-energized the Army, which had sunk to its lowest morale following the debacle of the 1971 war. The high defense expenditure took money from other development projects such as education, health care and housing.

Baloch nationalist uprisings

The Baloch rebellion of the 1970s, was the most threatening civil disorder to a United Pakistan since Bangladesh's secession. The Pakistan Armed Forces wanted to establish military garrisons in Balochistan Province, which at that time was quite lawless and run by tribal justice. The ethnic Balochis saw this as a violation of their territorial rights. Emboldened by the stand taken by Sheikh Mujibur Rahman in 1971, the Baloch and Pashtun nationalists had also demanded their "provincial rights" from then Prime minister Zulfikar Ali Bhutto in exchange for a consensual approval of the Pakistan Constitution of 1973. But while Bhutto admitted the NWFP and Balochistan to a NAP-JUI coalition, he refused to negotiate with the provincial governments led by chief minister Ataullah Mengal in Quetta and Mufti Mahmud in Peshawar.

Tensions erupted and an armed resistance began to take place.

Surveying the political instability, Bhutto's central government sacked two provincial governments within six months, arrested the two chief ministers, two governors and forty-four MNAs and MPAs, obtained an order from the Supreme Court banning the NAP and charged them all with high treason, to be tried by a specially constituted Hyderabad Tribunal of handpicked judges.

In time, the Baloch nationalist insurgency erupted and sucked the armed forces into the province, pitting the Baloch tribal middle classes against Islamabad. The sporadic fighting between the insurgency and the army started in 1973 with the largest confrontation taking place in September 1974 when around 15,000 Balochs fought the Pakistani Army, Navy and the Air Force. Following the successful recovery of the ammunition in the Iraqi embassy, shipped by both Iraq and Soviet Union for the Baluchistan resistance. The Naval Intelligence launched the investigation, and cited that arms were smuggled from the coastal areas of Balochistan. The Navy acted immediately, and jumped in the conflict. Vice-Admiral Patrick Simpson, commander of Southern Naval Command, began to launched the series of operation with also applying the naval blockage.

The Iranian military fearing a spread of the greater Baloch resistance in Iran also aided the Bhutto-sent Pakistan military in brutally putting down the insurrection. After three days of fighting the Baloch tribals were running out of ammunition and so withdrew by 1976. The army had suffered 25 fatalities and around 300 casualties in the fight while the rebels lost 5,000 people as of 1977.

Although major fighting had broken down, ideological schisms caused splinter groups to form and steadily gain momentum. Despite the overthrow of the Bhutto government in 1977 by General Zia-ul-Haque, Chief of Army Staff of Pakistan Army, calls for secession and widespread civil disobedience remained. The military government then appointed General Rahimuddin Khan as Martial Law Administrator over the Balochistan Province. The provincial military government under the famously authoritarian General Rahimuddin began to act as a separate entity and military regime independent of the central government.

This allowed General Rahimuddin Khan to act as an absolute Martial Law Administrator, unanswerable to the central government. Both General Zia-ul-Haq and General Rahimuddin Khan supported the declaration of a general amnesty in Balochistan to those willing to give up arms. General Rahimuddin then purposefully isolated feudal leaders such as Nawab Akbar Khan Bugti and Ataullah Mengal from provincial policy. He also militarily put down all civil disobedience movements, effectively leading to unprecedented social stability within the province. Due to Martial Law, his reign was the longest in the history of Balochistan (1977–1984).

Tensions have resurfaced recently in the province with the Pakistan Army being involved in attacks against an insurgency known as the Balochistan Liberation Army. Attempted uprisings have taken place as recently as 2005.

SECOND MILITARY RULE

During the 1977 elections, there were rumors of widespread voter fraud and as such the civilian government under Zulfikar Ali Bhutto was overthrown in a bloodless coup of July 1977 and the new ruler and Bhutto's own appointed Chief of Army Staff General Zia-ul-Haq became Chief Martial Law Administrator in 1978. General Zia-ul-Haq was appointed by this position by Bhutto after Bhutto forced seventeen senior general officers to retire from the army. General Zia appointed Mushtaq Hussain, chief jurist for Bhutto's case. Mushtaq Hussain was famously known in the public as extreme hater of Bhutto, and played a controversial role in Bhutto's removal as Foreign minister in 1965. Mushtaq Hussain, now judge, disrespected Bhutto and his hometown, and further denied any appeals. Under Zia's direction and Mushtaq's order, Bhutto was controversially executed in 1979 after the Supreme Court upheld the High Court's death sentence on charges of authorizing the murder of a political opponent. Under Zia's Martial Law military dictatorship (which was declared legal under the *Doctrine of Necessity* by the Supreme Court in 1978) the following initiatives were taken:

- Strict Islamic law was introduced into the country's legal system by 1978, contributing to current-day sectarianism and religious fundamentalism, as well as instilling a sense of religious purpose within the youth.

- Pakistan fought a war by proxy against the Communists in Afghanistan in the Soviet-Afghan War, greatly contributing to the eventual withdrawal of Soviet forces from Afghanistan.
- Secessionist uprisings in Balochistan were put down by the province's authoritarian Martial Law ruler, General Rahimuddin Khan, who ruled for an unprecedented seven years under Martial Law.
- The socialist economic policies of the previous civilian government, which also included aggressive nationalisation, were gradually reversed; and Pakistan's Gross National Product rose greatly.

General Zia lifted Martial Law in 1985, holding party-less elections and handpicking Muhammad Khan Junejo to be the Prime Minister of Pakistan, who in turn rubber-stamped Zia remaining Chief of Army Staff until 1990. Junejo however gradually fell out with Zia as his political and administrative independence grew. When Junejo asked his Minister of State Mr. Zain Noorani to sign the Geneva Accord by all means, which President Zia disliked. After a large-scale explosion at a munitions store in Ojhri, Junejo vowed to bring those responsible for the significant damage caused to justice, implicating several times the Inter-Services Intelligence (ISI) Director-General Akhtar Abdur Rahman.

President Zia, infuriated, dismissed the Junejo government on several charges in May 1988. He then called for the holding of fresh elections in November. General Zia-ul-Haq never saw the elections materialize however, as he died in a plane crash on August 17, 1988, which was later proven to be highly sophisticated sabotage by unknown perpetrators.

Under Zia, real defence spending increased on average by 9 percent per annum during 1977–88 while development spending rose 3 percent per annum; by 1987–88 defence spending had overtaken development spending. For 1980s as a whole, defence spending averaged 6.5 percent of GDP. This contributed strongly to large fiscal deficits and a rapid buildup of public debt.

1979–1999

Development of atomic bomb projects

Soon after Bhutto came to assumed the control of Pakistan, Bhutto made his move to established the nuclear weapons development. In January 20, 1972, Abdus Salam, after being request by Zulfikar Ali Bhutto, arranged and managed secret meeting of academic scientists and engineers, in Multan city, to meet with Zulfikar Ali Bhutto who assumed the control of his country shortly after the Indo-Pakistani war of 1971 and the Bangladesh Liberation War. It was here that Bhutto orchestrated, administrated, and led the scientific research on nuclear weapons as he announced the official nuclear weapons development programme. In 1972, Pakistan's core intelligence service, the ISI, secretly learned that India was close to developing an atomic bomb, under its nuclear programme. Partially in response, defence expenditure and funding of science under then-Prime minister Zulfikar Ali Bhutto increased by 200%. In the initial years and starting years, Dr. Abdus Salam, a Nobel laureate, headed the nuclear weapons program as he was the Science adviser to the Prime minister. He is also credited in bringing hundreds of Pakistani scientists, engineers, and mathematicians who would later go on to develop the nuclear weapons program and later on formed and headed "*Theoretical Physics Group*" (TPG), the special weapons division of Pakistan Atomic Energy Commission (PAEC) that developed the designs and completed the crucial mathematical and physics calculations of the nuclear weapons.

Throughout the time, the foundations were laid down to develop a military nuclear capability. This includes the nuclear fuel cycle and nuclear weapons design, development and testing programme. The fuel cycle program included the uranium exploration, mining, refining, conversion and Uranium Hexafluoride (UF_6) production, enrichment and fuel fabrication and reprocessing facilities. These facilities were established in the Pakistan Atomic Energy Commission or PAEC by its Chairman Munir Ahmad Khan. He was appointed as Chairman of Pakistan Atomic Energy Commission (PAEC) on January 20, 1972 at the Multan Conference of senior scientists and engineers. Earlier, Munir

Ahmad Khan was serving as Director of Nuclear Power and Reactors Division, IAEA. He was credited to be the *"technical father"* of Pakistan's atom project by a recent International Institute of Strategic Studies, London, (IISS) Dossier on history of the Pakistan's nuclear development, with Zulfikar Ali Bhutto as the father of Pakistan's nuclear developmental programme. Munir Ahmad Khan, an expert in Plutonium technology, had also laid the foundation and groundbreaking work for the Plutonium reprocessing technology. Khan, built the *New Laboratories*, a plutonium reprocessing plant located in Islamabad.

After Chief Martial Law Administrator (later President) and Chief of Army Staff General Zia-ul-Haq came to power , further advancements were made to enrich uranium and consolidate the nuclear development programme. On March 11, 1983, PAEC under Munir Ahmad Khan carried out the first successful cold test of a working nuclear device near at the Kirana Hills under codename *Kirana-I*. The test was led by CERN-physicist Dr. Ishfaq Ahmad, and was witnessed by other senior scientists belonging to Pakistan Armed Forces and the PAEC. To compound further matters, the Soviet Union had withdrawn from Afghanistan and the strategic importance of Pakistan to the United States was gone. Once the full extent of Pakistan's nuclear weapons development was revealed, economic sanctions were imposed on the country by several other countries, particularly United States. Having been developed under both Bhutto and Zia, the nuclear development programme had fully matured by the late 1980s. Dr. Abdul Qadeer Khan, a metallurgical engineer, greatly contributed to the uranium enrichment programme under both governments. Dr. A.Q. Khan established an administrative proliferation network through Dubai to smuggle URENCO nuclear technology to Khan Research Laboratories. He then established Pakistan's gas-centrifuge program based on the URENCO's Zippe-type centrifuge. Dr. Abdul Qadeer Khan is considered to be the founder of Pakistan's HEU based gas-centrifuge uranium enrichment programme, which was originally launched by PAEC in 1974.

The PAEC also played its part in the success and development of the uranium enrichment programme by producing the uranium hexafluoride gas feedstock for enrichment. PAEC was also responsible for all the pre and post enrichment phases of the nuclear fuel cycle. By 1986 PAEC Chairman Munir Ahmad Khan had begun work on the 50MW plutonium and tritium production reactor at Khushab, known as Khushab Reactor Complex, which became operational by 1998. After India, by the order of the Indian Premier Atal Vajpayee, successfully tested five underground nuclear tests (codename *Pokharan-II*) in Pokhran region in 1998. Pakistan, under Prime Minister Nawaz Sharif, to the distaste of the international community, successfully carried out six underground in Ras Koh region of the Chagai Hills on nuclear tests on May 28 (codename *Chagai-I*) and on Kharan region (codename *Chagai-II*) on May 30, proving Pakistan's nuclear capability. These tests were carried out by the supervision of the PAEC. These tests were supervised and observed by physicist Dr. Samar Mubarakmand and other senior academic scientists from PAEC and the KRL.

U.S. sanctions

U.S. Senator Pressler introduced the Pressler Amendment, which imposed an embargo on all economic and military aid to Pakistan for developing nuclear weapons. This whole episode caused very negative publicity in Pakistan towards the USA as many people in Pakistan as well as the Pakistani Armed Forces believed they had risked a great deal in helping the USA give the Soviet Union its own Vietnam in Afghanistan and when the task was done, Pakistan was promptly abandoned. Pakistan was hosting a very large Afghan refugee population and drugs from Afghanistan had infiltrated Pakistan and the use of heroin was growing to be a very widespread problem that further compounded the situation.

The embargo continued for five years and in 1995, the Brown Amendment authorised a one-time delivery of US military equipment, contracted for prior to October 1990, worth US$368 million. However, the additional 28 F-16 aircraft costing US$658 million and already paid for by Pakistan were not delivered. Unable to purchase American or NATO weaponry, Pakistan tried to develop an indigenous weapons industry, which has yielded some successes such as the development of the Al-Khalid Tank and JF-17 Strike Fighter.

Soviet-Afghan war

During the Soviet occupation of neighbouring Afghanistan, the alliance between USA and Pakistan was greatly strengthened as the USA needed Pakistan as a staging area from which to send weapons to the Mujahideens who were fighting the Soviets. Apprehensive of the threats on two front to Pakistan from India and from Soviet occupied Afghanistan, the U.S. in 1981 offered a military aid package of over $1.5 billion, which included 40 F-16 fighters, 100 M-48 tanks, nearly 200 artillery guns and over 1,000 TOW anti-tank missiles, which considerably enhanced Pakistan's defence capability. During the course of the war, Pakistan experienced several air intrusions by Afghan/Soviet pilots and claims to shooting down about 8 Afghan/Soviet aircraft over the years as well as losing one F-16 from its own fleet.

The Pakistani Military, aided by the United States and financed by Saudi Arabia, began helping the Mujahideen in setting up training camps and arming them. United States President Jimmy Carter had accepted the view that Soviet aggression could not be viewed as an isolated event of limited geographical importance but had to be contested as a potential threat to the Persian Gulf region. The uncertain scope of the final objective of Moscow in its sudden southward plunge made the American stake in an independent Pakistan all the more important.

Pakistan's Inter-Services Intelligence and Special Service Group now became actively involved in the conflict against the Soviets. Pakistan's SSG created a unit called the Black Storks who were SSG men dressed as Afghan Mujahideen during the Soviet-Afghan war. They were then flown into Afghanistan and provided the Mujahideen with support. After Ronald Reagan became the new United States President in 1980, aid for the Mujahideen through Zia's Pakistan significantly increased. In retaliation, the KHAD, under Afghan leader Mohammad Najibullah, carried out (according to the Mitrokhin archives and other sources) a large number of terrorist operations against Pakistan, which also suffered from an influx of weaponry and drugs from Afghanistan. Pakistan also took in 3 million Afghan refugees (mostly Pashtun) who were forced to leave their country due to heavy fighting including genocide by the communist forces of Soviet Union. Although the refugees were controlled within Pakistan's largest province, Balochistan, then under martial law ruler General Rahimuddin Khan, the influx of so many refugees - believed to be the largest refugee population in the world - into several other regions had a heavy impact on Pakistan and its effects continue to this day.

PLO and Lebanese weapons captured by the Israelis in their invasion of Lebanon in June 1982 were of Soviet origin and were then covertly transferred into Afghanistan through Pakistan. Later, when American support for the Mujahideen became obvious, Stinger Missiles and other high-technology American weaponry were transferred through Pakistan into Afghanistan. However some of these weapons may have been siphoned off by the ISI for reverse engineering purposes. The arrival of the new high-technology weaponry proved to be quite helpful in organizing stiff resistance against the Soviet Union. Many Army regulars fought in Afghanistan along with the resistance and were partly instrumental in the withdrawal of Soviet forces from Afghanistan in 1989.

1st Gulf War

When Iraq occupied Kuwait The Saudi government reached agreement with Pakistan to have several brigades brought into the country to help in its defense. These brigades were placed under the orders of the Ministry of Defense and deployed in Tabuk and Khamis Mushayt.

Taliban takeover of Afghanistan

After the Soviet withdrawal, Pakistan for the first time since 1947, was not concerned about a threat on two fronts. Further, the emergence of five independent Muslim republics in Central Asia raised hopes that they might become allies and offer Pakistan both the political support and the strategic depth it lacked. As long as Afghanistan was in chaos, Pakistan would lack direct access to the new republics.

Fighting between the Communist government in Kabul and the Mujahideen forces continued until 1992 when the Mujahideen forces, led by Ahmed Shah Massoud, removed the Soviet-backed government of Mohammad Najibullah. By 1993, the rival factions who were vying for power agreed on the formation of a government with Burhanuddin Rabbani as president, but infighting continued. Lawlessness was rampant and became a major hindrance to trade between Pakistan and the newly independent Central Asian states. Pakistan appointed the Taliban to protect its trade convoys because most of the Taliban were Pashtun and were trained by the ISI and CIA in the 1980s and could be trusted by Pakistan. With Pakistan's backing, the Taliban emerged as one of the strongest factions in Afghanistan. Pakistan then decided to the end the infighting in Afghanistan and backed the Taliban in their takeover of Afghanistan to bring stability to its western border and establish a pro-Pakistan regime in Kabul.

Pakistan solicited funds for the Taliban, bankrolled Taliban operations, providing diplomatic support as the Taliban's virtual emissaries abroad, arranged training for Taliban fighters, recruited skilled and unskilled manpower to serve in Taliban armies, planned and directed offensives, providing and facilitating shipments of ammunition and fuel, and on several occasions senior Pakistani military and intelligence officers help planned and execute major military operations. By September 1996, the Taliban under the leadership of Mullah Muhammad Omar seized control of Kabul. However, the stability in Afghanistan led to Osama bin Laden and Zawahiri to come to Afghanistan, which caused the Taliban to implement a very strict interpretation of Islamic law. The Taliban continued to capture more Afghan territory until by 2001 they controlled 90% of the country.

Siachen Glacier

After the 1971 war, another border flare-up occurred between India and Pakistan in 1984. The area of the dispute was the Siachen Glacier - the world's highest battlefield. The Glacier was under territorial dispute, but in the late 1970s and early 1980s, Pakistan began organizing several tourist expeditions to the Glacier. India, irked by this development, mounted Operation Meghdoot, and captured the top of the Glacier by establishing a military base that it still maintains to this day at a cost of more than US$1 million per day. Pakistan on the other hand spends just under US$1 million per day, though as a percentage of GDP Pakistan spends 5 times as the Indian Military does to maintain its share of the glacier. Pakistan tried in 1987 and in 1989 to retake the whole Glacier but was unsuccessful.

The Pakistanis control the glacial valley just five kilometers southwest of Gyong La. The Pakistani Army has been unable get up to the crest of the Saltoro Ridge, while the Indians cannot come down and abandon their strategic high posts.

The line between where Indian and Pakistani troops are presently holding onto their respective posts is being increasingly referred to as the Actual Ground Position Line (AGPL).

Kargil War

After the failure of the 1989 attempt to re-take the glacier, a new and much more daring plan was developed by the Pakistan Army to re-take the glacier by blocking the Indian supplies reaching the Indian base at the top of the glacier. The plan was ready in the late 1980s but was put on hold due to the fear that this operation could lead to an all out war with India. Pakistan had recently been placed under US military sanctions for developing Nuclear weapons and the Pakistani military hierarchy believed that they did not have the proper military deterrent if the situation escalated into an all out war with India.

In the winter of 1998, a modified version of the plan was approved due to the fact that months earlier both India and Pakistan had conducted nuclear tests. Pakistan believed that it now had a deterrent to prevent all out war with India and believed that once it had taken the Kargil hills, the international community, fearing a nuclear war, would urge a secession of hostilities. Pakistan would emerge with an improved tactical advantage along the LOC and bring the Siachen Glacier conflict to the forefront of international resolution.

Some elements of the Pakistani SSG Commandos, Northern Light Infantry Forces as well as Indian Kashmiri militants planned to take over the abandoned Indian bunkers on various hills that overlooked the vital Srinagar-Leh highway that serviced the logistics base from which supplies were ferried through helicopter to the Indian Army at the top of the Siachen Glacier. The Indian Army routinely abandoned the bunkers in the winter due to the cold and snow and re-occupied them in the spring.

The Pakistani backed forces took over the bunker complex around April and May 1999, but the winter snows had melted earlier than usual and an Indian reconnaissance team sent to inspect the bunkers was wiped out by them. The Indian Army, alerted to the presence of these militants, responded quickly, forcefully and massed a huge force of around 30,000 men to re-take the Kargil hills. The Pakistani backed forces were detected very early in the operation and were not adequately prepared as they still needed another month or so before they properly established themselves on the Kargil hills, as they were short on heavy weaponry, ammunition, food, shelter, and medicine. However Pakistani troops initially managed to retain most of the heights in spite of continuous Indian attacks. Two months into the conflict, Indian troops had slowly retaken most of the ridges that were encroached by the infiltrators; according to official count, an estimated 75%–80% of the intruded area and nearly all high ground was back under Indian control.

Faced with the possibility of international isolation, the already fragile Pakistani economy was weakened further. The morale of Pakistani forces after the withdrawal declined as many units of the Northern Light Infantry suffered heavy casualties. The government refused to accept the dead bodies of many officers, an issue that provoked outrage and protests in the Northern Areas. Pakistan initially did not acknowledge many of its casualties, but Sharif later said that over 4,000 Pakistani troops were killed in the operation and that Pakistan had lost the conflict.

1999-2008

Third military rule

Many people in Pakistan blamed Sharif for retreating from Kargil under American pressure. Growing fiscal deficits and debt-service payments mainly due to American sanctions after Pakistan tested its Nuclear Weapons in May 1998 as a response to India had led to a financial crisis. When asked about his reason for backing down from Kargil, Sharif said that Pakistan had only enough fuel and ammunition for 3 days and the nuclear missiles were not ready at that time. This comment made many Pakistanis brand Nawaz Sharif a traitor as Army doctrine called for having at least 45 days of fuel and ammunition and to have stand by nuclear missiles ready.

Fearing that the Army might take over, Sharif attempted to dismiss his own appointed Chief of Army Staff and Chairman of Joint Chiefs of Staff Committee General Pervez Musharraf and install an ISI director-general Lieutenant-General Ziauddin Butt as Chief of Army Staff.

General Musharraf, who was out of the country, boarded a commercial flight to return to Pakistan.

Senior Army generals refused to accept Musharraf's dismissal. Sharif ordered the Karachi airport to prevent the landing of the airline, which then circled the skies over Karachi.

In a coup d'état, the generals ousted Sharif's administration and took over the airport. The plane landed with only a few minutes of fuel to spare, and Musharraf assumed control of the government. Prime Minister Nawaz Sharif was put under house arrest and later exiled.

The coup d'état in Pakistan was condemned by most world leaders but was mostly supported by Pakistani populace. The new military government of Pervez Musharraf was heavily criticized in the United States, Saudi Arabia, United Kingdom and when President Bill Clinton went on his landmark trip to South Asia, he only made a last minute stop in Pakistan for a few hours but spent more than five days touring and visiting India. Pakistan was also suspended from the Commonwealth Nations while Musharraf pledged to clean corruption out of politics and stabilize the economy.

On 18 August 2008, General Pervez Musharraf resigned from the post of President under impeachment pressure from the coalition government. Consequently, his website was removed since he was no longer President. He was succeeded on 6 September 2008 by Asif Ali Zardari, duly elected as Pakistan's 11th President since 1956.

Standoff with India

In response to a militant attack on the Indian Parliament on December 13, 2001 during which fourteen people, including the five men who attacked the building, were killed. India claimed that the attacks were carried out by two Pakistan based militant groups fighting Indian rule in Kashmir, Lashkar-e-Taiba (LeT) and Jaish-e-Mohammad (JeM), both of whom, were backed by Pakistan's Inter Services Intelligence (ISI) agency, a charge Pakistan denied. This led to a military standoff between India and Pakistan that resulted in the amassing of troops on either side of the International Border (IB) and along the Line of Control (LoC) in the region of Kashmir. In the Western media, coverage of the standoff focused on the possibility of a nuclear war between the two countries and the implications of the potential conflict on the United States-led War on Terrorism. Tensions de-escalated following international diplomatic mediation, which resulted in the October 2002 withdrawal of Indian and Pakistani troops from the International Border.

Military assistance to Sri Lanka

Pakistan and Sri Lanka enjoy a strong relationship and Pakistan International Airlines planes ferrying Pakistan Army reinforcements to East Pakistan, now Bangladesh, refueled in Colombo after India denied Pakistan overflight permissions before the actual outbreak of the Indo-Pakistan war of 1971. Pakistan has sent military advisers, ammunition and other equipment to Sri Lanka during previous offensives against the LTTE. Many Sri Lankan officers are trained in Pakistan. Pakistan, by supplying high-tech military equipment such as 22 Al-Khalid main battle tanks, 250,000 rounds of 60 mm, 81 mm, 120 mm and 130 mm mortar ammunition worth and 150,000 hand grenades and along with positioning of some of its highly trained army officers in Sri Lanka, played a key role in the ultimate defeat of Tamil Tigers in May 2009. Back in 2000, when a LTTE offensive code-named Operation Ceaseless Waves overran Sri Lankan military positions in the north and captured the Elephant Pass Base and entered Jaffna, and it was being feared that the LTTE would run down thousands of Sri Lankan troops stationed in Jaffna, Pakistan supplied Multi-Barrel Rocket Launcher System and other high-tech weaponry, which halted the offensive.

War in the North-West region

After the September 11 attacks in the United States, Pakistan joined the US-led War on Terror and helped the U.S. Military by severing ties with the Taliban and immediately deploying more than 72,000 troops along Pakistan's western border to capture or kill Taliban and al-Qaida militants fleeing from Afghanistan.

Pakistan initially garrisoned its troops in military bases and forts in the tribal areas. After several high profile terrorist attacks inside Pakistan and assassination attempts on Pervez Musharraf that Pakistan in May 2004. As Chief of Army Staff, General Pervez Musharraf ordered XII Corps and XI Corps to be stationed in FATA region and take forceful action against al-Qaeda members in Pakistan's mountainous Waziristan area (in the Federally Administered Tribal Areas), which escalated into armed resistance by local tribesmen. On March 2004, a battle began to take place in Wana, South Waziristan. It was reported that Al-Qaeda's second-in-command dr. Ayman al-Zawahiri was among with these fighters. Pakistan responded to deploy its 10th Mountaineering Division under Major-General Noel Israel. After a week of fighting, the army suffered a major casualties with hundreds of fighters being captured. However, army was unable to Ayman al-Zawahiri as he either escaped or was never among these fighters.

Clashes erupted between the Pakistani troops and al-Qaeda's and other militants joined by local rebels and pro-Taliban forces. The Pakistani actions were presented as a part of the War on Terrorism, and had connections to the war and Taliban insurgency in Afghanistan. However, the offensive was poorly coordinated and the Pakistani Army suffered heavy casualties as well public support for the attack quickly evaporated.

After a 2-year conflict from 2004 until 2006, the Pakistani military negotiated a ceasefire with the Tribesmen from the region in which they pledged to hunt down al-Qaeda members, stop the Talibanization of the region and stop attacks in Afghanistan and Pakistan. However, the militants did not hold up their end of the bargain and began to regroup and rebuild their strength from the previous 2 years of conflict.

The militants emboldened by their success in FATA moved into Islamabad where they sought to impose an extremist Sharia government on Pakistan. Their base of operations was the Lal Masjid in Islamabad. After a 6-month standoff fighting erupted again in July 2007 when the Pakistani Military decided to use force to end the Lal Masjid threat. Once the operation ended, the newly formed Pakistani Taliban, an umbrella group of all militants based out of FATA vowed revenge and launched a wave of attacks and suicide bombings erupted all over North-West Pakistan and major Pakistani cities throughout 2007.

The militants then expanded their base of operations and moved into the neighboring Swat Valley and imposed a very harsh Sharia law on the scenic valley. The Army launched an offensive to re-take the Swat Valley in 2007 but was unable to clear it of the militants who had fled into the mountains and waited for the Army to leave to take over the valley again. The militants then launched another wave of terrorist attacks inside Pakistan.

The Pakistani government and military tried another peace deal with the militants in Swat Valley in 2008. This was roundly criticized in the West as abdicating to the militants. Initially pledging to lay down their arms if Sharia Law was implemented, the Pakistani Taliban used Swat Valley as a springboard to launch further attacks into neighboring regions and reached to within 60 km of Islamabad.

The public opinion turned decisively against the Pakistani Taliban when a video showing a flogging of a girl by the Pakistani Taliban in Swat Valley finally forced the army to launch a deceive attack against the Taliban occupying Swat Valley in April 2009. After heavy fighting the Swat Valley was largely pacified by July 2009 although there are isolated pockets of Taliban activity continues.

The next phase of Pakistani Army's offensive was the formidable Waziristan region. A US drone attack killed the leader of the Pakistani Taliban, Baitullah Mehsud in August in a targeted killing. A power struggle engulfed the Pakistani Taliban for the whole of September but by October a new leader had emerged, Hakimullah Mehsud. Under his leadership, the Pakistani Taliban launched another wave of terrorist attacks throughout Pakistan killing hundreds of people.

The Pakistani Army had been massing over 30,000 troops and 500 Commandos to launch a decisive offensive against the Pakistani Taliban's sanctuaries. After a few weeks of softening up the targets with air strikes and artillery and mortar attacks, the Army moved in a three pronged attack on South Waziristan. The fighting is currently continuing.

Since the conflict began, Pakistan has lost more than three times the number of its soldiers compared to the number of US troops killed in Afghanistan. However, as of 2009, the confirmed bodycount of militants killed by the Pakistan Army reached the 7,000 mark.

THE RESURGENCE OF PAKISTAN'S MILITARY

In a rare convergence of views, conservative religious political parties and mainstream liberals in Pakistan seem to agree it is a terrible idea to allow special military courts to try suspected terrorists. But they think so for different reasons, highlighting that once again Pakistan is both polarized and confused about how to respond to terrorism.

Last Tuesday, the National Assembly and the Senate unanimously adopted (with abstentions but no votes against) the 21st amendment to the Constitution: For two years, military courts will have authority to adjudicate cases involving civilians suspected of links to terrorist organizations. The president approved the law the next day.

This is the first major initiative the government has pushed through since the new National Action Plan to counter terrorism was drawn up last month. After the Pakistani Taliban's rampage on an army-run school in Peshawar on Dec. 16, the government's immediate, and vengeful, response was to lift a moratorium on the death penalty. But then it put forward a comprehensive program that goes well beyond the usual antiterrorist military operations. Among other measures, the National Action Plan calls for cracking down on hate speech and attacks on religious minorities and for regulating Islamic seminaries.

Both the public and parties across the political spectrum have hailed the plan for its holistic approach. Even the opposition party Pakistan Tehreek-e-Insaf, or P.T.I., which has led antigovernment protests for months and is generally reluctant to condemn Islamists, came out in support of the government's new counterterrorism strategy.

But what did the government do last week by passing the constitutional amendment? Instead of revamping the criminal justice system, as the new action plan called for, it cited the failings of civilian courts, such as backlogs and corruption, to increase the remit of military courts: In other words, it ceded yet more control to an armed services that already dominates security and foreign policy making. And with that, it crushed hopes that Pakistan — which has spent half of its history under martial law — was undergoing a democratic transition after the May 2013 election, the first in which power was transferred from one civilian government to another through the ballot box.

Last week's amendment to the Constitution is a step backward; civilian courts had been enjoying unprecedented independence in recent years, after a long history of operating at the military's behest and on occasion providing it legal cover for unconstitutional takeovers. The move also increases the risk of human rights violations against terrorist suspects since the special military courts' decisions will not be subject to appeal.

Like other progressive Pakistanis, I was even more dismayed to realize that political parties with purportedly liberal agendas supported the amendment, and despite understanding it would be a setback for democracy. Members of the opposition Pakistan Peoples Party refused to vote for the law on Monday, Jan. 5, because that was the birthday of the party's founder, Zulfikar Ali Bhutto, a former prime minister and president of Pakistan who is seen as an icon of democracy. They just voted for it the next day. One P.P.P. leader said he had done so against his conscience. Another called the amendment a "bitter pill" that was required to save the country.

Some parties abstained, such as the right-wing religious groups Jamaat-e-Islami and Jamiat Ulema-e-Islam. But this was not in the interest of democracy; it was because the amendment applies to "any terrorist group, armed group, wing and militia or their members using name of religion or a sect." These religious parties, which are accused of maintaining links with the Taliban and Al Qaeda, fear that the new law will mean more security crackdowns on religious groups and seminaries.

The already confused and confusing debate about extremism in Pakistan has just become even more fraught. In the name of keeping the military out of civilian affairs, Pakistani liberals now find themselves having to defend a criminal justice system they have been criticizing for being sympathetic to extremist groups. (In the past Pakistani lawyers have feted the assassin of a politician critical of anti-blasphemy laws, and banned the sale at bar association canteens of drinks made at factories owned by Ahmadi Muslims, a sect they consider heretical.) And conservative religious political parties are having to take a stance against the military, even though historically they have enjoyed its patronage and formed governments with its backing as part of a strategy to sideline secular political parties.

Yet the greatest contradiction of all is that so many parliamentarians — including 247 members of the National Assembly — would vote to empower the military when many of them distrust it. Journalists and politicians, including the former head of P.T.I., believe the military may have orchestrated the antigovernment protests last year in the hope of triggering early elections. But now some of these politicians appear to be kowtowing to the army, presumably so they can complete their terms in office.

They seem to think they must sacrifice democracy in order to save it. But how soon will there be too little of it left to save?

THE ROLE OF MILITARY IN POLITICS

It is axiomatic that military has no political role in any democratic country. Unfortunately, a weak political system allowed the Pakistan military to manipulate events, and, ultimately, hijack the state.

The military has cast a long shadow over politics in Pakistan even during the period of civilian rule. Repeated army intervention in the politics of Pakistan has been a recipe for disaster. It has thwarted the growth and development of parliamentary democracy and destroyed whatever little faith people had in their political institutions. What is worse, it has eroded people's faith in themselves as citizens of a sovereign, independent, democratic country.

Marx once said: "Neither a nation nor a woman is forgiven for an unguarded hour in which the first adventurer who comes along can sweep them off their feet and possess them". October 7, 1958, was our unguarded hour when democracy was expunged from the politics of Pakistan with scarcely a protest.

The result is the mess we are in today. As a direct consequence of military intervention in the politics of Pakistan in 1958, we lost half the country in 1971. Our Bengali compatriots parted company with us when we drifted away from the democratic path.

They saw no future for themselves in a military – dominated Pakistan and broke the country in two. We lost half the country but learned nothing. 33 years after that traumatic experience, a General in uniform rules Pakistan. Some lessons of history, they say, take time to have an effect.

It is now abundantly clear, except to those who are blind, or on drugs, that Pakistan cannot survive if army is not taken out of the turbulent arena of political conflict. Pakistan cannot survive under military rule, with or without a civilian façade, because military rule lacks legitimacy and is an anachronism in a world of global markets, information and media.

Pakistan cannot survive under military rule because military rule symbolizes the hegemony of Punjab over the smaller federating units. Pakistan cannot survive under military rule because experience has amply demonstrated that military rule is a recipe for disaster. Army is the only shield we have against foreign aggression. Why involve it in politics?

On August 14 / 15 1947, both Pakistan and India emerged as sovereign, independent, democratic countries with great hopes and high expectations. 57 years after independence, the Indian army remains bound by tight constitutional and political constraints. There has been no coup, no colonels or brigadiers conspiracy to seize power. The Indian army has not intervened in politics. De Tocqueville and other theorists have argued that democracy and a large standing army were incompatible, but India has managed both. Indian democracy has stood the test of time.

The constitution has kept the country united, allowed its democracy to survive and kept the armed forces at bay. The structure of the Indian civil-military relationship is still intact largely because the legitimacy of the political system remains high. The British tradition of separate spheres of military and civil authority has carried over. Indian officers like to boast that politics and military do not mix; that the two are immutably different and separate. Junior officers are taught to be political illiterates. Tragically, Pakistan army followed a different path with disastrous consequences for the country.

The engine of history is moving Pakistan backwards. If we are not vigilant, our fledging democracy may, after all, turn out to have been a historical accident and a parenthesis that is closing before our eyes. Today Pakistan has no choice: It is condemned either to be part of the democratic world or not to be at all. Pakistan will never be all it can be, let alone all it need to be, if army is not taken out of the arena of political conflict and civil administration.

Asghar Khan is right when he says that, "Only powerful public pressure to restrict the armed forces to their defense responsibilities under political direction can bring about a change". This task must be undertaken today. Tomorrow will be too late. Today our fate is still in our hands, but soon it may pass beyond control.

DEMOCRACY AND DICTATORSHIP IN PAKISTAN

The wheel of military coups turned once again in Pakistan on October 12, 1999 and brought the entire country under direct military rule for the fourth time. I was reminded of a retired colonel who had once confided that a manual on how to stage bloodless coups has been in circulation among the officer corps of the Pakistan army for a long while. So it was small wonder that when time came Gen. Parvez Musharraf's men seized power with textbook precision. The only thing new about this coup was the theatrics staged by Prime Minister Nawaz Sharif in his attempt to remove the Chief of Army Staff (COAS), appointed by himself a few months earlier, which backfired.

In contrast to the banality of the event the media commentary and international reaction that followed attached great significance to the military takeover, but on the basis of two opposite perceptions both of which missed the central point of the reality of Pakistani state. The first perception originating mainly with the media commentators and political analysts within Pakistan blamed Prime Minister Nawaz Sharif's increasingly corrupt, manipulative and oppressive government for the latest military intervention, while at the same time raising hopes that the coup makers will return the country to democracy "after cleaning up the mess." This view was reinforced by the calmness, even a sense of relief, that characterised the response of a cynical public to the dismissal of Nawaz Sharif's elected but much discredited government.

The second perception was revealed in the form of a strong and swift international reaction to the military coup in Pakistan. The United States, having backed every ruthless dictatorship in the past was quick to disapprove the removal of Nawaz Sharif's civilian government as a serious deviation from democratic norms and threatened the continuation of sanctions imposed earlier at the time of Pakistan's nuclear tests. The IMF hinted at suspension of its loan installments to the military regime. The British Commonwealth and the European Union decided to dispatch high-profile delegations to investigate the situation and to urge prompt restoration of civilian rule within a fixed time frame or face ostracisation.

But it so happens that none of these perceptions of the October 12 coup are correct and as a consequence any course of action based on these perceptions for the restoration of democracy in Pakistan is a mere illusion. In order to understand the reasons for the failure of parliamentary democracy to take root in Pakistan one has to understand the central reality of the Pakistani state. To put it in a few words, the state in Pakistan has evolved into a highly centralized, unitary and oligarchic instrument which continues to operate in a neo-colonial framework.

THE CENTRALISATION OF STATE POWER

The history and the genesis of rise to power of a military-bureaucratic oligarchy in Pakistan from the early 1950s and the centralization of state power in the hands of this oligarchy, predominantly native to or domiciled in Punjab, is well researched and documented by the country's own reputable scholars from Hamza Alavi to Ayesha Jalal. What is conveniently overlooked for ideological reasons or just poverty of imagination is the fact that many of Pakistan's grave political, economic and social problems, including the failure of parliamentary democracy to take roots, emanate from this unitary, highly centralized, patriarchal and authoritarian structure of the state and the forces that sustain this structure. The corruption and misdeeds of the civil politicians elected to high state offices are not primary factors leading to direct military interventions and martial rule. They are rather integral to the capitalist system globally and only more visibly blatant in instances where bourgeois legalisms regulating private property relations are underdeveloped and inadequately enforced.

On the other hand democracy, indeed the vibrancy of the civil society itself, is the first casualty of a highly centralised oligarchic state. It makes little difference if such a state maintains a facade of parliamentary democracy or its affairs are conducted by its military and bureaucratic arms directly in the absence of any democratic procedures and structures.

What we see in the first quarter century of Pakistan's existence is an uninterrupted process of concentration of power at the centre of the federal state through the agency of a military bureaucratic oligarchy unresponsive to the basic needs of people and riding rough shod over the interests and aspirations of the culturally and linguistically diverse federating units. The decade long rule of Field Marshal Ayub Khan (1958-1968) was the first substantive outcome of this process during which the relationship between the Pakistani state and civil society came to be defined. The state emerged as an institution above society assuming the role of the guardian of public interest and national purpose. The regime derived its main sustenance from the neo- colonial links established with the United states and its global defense treaty system aimed at containing the influence of the "communist block." Western style parliamentary democracy was declared contrary to the "genius" of the people of Pakistan by Ayub Khan who, with the help of his bureaucrat advisors, devised a system of party-less indirect elections named "basic democracy." The provinces of West Pakistan were amalgamated into one administrative unit and a movement for autonomy that arose in the tribal areas of Baluchistan was crushed with a massive military crack down. Political parties were banned, and severe restrictions were placed on labour unions, civil liberties and freedom of the press.

The basic model of Pakistan's economic development was also formulated during this period. Rapid capital accumulation or maximization of profits at the cost of economic equality and social justice was the central goal of the model and its success was measured exclusively in rates of economic growth. The state elite and US experts rather than the people in general were to play the central role in the planning and execution of the development process. It is interesting to note that this was the same time when the late Akhter Hamid Khan working, at the periphery of the state activities, was successfully demonstrating that people power was more effective in developing prosperous communities through his Comila project. But such initiatives had to be ignored as they were threatening to elitist control.

General Elections After 24 Years. When the Ayub regime fell apart as a result of popular uprising spurred by political repression and aggravation of class and regional inequalities, Gen. Yahya Khan took over at the head of another martial law regime. This regime finally allowed general elections to be held on the basis of universal adult franchise in 1970, twenty four years after the creation of Pakistan.

The results of these elections required the transfer of power to the Awami League which took a majority of the national assembly seats by its land slide victory in East Bengal, a prospect threatening to the power of the central state dominated by a predominantly Punjabi military- bureaucratic establishment. The refusal of this establishment to honour the verdict of these elections, the military crack down in East Bengal, the 1971 war with India and the secession of East Pakistan is now history. What is significant is that at least after these events the first long stretch of military rule ended in the territorially diminished Pakistan and a civilian politician, Zulfiqar Ali Bhutto, who had won a majority of the parliamentary seats in West Pakistan as the leader of Pakistan Peoples Party (PPP) emerged as the first directly elected prime minister of the country.

The populist manifesto of the PPP, embellished with Bhutto's rhetoric of "all power to the people" and "socialism" generated much hope that Pakistan was now on its way to democracy. However, Bhutto found a coercive, alienated, and neo-colonial state structure, in which his political career was nurtured within the Ayub regime, much more congenial to his temperament than the image of the "man of the masses" he had projected for himself during his election campaign. Once in office, he made all the right noises about the inordinate power enjoyed by the military and the bureaucracy, but went no further than effecting a few cosmetic changes in the structure of these institutions. The armed forces continued to swallow as much as 40 percent of the national revenues and an expensive nuclear programme was initiated to build a bomb to counter the perennial "threat" from India. A new paramilitary force , the Federal Security Force (FSF) was also created to suppress any emergent civil unrest or challenge to his regime.

Bhutto also demonstrated that the central state's writ will prevail within the federation by dismissing the non-PPP governments of the smaller provinces of NWFP and Balochistan and prosecuting their leaders for anti-state activities. And as far as the socialist goals of his party were concerned, those of his close circle who took this project seriously soon fell by the wayside and their places were taken by eulogists and sycophants. When the factory workers who had rallied behind his election campaign came out to protest the broken promises, they were warned that the "power of the street will be met with the power of the state." Zulfiqar Ali Bhutto must of course be given the credit for using his legislative majority to enact for Pakistan a standard parliamentary democratic constitution in 1973, which even contained a specific clause making military coups illegal. But a social democrat as he claimed to be, Bhutto should have known that mere paragraphs in constitutions are not enough to ensure a democratic order.The best assurance for the survival of democracy is its work, the work that secures the essentials of a civilized existence for people and respect for their dignity as human beings.

Missing this point, Bhutto continued to strengthen the institutional power of the central state hoping that this will secure his personal civilian rule, a mistake he had to discover at his own peril.

The Islamic Military State

In 1977 as Zulfiqar Ali Bhutto faced a storm of political protest at the alleged rigging of his second term elections, his obsequious chief of the armed forces, Gen. Ziaul Haq, staged his coup promising to hold "fair and free" elections within 90 days. But he soon settled down to rule Pakistan with an iron hand until his death in 1988. His regime was fully supported by the United States and its allies militarily and financially for taking on the Russians in Afghanistan. Except for a short lived and vacillating period towards the end of his rule, Zia made no pretense of ruling by popular consent. His brutally repressive regime in known for many novelties but viewed in its entirety his genius, if we can call it that, comprised in taking all those pre-existing ideological elements, distortions and practical devices from the political history of Pakistan that had been used to legitimise authoritarian regimes in the past and simply perfecting their application to his own ends.

One can take the example of Zia's prime mission to "Islamise" the Pakistani society. The use of the name of Islam and "Islamic ideology" was quite common among the previous regimes to oppose movements for social equality as "godless socialism" and to counter the demands for linguistic rights and provincial autonomy as disruptive of Islamic solidarity. In Zia's hands Islam and Islamic ideology became a versatile tool for the extension of state control in the domain of personal and private lives of citizens as well as their public, political, professional and cultural activities. Borrowing from the Jamat-e-Islami's exposition of the Islamic state and its righteous ruler, the amir-ul-momineen, Zia vested in himself limitless prerogatives to define and enforce , through martial law and presidential ordinances, what was to be proper or improper conduct and thought for men and women. The introduction of the patriarchal medieval Islamic code, the shari'a law, was part of this exercise, which for better or worse, remains the law of modern Pakistan. In the end Zia dug up the Objectives Resolution, a relic of Pakistan's initial failed attempts to frame an "Islamic" constitution for the country, and enshrined it in the 1973 constitution. The highlight of the Objectives Resolution is the proclamation that sovereignty in Pakistan belongs to Allah, contrary to the usual attribution of sovereignty in democratic state constitutions to the people. Never mind whether Allah, the Beneficent, would care to be recognized as sovereign of what has turned out to be one of the most corrupt countries in the world; what is significant here is the implicit denial of the principle of popular sovereignty.

Democracy Under the Military's Shadow

On Gen. Ziaul Haq's demise in 1988, the military high command, greatly enhanced in its sphere of power and somewhat sobered by the excesses of the previous regime, allowed formal parliamentary democracy to return by permitting party-based elections to be held under the 1973 constitution which now stood heavily amended and distorted, especially with its 8th amendment giving the president power to dismiss the directly elected prime minister and dissolve the parliament.

Benazir Bhutto as leader of the PPP formed the first post-Zia elected government but with less than a clear majority in the parliament and not before she had made all the right moves to receive the endorsement of the army, the bureaucracy and the US administration. By this time the balance of power had tilted so much in favour of the military-bureaucratic oligarchy that we forewarmed not to expect that "the death of Zia has cleared the way for transition to a new era of unfettered democratic rule and popular determination of the national and international orientations of the Pakistani state (Gardezi, H. N., Understanding Pakistan, Lahore, 1991, p. 120). We also noted at the time that the degree of "the military's defacto involvement in the affairs of the state had increased so much that the imposition of another martial law was unnecessary, at least in the short run."

That short run lasted for 11 years during which three elected governments were dismissed by presidential edicts alternating between Bhutto and Sharif. The fourth elected government led by Nawaz Sharif could perhaps have lasted for a little longer had he reined in his ambitions and not taken on the military in the manner he did after clipping the wings of the presidency and humiliating the higher judiciary.

Nevertheless, it had become evident over those 11 years of the elected governments of Benazir Bhutto and Nawaz Sharif that they could hardly be regarded as functional democracies. Ushered in and out of office without completing their constitutionally allotted tenures and operating under the shadow of a powerful military establishment, they were trapped in such internal and external structural constraints that their ability to deal with the cumulated burden of Pakistan's problems was seriously impaired.

Unable even to guarantee the basic livelihood and physical safety of the citizens, the leaders of these elected govenments remained preoccupied in victimizing their political opponents, silencing the voices of dissent from the civil society, warding off threats to their rule from within the state institutions, and of course, amassing private fortunes while the opportunity was there.

To make matters worse for both Bhutto and Sharif administrations, the restoration of parliamentary democracy in 1988 coincided with a new stage of world imperialism, designated as globalisation, that posed new and more serious problems for Pakistan's model of dependent development. In order to enforce conformity to the agenda of globalization the IMF and World Bank loans now came with new conditionalities the brunt of which was to be borne by the already poverty stricken people of Pakistan. These conditionalities, euphemistically called structural reforms, require the dependent economies to privatise state assets, deregulate, downsize, introduce regressive sales taxes, eliminate state subsidies for essential consumer goods and public utilities, devalue national currencies and so on. These measures played havoc with the lives of the low and subsistence wage workers as jobs disappeared, wages were reduced, prices rose, and access to essential services such as health, housing, transportation and education were further limited. During her second term in office Benazir Bhutto's government had to accept such stringent conditionalities to qualify for a $1.5 billion World Bank loan creating severe hardships for the people.

The result was that in the following election in 1997 her party supporters sat home as Nawaz Sharif marched to a big victory on the basis of very low voter turn-out. The implementation of the IMF/Word Bank structural reforms continued during his government and in combination with the infliction of additional austerities on the public, triggered a spectacular spate of economic suicides by people driven insane with poverty.

But even such screams of public agony failed to move any collective consciousness or produce any policy response at the official level. Confident in his "heavy mandate" Nawaz Sharif ruled merrily hounding his political opponents and public critics, demolishing judicial constraints to the exercise of his power and playing cricket in front of his TV audiences until ousted by Gen. Musharraf's military coup.This was "sham democracy," declared Gen. Musharraf as he took over and promised to lead the country to "true democracy" in his post-coup address to the nation on October 17, 1999.

What Is To Be Done

The lesson that follows from any objective sketch of the political realities of Pakistan, with more than half a century of history behind them, is quite clear - democracy in any form or substance cannot coexist with a state in which all power is centralized and which is thoroughly alienated from the civil society. If this lesson is received seriously it also suggests what will have to be done if Gen. Pervez Musharraf is to succeed in "ending the era of sham democracy" in Pakistan and directing Pakistan to the path of "true democracy."

First and foremost a bold and concrete plan will have to be put into effect to dismantle the highly centralised, unitary and authoritarian structure of the Pakistani state. As noted earlier the concentration of power in the central state has been its own justification for attempting to resolve all types of national issues by application of coercive force, rather than political negotiation and democratic consensus building, with disastrous social and political consequences.

A prime example is the frequent use of central authority in the form of military and police action, as well as constitutional and extra-constitutional dismissals of the elected provincial governments, to promote national unity. The results of all such exercises proved to be counterproductive, leading to the dismemberment of Pakistan in 1971 and in subsequent years giving rise to what Gen. Musarraf in his October 17 address called "provincial disharmony" and "cracks in the federation." A truly democratic state must be firmly based on the principle of consent rather than coercion at all levels. One of these critical levels is that of linguistically and culturally identifiable sub-national groups that roughly comprise the provinces of Pakistan today. These groups must be accommodated in the federation as free and equal partners in law.

Within the existing setup of Pakistan this means downward devolution of power by the central government to the provincial governments, as well as divisional, district and tehsil administrations. But such devolution of power to the local levels should not be a cynical device to legitimise the central rule corresponding to the schemes employed by the previous military regimes, the so called basic democracy of Ayub Khan and the party-less local bodies elections of Ziaul Haq. To set up networks of locally elected bodies without empowering the local people to exercise their choices freely, and control the bodies so created, amounts to a sham of grass root's democracy. The outcome of such exercises may reflect the existing power structures based on class, caste, biradri (kinship) etc., but it does not reflect "people power." It is often repeated as a truism in Pakistan that feudalism is a major obstacle to the working of democratic institutions. But to make such broad statements is not very helpful. Much change has taken place in the agrarian relations of production in the country over the last few decades.

Most peasants in the countryside are no longer sharecroppers bound to the so called feudals by traditional bonds and extra-economic coercion. If they are empowered through organisation and meaningful participation, economic security and freedom from intimidation not only by influential land lords and tribal lords but also by the state police and religious zealots, they can make wise and independent political choices affecting their collective welfare. One can recall how Zulfiqar Ali Bhutto had just by his rhetoric of equality infused enough confidence among the under classes and oppressed groups that they had begun to stand up for their rights and challenge their traditional masters and bullies. Unfortunately all that was reversed when Zia brought back the politics of influence paddling and the PPP itself betrayed its constituency of the underprivileged.

The empowerment of people, of course, has to be an integral part of the overall project of strengthening the civil society visa-vis the state. The democratically organised political parties, independent and free press and electronic media, advocacy groups, wokers and peasants groups are prerequisites of the civil society. Its essence lies in the existence of a plurality of open and secular voluntary associations where people come together as coequals to debate and define the issues that concern their lives such as work, health, education, housing, environment, gender equality, human rights, violence and so forth; they mobilise their resources to deal with these issues and mediate in the policy processes of the state. For too long the authoritarian state elite, not only in Pakistan but in all of South Asia, have tried to do all these things for the people with a miserable record of achievement tarnished with corruption and patronage. The state can serve the people better, while at the same time strengthen the culture of democracy, by letting people decide for themselves what their needs are in all these areas and how they are to be met, reconstituting the role of its officials to providing financial, legal and technical expertise as required. Some of the more imaginative and well functioning non-governmental organizations or NGOs have already demonstrated how even the economically and socially marginalised groups can organise to solve their problems more effectively than the state bureaucracies. A specific example of what people themselves should be able to do much better than state bureaucracies is the grandiose housing project floated by the defunct Nawaz Sharif government under the label of "Mera Ghar." To be implemented by a bureaucracy out of touch with the lives of the people, it is bound to fail leaving behind a trail of waste and disillusionment, unless thoroughly redesigned on the pattern of something like the Orangi project of Karachi, developed and implemented with full community involvement and participation.

State policy

The opportunities and possibilities of what people can accomplish for their communities depends also on the overall state policy in various sectors of national administration. Two such important sectors in which state policy has seriously affected the lives of the people of Pakistan are the economy and the country's foreign relations both of which are closely interrelated.

What is striking in the economic sector is that distributive justice has never been a recognised and actively pursued goal of development policy and planning since its blue print was laid out during the Ayub era. Although there was an underlying assumption that the fruits of development will one day trickle down to the poor and the working classes, that trickle down never took place until a combination of excessive external borrowing, heavy defense spending and mismanagement landed the Pakistani state into a full blown fiscal crisis. With over 60 percent of the annual revenues going to debt servicing and 45 percent allocated to defense (1999-2000 budget) there is little left to finance the development sector any more. To add to the misery of the poor and the working classes the IMF/World Bank conditionalities now prohibit the subsidizing of food and other essential items as noted earlier. No political system, least of all a democratic one, can remain stable under these conditions.

Pakistan's economy is indeed in "deep trouble" to use Gen. Musharraf's words from his October 17 speech. The question now is what can be done to "revitalize" it ? The measures being suggested by Gen. Musharraf and his cabinet amount to doing more of the same thing, which combined with the operation to recover defaulting bank loans and the embezzled wealth of the country, if successful, may buy some time but will not turn things around unless there is a fundamental change in the existing economic priorities. In fact the entire model of Pakistan's economic development requires radical change so that the welfare of the people and their participation acquires a place at the centre of the development process. But even without waiting for a major change in the development paradigm , a beginning can be made to redress the serious imbalances in the existing allocation of resources.

Obviously a major drain on the country's economic resources is the very heavy expenditure on defense, combined now with the added cost of nuclear armament, which has grown out of all proportion to other investments necessary for building a minimally prosperous and stable society. Although a symbolic cut in the defense expenditure announced by the present military government in the economic reforms package unveiled on December 15, 1999 is in the right direction, this reduction has to be more substantial and Gen. Musharraf is in a good position to initiate this task for several reasons. He is said to enjoy a high degree of support within the armed forces; he has direct and open lines of communication with the rank and file of the armed forces to sell the idea of cuts in defense expenditure; he is privy to the detailed break down of the defense budget and as such in a position to determine where the cuts can be made most prudently. Besides, he has assumed the position of the head of state at a time when the aftermath of the May, 1998 India-Pakistan nuclear tests produced a wide-spread peace movement in the subcontinent which can counter the right-wing militant formations whose business it has been to keep alive costly tensions between the two neighbours.

An effective downsizing of the defense establishment will no doubt necessitate a change and a fresh perspective in Pakistan's traditional foreign policy which has been based too narrowly on a single minded preoccupation with the "Indian threat," at the core of which lies the Kashmir conflict. For too long the civil and military rulers of Pakistan have used this Indian equation to justify the building of a military power far beyond the capacity of available national resources to support it, going even to the extent of serving the Cold War interests of the United States in return for military and economic aid. It is about time to admit that the results of this policy have been catastrophic for Pakistan. No wars with India have been won on the battlefield leading only to tragic losses of military and civilian lives on both sides, the Kashmir conflict is no closer to settlement, and proxy engagements on behalf of the United States in Afghanistan have subverted the internal peace and security of Pakistani society.

There are precious resources tied up in maintaining an adversarial relationship with a neighbour manifold larger in size and means of waging war. Peace with India will not only release these resources for more productive use and social uplift; it will yield additional economic dividends by opening up mutually beneficial trade and commerce between the two countries. In short Pakistan has much to gain economically and politically by adopting a pro- active policy of improving its relations with India.

The related issue of Kashmir also demands a fresh approach. Officially, Pakistan has always maintained the justifiable position that the people of Kashmir have the right of self- determination. Yet it is ironic that the successive governments of the country have been totally negligent of consulting the people of Kashmir under Indian control or their leaders before launching strategic operations to "liberate" them. While each of such operations has failed in its objectives, as did the latest Kargil move, they have brought massive Indian retaliations and untold misery to the people of Kashmir. It may be best as a first step to leave the Kashmiris alone for a change so that they can themselves determine the course of their struggle for self- determination. Abdul Ghani Lone, a leader of of the All Parties Hurriyat Conference (APHC) on a visit to New York after the Kargil fiasco told Pakistani journalists that APHC wants "no help from Pakistan politically, financially and militarily (Herald, October, 1999, p. 23). He does make a lots of sense. Pakistan can play a much more constructive role in helping the people of Kashmir through quiet diplomacy and negotiations, from which the representatives of the people of Kashmir are not excluded.

The problem is that Pakistan's jingoistic foreign policy towards India, and by implication its stand on the Kashmir issue has been closely tied to the ideology of monolithic Islamic nationalism adopted and promoted by the state for its strategic purposes. The operative logic of this ideology is based on a simplistic dichotomy between "We" and the "Other." The collective solidarity of "We", the Muslim Pakistanis, needs to be constantly nourished by hostility towards the "Other", the Indian Hindus.

For the state this ideology of monolithic Islamic nationalism has served two main strategic functions. First, it has served as a justification for maintaining a well financed and sacrosanct sphere of military power as a defense against an identifiable "Other." Secondly it has been used to deny the cultural and linguistic plurality of Pakistan's nationhood. Those within "We" who individually or collectively assert an identity as Sindhi, Siraiki, Balochi etc. are disruptive of Islamic solidarity and therefore a challenge to national unity. The use of force is justified to bring them back to the fold. That this logic has never worked is another matter.

In reality this brand of nationalism that has come to define Pakistan's nationhood exclusively in terms of Islamic identity is patently undemocratic. It has no foundation in the ethos of a majority of Muslims in Pakistan, especially in the vast southern regions of the country where people follow the Sufi tradition of tolerant, syncretic Islam. It is the creation of politico- Islamic parties led by articulate orthodox Sunni clerics or ulema. Whenever such parties havefielded candidates in Pakistan's national elections they have done poorly. That is why these parties have to use psychological and physical intimidation or state patronage to promote their objectives.

Given the imperatives of the authoritarian Pakistani state all government leaders whether military or civilian have accommodated these politico-Islamic parties regardless of their popular support. But their influence on Pakistan's politics and civil society has increased tremendously since the late 1970s when the Zia regime drew them into active collaboration with the army's US supported operations in Afghanistan. Now they are an important link in Pakistan's support for the Taliban rule in Afghanistan and have at the same time acqired an independent power base that cross-cuts the border between the two countries. Integrared into this power base are their religious schools and military training camps that supply young fighters to the Taliban and Kashmiri mujahideen, the operations of the truck and transport mafias that smuggle consumer goods, narcotics and guns between Pakistan and the central Asian states, the armed gangs that kill members of minority Muslim sects, the terrorists who explode bombs and lauch rockets in the major cities of Pakistan including the federal capital of Islamabad killing innocent civilians and disappear without a trace while the government officials dutifully blame all this to the Indian agents.

To conclude, we have identified some of the major, and no doubt complex, problems that stand in the way of democracy and economic revival in Pakistan. If any credible agenda is to be laid out for restoring the economic and political health of the country these problems will have to be addressed. Otherwise one cannot realistically expect that the latest military regime is going to "clean up the mess" and return the country to democratic governance. As far the concern of Pakistan's Western well-wishers, particularly the United States, for restoration of civilian rule in Pakistan is concerned, it will be well for them to remember that they have been part of the political and economic problems that afflict Pakistan today.

MILITARY MODERNIZATION AND THE FUTURE OF WARFARE IN ASIA

In 1999, the American nuclear strategist Paul Bracken heralded "the second nuclear age" in Asia. Since then, the continuing rise of China has fueled expectations of a shift in the Asian balance of power, and the continent's major powers have added significant new conventional military capabilities. What does this military modernization say about the future of warfare in the region? Below I offer five different ways to look at Asian military modernization.

Five expectations

First, Asian states expect nuclear deterrence to work. India and Pakistan conducted nuclear tests in 1998, and North Korea tested its own device in 2006. Iran has sought nuclear capability at considerable cost to its economy and international position. China has advanced its nuclear warhead design and missile technology. Beijing has acquired a robust ability to launch ballistic missiles from its submarines and is reportedly working on a nuclear-capable cruise missile. In 2013, Pakistan announced its tactical nuclear capability and India is now believed to be working on multiple warhead missiles (MIRV).

The one partial holdout on nuclear deterrence is Japan. Although Tokyo generally eschews nuclear weapons and does not expect nuclear deterrence to be effective vis-à-vis North Korea, it fully expects the American nuclear umbrella to deter China. This anomaly is a consequence of regional politics. North Korea is seen as having a volatile and unpredictable regime, which might attack Japanese cities even at the cost of its own destruction, but military competition with the Chinese is limited to the unpopulated Senkaku/Daiyou Islands. Even the most hawkish Japanese are not concerned about the prospect of Chinese nuclear attacks on Japanese cities. Consequently, the Japanese have sought a limited area, sea-based ballistic missile defense system to identify and destroy North Korean missiles close to launch. Further, the Japanese government has sought legal authority to target North Korean missiles bound for the United States. The Japanese constitution defines self-defense narrowly, prohibiting military action even in cases of attacks against Japanese allies.

Second, Asian states expect their conflicts to remain limited to their particular regional security complexes of East, Southeast, South, and West Asia. The idea of Asia itself is ambiguous. The continent stretches from the Persian Gulf to Japan and Siberia to Indonesia, but practically no government sees these diverse parts of the world in the same frame. Despite the structural changes brought on by globalization and the rise of China, Asia has not become a singular strategic entity. Consequently, balance-of-power calculations in Asia remain generally contained to regions.

Although there have been reports of the long arc of Chinese aggressiveness from the Senkaku Islands to the Bay of Bengal, Chinese military modernization, with the exception of nuclear weapons and delivery, is largely focused on East Asia, and in particular on denying American military influence in the region. China's controversial Air Defense Identification Zone is notably limited to the region. Similarly, Japan remains focused on East Asia, somewhat less interested in South China Sea, and practically not at all interested in Chinese activity in the Bay of Bengal. Vietnam and the Philippines are faced with Chinese aggression in the South China Sea, which has brought the ASEAN states closer, but the region has had difficulty persuading India to become interested in the South China Sea. India has territorial disputes with China, but its security focus has been to the west, on Pakistan. Japan has little interest in the India-China territorial dispute. West Asia remains the most distinct security complex on the continent. Few other Asian states want to become involved in its violence.

Third, Asian states expect war to occur at a distance from population centers—at sea, on unpopulated islands, in mountains and deserts. These conflicts will have economic and symbolic consequences, but their human cost should be significantly lesser than "the people's wars" or "war of the cities" of the past.

With the exception of its dispute with Taiwan, China's territorial conflicts all focus on sparsely populated territory, which shapes Chinese military modernization. The rearmament of the People's Liberation Army Navy (PLAN) outstrips the effort expended on the strategic forces of the Second Artillery Corps. The PLAN has its own air force that is comparable in size and capability to the PLA Air Force. A new aircraft carrier, several new amphibious landing ships and new submarines, and advanced missile and radar technology is expected not only to give China blue water capabilities after 800 years but also to push war away from continental China, after 250 years.

The military invasion of Taiwan by China was the last real possibility of triggering a people's war in East Asia. Not only have relations between the two Chinas improved, but their military balance has also changed. In the 1990s, Taiwanese military officials estimated that they would be able to hold out against an invasion for three months. Recently, a Taiwanese official reported that the holdout time was down to one month, suggesting that the prospect of a Chinese invasion is fading.

The people's wars should continue in parts of South and West Asia, but these conflicts will occur in the form of insurgency, terrorism, and proxy wars. Military modernization efforts in South and West Asia do address subconventional conflicts, but the spending on counterterrorism and counterinsurgency remains significantly less than on advanced conventional weapons, indicating a mismatch between security threats and military preparation. Governments and armed forces expect that preparing for higher intensity conflicts will automatically address lower intensity conflicts, but military power is not always as fungible. The consequence of the mismatch for the future of warfare in South and West Asia is that these conflicts are likely to endure as low-intensity conflicts.

Wars of the cities remain a concern in East Asia to the extent that North Korea poses a threat to South Korean and Japanese cities. War of the cities is also a possibility in West Asia, where it is fueled by regional politics and military asymmetry between competing armed forces. In contrast, South Asia has set a new norm for fighting away from cities. Despite the intensity of their rivalry, India and Pakistan have stayed away from bombing each other's cities in past wars going back to 1965. Pakistan's most vital city, Lahore, is 14 miles from the Indian border, but it has not been attacked since 1947.

Drone warfare represents an opportunity to make war more distant from the population but also decreases the cost of bringing of war back to population centers. Unmanned drones remove human presence from the weapons platform, but in doing so reduce the cost of more dangerous missions, thereby risking greater damage and escalation.

Asian states have been acquiring drones in large numbers, but most appear to be for surveillance rather than lethal use of force. This will change with time, which brings us to the role of technology in Asia's military modernization.

Fourth, Asian states expect conflict to occur away from populations in another way—on the internet and in outer space. In cyberspace, China has developed a sophisticated ability to infiltrate and disrupt foreign computer systems. In space warfare, Beijing is developing the capability to collide ballistic missiles with enemy satellites. Recently, Japan and India have established cyber warfare units as part of their armed forces. Singapore and Australia already have advanced cyber capabilities.

Although cyber and space warfare can cause enormous economic damage and deny military advantage in air, space, and sea—the global commons—to others, they do not yet threaten human life directly. The economic damage caused by cyber and space warfare may lead to reprisals or other second-order consequences that result in human deaths, but the relative non-lethality of cyber and space warfare serves as an interesting new limit on war itself. Cyber and outer space may not remain clearly delineated from the physical world in the future, but Asian states do not seem to be at the cutting edge of developing the kind of technological breakthrough that would blur those lines.

Fifth, Asia's new cyber and space warfare capabilities reflect a strategic preference for deception and denial rather than confrontation and attrition. Apart from nuclear weapons, the navy, and the naval air force, Asian states have focused on advancing their radar and stealth capabilities.

Western military doctrine and equipment has long set the benchmark for mobility and standoff warfare, including the use of technology for deception and denial. Asia's adoption of Western concepts of deception and denial—and military technology in general—demonstrates the lasting influence of Schelling's nuclear brinksmanship tactics of "fighting without fighting" as well as Asia's growing technological and financial capacity.

There are huge disparities among Asian states, in terms of their technological and financial ability. Japan has both, China has financial capacity but limited access to foreign technology, and India has relatively poorer financial ability, but better access to foreign technology. Saudi Arabia has money but not the ability to absorb and integrate technology into its armed forces. Singapore has both resources and great ability to absorb technology, but is limited by its size. These differences determine the deception and denial capabilities of Asian states, suggesting technological and financial determinism, especially when it comes to advanced technology weapons and the future of warfare.

To the extent that technology and financial capability drive further military modernization, Schelling should prove to be right: Asia will have arms races but not outright war and the possibility that accidents could happen would make Asian states exercise greater self-control in war decisions.

2

History of the Pakistan Air Force

The history of the Pakistan Air Force (PAF) began when it was established in 1947 following the independence of Pakistan.

BRITISH ERA

In 1933, the British colonial government established the first Air Force station in the South Asia near Drigh Road, now called PAF Base Faisal in Karachi. In 1934, this element of the Royal Indian Air Force (RIAF) was extended to the north for operations in North-West Frontier Province. The RIAF had also contributed to the defeat of Japanese invasion during World War II.

1947–1950: FORMATIVE YEARS

The Royal Pakistan Air Force (RPAF) was established on 14 August 1947 with the independence of Pakistan from British India. The RPAF began with 2,332 personnel, a fleet of 24 Tempest II fighter-bombers, 16 Hawker Typhoon fighters, two H.P.57 Halifax bombers, 2 Auster aircraft, twelve North American Harvard trainers and ten de Havilland Tiger Moth biplanes. It also got eight C-47 Dakota cargo planes which it used to transport supplies to soldiers fighting in the 1947 War in Kashmir against India. All received allotted at the time of independence of Pakistan from British India. It started with 7 operational airbases scattered all over the provinces.

Operating these inherited aircraft was far from ideal in Pakistan's diverse terrains, deserts and mountains; frequent attrition and injuries did not make the situation any better. However, by 1948 the air force acquired better aircraft such as the Hawker Sea Fury fighter-bomber and the Bristol Freighter. These new aircraft gave a much-needed boost to the morale and combat capability of the Royal Pakistan Air Force; 93 Hawker Fury and roughly 50-70 Bristol Freighter aircraft were inducted into the RPAF by 1950.

1950–1958: THE JET AGE

Although the Royal Pakistan Air Force had little funds to use and markets to choose from, it entered the jet age quite early. Initially it had planned to acquire US-built F-94Cs, F-86s, or F-84s and produce its order in Pakistan. However, lack of funds and strong British pressure persuaded the PAF to acquire the British Supermarine Attacker. The first squadron equipped with these aircraft was the Number-11 "Arrow". The Supermarine Attacker had a rather unsatisfactory service in the Royal Pakistan Air Force with frequent attrition and maintenance problems. The prefix Royal was removed when Pakistan became a republic on 23 March 1956. It has since simply been called the *Pakistan Air Force* (PAF).

In 1957 the Pakistan Air Force received 100 American-built F-86 Sabres under the U.S. aid programme. Squadron after squadron in the PAF retired its Hawker Furys and Supermarine Attackers, and replaced them with F-86 jet fighters. In 1957 thirty-six-year-old Air Marshal Asghar Khan became the Pakistan Air Force's first commander-in-chief.

1959–1964: CONFLICTS WITH INDIA

On 10 April 1959, on the occasion of the Islamic Eid ul-Fitr festival holiday in Pakistan, an Indian Air Force (IAF) English Electric Canberra intruded into Pakistani airspace on a photo reconnaissance mission. Two PAF F-86F Sabres from No. 15 Squadron on Air Defence Alert (ADA) were scrambled from Peshawar Air Base to intercept the IAF intruder. The Sabre pilots were Flt. Lt. M. N. Butt (leader) and Flt. Lt. M. Yunus (wingman)(Later Air Vice Marshal) whereas Pilot Officer Rab Nawaz was the on-duty Air Defence Controller for this mission. Nawaz successfully vectored both Sabres to the location of the high-flying Canberra. Butt attempted to bring down the Canberra by firing his Sabre's machine guns but the Canberra was flying at an altitude of more than 50,000 feet - beyond the operational ceiling of the F-86F. When Yunus took over from his leader, the Canberra suddenly lost height while executing a turn over Rawalpindi. Yunus grabbed this opportunity and fired a burst from his 12.7 mm guns that struck the Canberra at an altitude of 47,500 feet and brought it down over Rawat, near Rawalpindi. Thus, PAF drew 'first blood' against the IAF. '55-5005' was the serial number of the F-86F Sabre that was flown by Flt. Lt. Yunus that day. Both the occupants of the IAF Canberra, namely Sqn. Ldr. J.C. Sen Gupta (pilot) and Flt. Lt. S.N. Rampal (navigator) from the IAF's No. 106 Sqn., ejected and were taken prisoner by Pakistani authorities and were subsequently released after remaining in detention for some time.

1965 INDO-PAKISTAN WAR

Rann of Kutch border skirmish

In June 1965, prior to the outbreak of the 1965 India-Pakistan War, India and Pakistan had a border skirmish in the Rann of Kutch region near the south-eastern coastline of Pakistan. The PAF was tasked with providing point-defence to the Rann of Kutch region to prevent the Indian Air Force (IAF) from intruding into Pakistani airspace and attacking Pakistan Army positions. On 24 June 1965, an IAF Ouragan fighter (Serial No. IC 698), flown by Flt. Lt. Rana Lal Chand Sikka of No. 51 Auxiliary Squadron from the IAF's Jamnagar Air Station intruded into Pakistani airspace. A PAF F-104A Starfighter from No. 9 Squadron intercepted the IAF fighter near Badin in Sindh, Pakistan. Just as the PAF pilot locked on to the Indian fighter and was about to release his AIM-9B Sidewinder Air-to-Air Missile (AAM), the Indian pilot lowered his aircraft's landing gear (an internationally recognized sign of aerial surrender). The IAF pilot landed at an open field near Jangshahi village near Badin. The IAF pilot was taken prisoner and released on 14 August 1965 - as a goodwill gesture on the 18th Anniversary of Pakistan's Independence Day - minus the IAF Ouragan fighter, which was retained by the PAF as a trophy and flown by a PAF pilot to an airbase in Karachi.

Outbreak of war

The PAF fleet at the time consisted of 12 F-104 Starfighters, some 120 F-86 Sabres and around 20 B-57 Canberra bombers. The PAF claims to have had complete air superiority over the battle area from the second day of operations. It is believed that the Indian Army would agree. Close air support to the Pakistan Army was unexpectedly effective and the PAF is widely considered to have single-handedly neutralised the large difference in military strength of India and Pakistan.

Many publications have credited the PAF's successes to U.S. equipment, claiming it to be superior to the aircraft operated by the IAF and giving the PAF a "qualitative advantage". However some people refute this argument. As per them, the IAF's MiG-21, Hawker Hunter and Folland Gnat aircraft had better performance than the PAF's F-86 fighters. According to Air Cdre (retired) Sajad Haider, the F-86 Sabre was inferior in both power and speed to the IAF's Hawker Hunter.

According to Air Commodore (retired) Sajjad Haider who flew with No. 19 squadron, the F-104 Starfighter did not deserve its reputation as "the pride of the PAF" because it "was unsuited to the tactical environment of the region. It was a high-level interceptor designed to neutralise Soviet strategic bombers in altitudes above 40,000 feet." Nevertheless the IAF is believed to have feared the Starfighter although, according to some, it was not as effective as the IAF's Folland Gnat. The F-86F performed reasonably well over IAF's Hawker Hunters but had trouble in dealing with the Gnats, which earned the nickname *Sabre Slayers.*

Post-war sanctions and acquisitions

After the 1965 war the U.S. placed an arms embargo on Pakistan and the PAF was badly affected. Its entire fleet was of U.S. origin and spare parts could not be sourced from the United States.

The PAF began searching for new combat aircraft. China was approached and agreed to supply an initial 72 Shenyang F-6 fighters and it was inducted on 30 December 1965. China also supplied a squadron of Harbin B-5 bombers which the PAF was not satisfied with due to their lack of a modern bomb aiming system. These were later returned to China in exchange for more Shenyang F-6.

In 1968 the PAF's No. 5 Squadron started converting to the Dassault Mirage IIIEP. As the F-6 was a short range air defence fighter, the Mirage III was the PAF's main offensive weapon. Even still, the Mirage was not equipped with modern munitions such as anti-runway bombs for attacking airbases, cluster bombs for attacking armoured formations or anti-ship weapons because such weapons could not be sourced from the U.S. or Europe. The Mirage was also restricted by lack of equipment such as bomb pylons and missile launchers, which meant the Mirage III fleet was limited in terms of weapon configurations.

1971 INDO-PAKISTAN WAR

Build-up to war

In the late 1960s, many East Pakistanis believed that their wing of the country was being exploited economically by West Pakistan. They also saw that the military in East Pakistan was very low in numbers and had seemingly left East Pakistan defence less. An election in 1970 resulted in a win for the Awami League, a popular East Pakistani party. However the governing Pakistan Peoples Party (PPP) refused to allow the Awami League to take over governance of Pakistan. At the time Pakistan was ruled by a military President who did not move to resolve the political conflict, resulting in uprisings springing up in East Pakistan. In March 1971 the government in West Pakistan decided to use military force to quell the uprisings, resulting in a civil war in East Pakistan. India claimed that 10 million refugees had entered its territory, using this as an excuse to assist the East Pakistani rebels and later invade the country to ensure its secession and independence from Pakistan. India's alliance with the Soviet Union ensured full backing of the superpower.

Disparity in equipment and numbers

In December 1971, India and Pakistan went to war over East Pakistan. At the start of the war, the PAF inventory contained around 270 combat aircraft while the IAF had over 1,200 -

outnumbering the PAF 4:1 in West Pakistan and 10:1 in East Pakistan.

At the end of the war, the Indian Air Force claimed it had shot down 94 PAF aircraft, including 54 F-86 Sabres. According to some sources, the overall attrition rate (losses per 100 sorties) was 0.48 for the IAF and 1.42 for the PAF, the PAF flying 2914 combat sorties while the IAF flew 7,346 combat sorties during the conflict.

1972–1979

In 1979, the PAF's Chief of Air Staff, Air Chief Marshal Anwar Shamim, was told by then President, and Chief of Army Staff General Zia ul Haq that Pakistan had reliable information of Indian plans to attack and destroy the Pakistani nuclear research facilities at Kahuta. ACM Shamim told General Zia that Indian aircraft could reach the area in 3 minutes whereas the PAF would take 8 minutes, allowing the Indians to attack the facility and return before the PAF could defend it. Because Kahuta was too close to the Indian border to be effectively defended it was decided that the best way to deter an Indian attack would be to procure new advanced fighters and weaponry. These would be used to mount a retaliatory attack on India's nuclear research facilities at Trombay in the event of an Indian attack on Kahuta. It was decided the most suitable aircraft would be the F-16, which the United States eventually agreed to supply after the PAF refused to buy the F-5E and F-5G. In 1983, when the first batch of F-16s reached Pakistan, ACM Shamim informed Zia of the PAF's capability to respond to an attack on the nuclear research facilities at Kahuta.

1979–1988: SOVIET-AFGHAN WAR

The Soviet invasion of Afghanistan in 1979 in support of the pro-Soviet government in Kabul, which was being hard-pressed by Mujahadeen rebel forces, marked the start of a decade-long occupation. Mujahadeen rebels continued to harass the occupying Soviet military force as well as the forces of the Afghan regime that it was supporting. The war soon spilled over into neighbouring Pakistan, with a horde of refugees fleeing to camps across the border in an attempt to escape the conflict. In addition, many of the rebels used Pakistan as a sanctuary from which to carry out forays into Afghanistan, and a steady flow of US-supplied arms was carried into Afghanistan from staging areas in Pakistan near the border. This inevitably resulted in border violations by Soviet and Afghan aircraft attempting to interdict these operations.

The PAF is believed to have evaluated the Dassault Mirage 2000 in early 1981 and was planning to evaluate the General Dynamics F-16 Fighting Falcon afterwards.

A letter of agreement for up to 28 F-16A and 12 F-16B was signed December 1981. The contracts, *Peace Gate I* and *Peace Gate II*, were for 6 and 34 Block 15 models respectively which would be powered by the F100-PW-200 engine. The fist *Peace Gate I* aircraft was accepted at Fort Worth in October 1982.

Two F-16A and four F-16B were delivered to Pakistan in 1983, the first F-16 arriving at PAF Base Sargodha (now known as PAF Base Mushaf) on 15 January 1983 flown by Squadron Leader Shahid Javed.

The 34 remaining *Peace Gate II* aircraft were delivered between 1983 and 1987. Six F-16A and four F-16B Block 15 OCU models were ordered as attrition replacements in December 1988 under the *Peace Gate III* contract. Another 60 F-16A/B were ordered in September 1989 under *Peace Gate IV*. These were later embargoed.

Between May 1986 and November 1988, PAF F-16s have shot down at least eight intruders from Afghanistan. The first three of these (one Su-22, one probable Su-22, and one An-26) were shot down by two pilots from No. 9 Squadron. Pilots of No. 14 Squadron destroyed the remaining five intruders (two Su-22s, two MiG-23s, and one Su-25). Most of these kills were by the AIM-9 Sidewinder, but at least one (a Su-22) was destroyed by cannon fire. Flight Lieutenant Khalid Mahmood is credited with three of these kills. One F-16 was lost in these battles during an encounter between two F-16s and six Afghan Air Force aircraft on 29 April 1987, stated by the PAF to have been an "own-goal" because it was hit by an AIM-9 Sidewinder fired from the other F-16. The pilot, Flight Lieutenant Shahid Sikandar Khan, ejected safely. Most of these air kills were achieved within Pakistani borders. No.9 Sqn was credited with 3 kills, where as No.14 Sqn was credited with 5 kills.

Project Sabre II was initiated by the PAF in 1987 and was aimed at developing a replacement for the ageing Shenyang F-6 fleet. After a design study by Grumman Aerospace determined it would be to financially risky, it was abandoned by PAF and the Chengdu F-7P was introduced in 1988 to replace the F-6.

1989–2001: SANCTIONS AND THE 'LOST DECADE'

After the Pressler Amendment was passed, the U.S. placed sanctions and an arms embargo on Pakistan on 6 October 1990 due to the country's continued nuclear weapons programme. All eleven *Peace Gate III* F-16s, along with 7 F-16A and 10 F-16B of the 60 *Peace Gate IV* F-16s, which had been built by the end of 1994 were embargoed and put into storage in the United States.

Desperate for a new high-tech combat aircraft, between late 1990 and 1993 the PAF evaluated the European Panavia Tornado MRCA (multi-role combat aircraft) and rejected it.

The Mirage 2000E and an offer from Poland for the supply of MiG-29 and Su-27 were also considered but nothing materialised. In 1992 the PAF again looked at the Mirage 2000, reviving a proposal from the early 1980s to procure around 20-40 aircraft, but again a sale did not occur because France did not want to sell a fully capable version due to political reasons. In August 1994 the PAF was offered the Saab JAS-39 Gripen by Sweden, but again the sale did not occur because 20% of the Gripen's components were from the U.S. and Pakistan was still under U.S. sanctions.

In mid-1992 Pakistan was close to signing a contract for the supply of 40 Dassault Mirage 2000, equipped with Thomson-CSF RDM/7 radars, from France but the deal was never signed. In mid-1994 it was reported that the Russian manufacturers Sukhoi and Mikoyan were offering the Su-27 and MiG-29. But Pakistan was later reported to be negotiating for supply of the Dassault Mirage 2000-5. French and Russian teams visited Pakistan on 27 November 1994 and it was speculated that interest in the Russian aircraft was to pressure France into reducing the price of the Mirage 2000. Stated requirement was for up to 40 aircraft.

In 1996 it was reported that Pakistan was negotiating a $160 million contract for missiles with South Africa, believed to be for the Kentron (now Denel) U-darter imaging-infra-red short range air-to-air missile.

1999 Kargil Conflict

The Pakistan Air Force (PAF) did not see active combat during the low-intensity Kargil Conflict between India and Pakistan during the summer of 1999 but remained on high air defence alert (ADA) and performed F-16 and F-7MP combat air patrols (CAPs) near the eastern border with India. The PAF closely monitored and tracked the IAF's movements near the Line of Control in Kashmir as well as the India-Pakistan international border.

2001–2011: WAR ON TERROR AND 'NEW DAWN'

Counter-insurgency operations

The Pakistan Army faced several problems during its 2009 offensive against the Taliban in north-west Pakistan. Hundreds of thousands of Pakistanis fled the area when the offensive was announced and, eventually, over 2 million had to be accommodated in refugee camps. The offensive was to be completed as quickly as possible to allow the refugees to return to their homes but the army's fleet attack helicopters were not sufficient to provide adequate support to the infantry. The PAF was sent into action against the Taliban to make up for the lack of helicopter gunships. Because the PAF was trained and equipped to fight a conventional war, a new "counter-terrorist doctrine" had to be improvised.

The PAF's *Saffron Bandit 2009/2010* exercise focused on extensive training of combat personnel to undertake COIN operations. New equipment was inducted to improve the PAF's joint intelligence, surveillance and reconnaissance (ISR) capabilities. A C-130 transport aircraft was indigenously modified for day/night ISR operations.

The PAF had been forced to use Google Earth for reconnaissance imagery until high resolution infra-red sensors were provided by the U.S. prior to the army's 2009 campaign in the Swat valley. These were installed on around 10 of the PAF's F-16 fighters and used to gather detailed reconnaissance imagery of the entire valley. Use of laser-guided bombs was increased to

80% of munitions used, as compared to 40% in the previous 2008 Bajaur campaign. A small corps of ground spotters were trained and used by the PAF, in addition to PA spotters, to identify high value targets.

Prior to the PA's offensive into South Waziristan the PAF attacked militant infrastructure with 500 lb and 2000 lb bombs.

After the Mumbai attacks and threats made by India PAF was put on high alert. Pakistani press reported an outstanding order to launch a counterattack in case of an air attack from India after Indian Foreign Minister Pranab Mukharjee threatened Pakistani President in rough tone. On the morning of 14 December Indian aircraft started moving towards Pakistan,PAF moved swiftly and intercepted them before they entered international borders. Two of the aircraft did cross the border but Indian aircraft managed to turn back. PAF was ordered to carry on the defensive combat patrols but avoid hostile action unless further hostile action was to take place.

A number of civilian deaths occurred during PAF air strikes on 10 April 2010 in the Khyber tribal region. According to a Pakistani military source, the first bombing was targeted at a gathering of militants in a compound. Local people, who had quickly moved onto the scene to recover the dead and wounded, were then killed during a second air strike. There was no confirmed death toll but at least 30 civilian deaths had occurred according to the military source, whereas a local official stated at least 73 locals, including women and children, were killed. A six-member committee of tribal elders from the area, tasked with finding the exact number of civilian casualties, reported that 61 civilians were killed and 21 wounded. This was not confirmed by military or political leaders but Pakistan's Chief of Army Staff, General Ashfaq Kayani, gave a public apology on 17 April. It is reported that BBC news and several other media correspondences were not allowed to take interviews from injured which makes the whole episode more mysterious.

On 22 May 2011 it was reported that the PAF had retaliated against attacks by Afghan mortar and machine gun positions on the Pakistani posts at Miskinai and Sangpura in the Bajaur area.

It was stated that since 19 May, around 1000 Afghan Askaris had entered the Bajaur area at Sahi as well as Miskinai and Sankpura. The Afghan forces had been firing at the posts during night and, after reconnaissance sorties, PAF aircraft destroyed the Afghan positions.

Modernisation and acquisitions

In light of Pakistan's significant contribution to the War on Terror, the United States and Western European countries, namely Germany and France, lifted their defense related sanctions on Pakistan; enabling the country to once again seek advanced Western military hardware. Since the lifting of sanctions, the Pakistan Air Force (PAF) became heavily active in evaluating potential military hardware such as new fighter aircraft, radars and land based air-defense systems. However the urgent relief needed in Kashmir after the 2005 Kashmir earthquake forced the Pakistani military to stall its modernisation programme so it could divert its resources for fuel and operations during the rescue efforts.

The modernisation stall would end in April 2006 when the Pakistani cabinet approved the PAF's proposals to procure new aircraft and systems from several sources, including modern combat aircraft from the U.S. and China. The AFFDP 2019 (Armed Forces Development Programme 2019) would oversee the modernisation of the Pakistan Air Force from 2006 to 2019.

The Bush administration on 24 July 2008 informed the US Congress it plans to shift nearly $230 million of $300 million in aid from counterterrorism programs to upgrading Pakistan's aging F-16s. The Bush administration previously announced on 27 June 2008 it was proposing to sell Pakistan ITT Corporation's electronic warfare gear valued at up to $75 million to enhance Islamabad's existing F-16s. Pakistan has asked about buying as many as 21 AN/ALQ-211(V)9 Advanced Integrated Defensive Electronic Warfare Suite pods, or AIDEWS, and related equipment. The proposed sale will ensure that the existing fleet is "compatible" with new F-16 Block 50/52 fighters being purchased by Islamabad.

After the September 11 attacks in 2001, the U.S. and Pakistan began discussing the release of the embargoed F-16s and a purchase of new aircraft. Of the 28 F-16A/B built under the *Peace Gate III/*

IV contracts and embargoed in 1990, 14 delivered as EDA (Excess Defense Articles) from 2005 to 2008., two of which were delivered on 10 July 2007.

Between 2005 and 2008, 14 F-16A/B Block 15 OCU fighters were delivered to the PAF under renewed post-9/11 ties between the U.S. and Pakistan. These had originally been built for Pakistan under the Peace Gate III/IV contracts but were never delivered due to the U.S. arms embargo imposed in 1990.

To upgrade the F-16A/B fleet, 32 Falcon STAR kits were purchased for the original *Peace Gate I* aircraft and 35 Mid-Life Update (MLU) kits were ordered, with 11 more MLU kits optional, in . 4 F-16A/B being upgraded in the U.S. to F-16AM/BM, delivery expected December 2011. F-16A/B in PAF service to be upgraded starting October 2010 by Turkish Aerospace Industries, 1 per month.

The *Peace Drive I* contract for 12 F-16C and 6 F-16D Block 52+ (Advanced Block 52) aircraft, powered by F100-PW-229 engines was signed on 30 September 2006. The first F-16 to be completed, an F-16D, was rolled out on 13 October 2009 and began flight testing. The first batch of F-16C/D Block 52+, two F-16D and one F-16C, landed at PAF Base Shahbaz, Jacobabad, on 26 June 2010 and one more F-16C was received by 5 July 2010.

On 19 May 2006 the PAF inaugurated a refurbished Sector Operations Centre at PAF Base Mushaf (Sargodha) which had been installed with a Pakistani-developed air defence automation system for command and control. An old air defence system installed in the 1980s was replaced.

During talks with a delegation from the French Senate on Monday 28 September 2009, Prime Minister Yousuf Raza Gilani stated that the PAF had used most of its stockpile of laser-guided munitions against militants in the Malakand and FATA regions and that replacements for such types of equipment were urgently required.

In December 2009 the PAF's first Saab 2000 Erieye AEW&C was delivered from Sweden and Il-78MP Midas aerial refuelling tanker/military transport aircraft from Ukraine.

The PAF is reported to be considering purchasing the Hongdu L-15 advanced jet trainer to train pilots for high-tech fighters such as the FC-20. Extensive evaluations of the aircraft took place in Pakistan during December 2009.

On 26 June 2010 the first batch of 3 F-16C/D Block 52+ fighters were delivered to PAF Base Shahbaz, Jacobabad. According to Air Chief Marshal Rao Qamar Suleman the new fighters would eliminate the PAF's limitations in precision night-time strike operations, the existing capability being based on around 34 Dassault Mirage 5 fighters upgraded with new avionics for night-time precision strike missions under the Retrofit Of Strike Element (ROSE) programme during 1999-2004.

It was reported in 2010 that the R-Darter, an active radar homing beyond visual range air-to-air missile, is being operated by the Pakistan Air Force.

2008 air alert

On 13 December 2008, the Government of Pakistan stated that two Indian Air Force aircraft were intercepted by the PAF kilometres within Pakistani airspace. This charge was denied by the Indian government.

Introduction of female engineers and pilots

Previously, women had been employed by Pakistan's armed forces in non-combat roles only, such as the medical corps, and the PAF had remained all-male throughout its history. However, in 2003 women were allowed to enroll in the aerospace engineering and other programs of PAF Academy Risalpur, including fighter pilot training programmes. It was stated that standards would not be compromised for women and those who did not achieve the same performance as their male counterparts would be dropped from the course. A level of segregation between the genders is maintained. For example, early-morning parades are performed together but some parts of training, mainly physical exercises, are done with males and females separated. According to Squadron Leader Shazia Ahmed, the officer in charge of the first female cadets and a psychologist, this also improves confidence of the women.

In 2005 it was reported that two batches in the Air Force Academy's flying wing contained 10 women, with many more in the engineering and aerospace wings. Cadet Saba Khan, from Quetta in Balochistan, applied after reading a newspaper advertisement seeking female cadets. She was one of the first four women to pass the first stages of flying training on propeller-driven light aircraft and move onto faster jet-powered training aircraft.

In March 2006, the PAF inducted a batch of 34 fighter pilots which included the organisation's first four female fighter pilots. Three years of training had been completed by the pilots at PAF Academy Risalpur before they graduated and were awarded their Flying Badges during the ceremony. Certificates of honour were handed to the successful cadets by a "delighted" General Ahsan Saleem Hayat, vice chief of the Pakistan Army, who acknowledged that the PAF was the first of the Pakistani armed forces to introduce women to its combat units. One of the women, Flying Officer Nadia Gul, was awarded a trophy for best academic achievement. The other female graduates were Mariam Khalil, Saira Batool and the above-mentioned Saba Khan. A second batch of pilots, including 3 female pilots, graduated from the 117th GD(P) course at PAF Academy Risalpur in September 2006. The Sword of Honour for best all-round performance was awarded to Aviation Cadet Saira Amin, the first female pilot to win the award. Aviation Cadet Saira Amin won the Asghar Hussain Trophy for best performance in academics. In September 2009 it was reported that seven women had qualified as operational fighter pilots on the Chengdu F-7, the first female combat pilots in the PAF's history, one of them being Ambreen Gull. Commanding Officer Tanvir Piracha emphasised that if the female pilots "are not good enough as per their male counterparts, we don't let them fly." It was noted that some of the female pilots wear the hijab while others do not.

Exercises

In September 2004 a PAF contingent of six F-16A/B arrived in Turkey to take part in the international Anatolian Eagle 2004 exercise. As well as the Turkish Air Force, the air forces of Germany, Holland, Italy and the United States also participated.

After around a year of planning, in 2005 the PAF launched the High Mark 2005 exercise which lasted for one month and also involved the Pakistan Army and Pakistan Navy. In the scenario, two opposing forces, Blueland and Foxland, engaged in simulated combat involving both offensive and defensive operations. All of the PAF's resources, including aircraft, avionics, weapons systems and ground based radars were involved. It was stated that the exercise would have three stages and PAF aircraft would fly 8200 sorties.

The exercise would take place right across Pakistan, from the northern areas of Skardu and Gilgit to the central and southern areas including the Arabian Sea. The exercise was designed to validate the PAF's operational concepts and would be used to further improve the PAF's training regimes and future force employment concepts. The PAF's F-16 fighters would fly in offensive and defensive air superiority roles, with F-7P/PG providing air defence. The Mirage 3/5 was to be used in the strike role and the A-5C would provide air support to the army units involved. Involvement of army and navy units was aimed at providing more realistic operational scenarios. High Mark 2005 followed the Tempest-1 exercise which was focused purely on air power but differed in terms of duration, intensity and complexity of air operations.

A PAF contingent of six F-16A/B fighters was sent to the international Anatolian Eagle 2006 exercise, which also involved the U.S. and Israeli as well as the Turkish air forces. Operation Indus Viper 2008, a joint exercise involving PAF and the Turkish Air Force, began on 21 April 2008 at PAF Base Mushaf (Sargodha) and was scheduled to last 10 days. Five Turkish F-16C/D fighters and 50 personnel of 191 *Kobras* Filo (191 *Cobras* Squadron) attended.

In the summer of 2005 a PAF team of 20 airmen, including pilots, navigators, engineers, maintenance technicians and a C-130E was sent to the U.S. to take part in the AMC (Air Mobility Command) Rodeo. The team, lead by Wing Commander Akbar Shoaib, was expected to score well in the paratrooping, spot landing and short-field landing events. The PAF later took part in the July 2007 AMC Rodeo.

In 2009, while undertaking combat operations against militants in FATA and Swat, the PAF initiated the Saffron Bandit exercise with the aim of training the PAF's entire combat force to undertake such anti-terrorist operations.

In December 2009 the PAF sent six Chengdu F-7PG fighters, of No. 31 Wing based at PAF Base Samungli, to the United Arab Emirates to take part in the Air Tactics Leadership Course (ATLC) at Al Dhafra Air Base. Al Dhafra Air Base hosts Dassault Mirage 2000-9 and F-16E/F Block 60 fighters of the UAEAF. Also participating were six F-16s of the Jordanian No. 1 Squadron, six Dassault Rafales of the AdlA, six Eurofighter Typhoons of the Royal Air Force No. 3 Squadron and six F-16CJ Block 52 fighters of the USAF 169th Fighter Wing. Six F-22A fighters of the USAF 1st Fighter Wing also flew training sorties with some of the air forces at Al Dhafra but did not take part in the main exercise. The U.S. units called the exercise *Operation Iron Falcon*. Most of the participants took turns flying as *Red Air* and were described by a USAF F-16 pilot as being "very competent" and posing "significant tactical problems to solve."

The PAF's *High Mark 2010* exercise was launched on 15 March 2010, the first time a *High Mark* exercise had been conducted since 2005, after all PAF received their Air Tasking Orders (ATO). The country-wide exercise involved units based all over Pakistan, from Skardu to the Arabian Sea, at all Main Operating Bases and Forward Operating Bases. Joint operations involving the Pakistan Army and Pakistan Navy were also conducted, aiming to test and improve integration and cooperation between the three arms. Operations emphasised a near-realistic simulation of the war-time environment, exposure of PAF aircrews to contemporary concepts of air combat, new employment concepts and joint operations between air force, army and navy. New inductions such as the JF-17 Thunder fighter, Saab 2000 Erieye AEW&C and Il-78 Multi-Role Tanker Transports also took part.

On 6 April 2010 the end of the first phase of exercise *High Mark 2010* was celebrated with a firepower demonstration at the PAF's firing range facility in the deserts of Thal. The 90-minute demo began with a sonic boom from a Mirage fighter flying past at supersonic speed, followed by various PAF combat aircraft attacking targets with a wide range of live weaponry. The newly inducted JF-17 Thunder was shown hitting targets with bombs and the new Saab 2000 Erieye AEW&C and Il-78 MRTT were also displayed to the public for the first time during the demo. The Il-78 performed an in-flight refuelling operation with two Mirage fighters. The H-2 SOW (Stand-Off Weapon) was also shown to the public for the first time, being launched from around 60 km away before hitting its target.

The demo also involved a mock counter-insurgency operation with troops raiding a compound, a search-and-relief operation, an air-drop of heavy equipment by transport planes and the use of unmanned aerial vehicles. The demo heralded the beginning of High Mark 2010's second phase where the PAF would practice joint operations with the Pakistan Army during the army's exercise *Azm-e-Nau-3* (New Resolve 3).

During *High Mark 2010* a Chengdu F-7 and Mirage 5 fighter (flown by Squadron Leader Nasir Mehmood and Wing Commander Atta ur Rehman respectively) practised landing, refuelling and take-off operations from a Pakistani motorway. It was reported that the PAF is in negotiations with the Ministry of Communications to set up all required facilities for Air Force operations on the motorways and highways of Pakistan.

In July 2010 the PAF sent six F-16B fighters of No. 9 *Griffins* Squadron and 100 PAF personnel to Nellis Air Force Base in the U.S. to participate in the international Red Flag exercise for the first time. During the exercise the PAF pilots practised in-flight refuelling of their F-16s with the KC-135 Stratotanker.

In October 2010 the PAF's No. 7 *Bandits* Squadron sent a team of its Dassault Mirage III ROSE fighters to Jordan to participate in the Falcon Air Meet 2010 exercise. The event took place at Azraq Royal Jordanian Air Base and involved teams from the U.S. Air Force, U.S. Navy and the United Arab Emirates as well as the Royal Jordanian Air Force.

In January 2011 a PAF contingent of F-16A/B and Dassault Mirage fighters took part in the Al-Saqoor II exercise in Saudi Arabia with the Royal Saudi Air Force. The exercise lasted from 6 January to 19 January 2011 and the PAF Chief of Air Staff, ACM Rao Qamar Suleman, also flew during the exercise.

In March 2011 a joint Sino-Pakistani exercise, Shaheen 1, was conducted involving a contingent of Chinese aircraft and personnel from the PLAAF. Information on which aircraft were used by each side in the exercise was not released, but photos of Pakistani pilots inspecting what appeared to be Chinese Shenyang J-11B fighters were released on the internet. The exercise lasted for around 4 weeks and was the first time the PLAAF had deployed to and conducted "operational" aerial maneuvers in Pakistan with the PAF.

3

Historical Background of Pakistan Army

The Pakistan Army is the land-based service branch of the Pakistan Armed Forces. It came into existence after the independence of Pakistan in 1947. The Pakistan Army is a volunteer professional fighting force. According to the International Institute for Strategic Studies (IISS) it had an active force of 642,892 personnel as of 2012. In addition there were around 500,000 reserves bringing the total available troops to 1,142,000. The Constitution of Pakistan contains a provision for conscription for times of possible need, but it has never been imposed.

Since its establishment in 1947, the Army (along with its inter–services: the Navy, the Marines and the Air Force) has been involved in three wars with neighbouring India and several border skirmishes with Afghanistan. Since 1947, it has also maintained a strong presence along with its inter-services in the Arab states during the past Arab-Israeli Wars, and aided the coalition in the first Gulf War. Recently, major joint-operations undertaken by the Army include Operation Toar-e-Tander (Black Thunderstorm) and Operation Rah-e-Nijat (Path to Salvation). Apart from conflicts, the Army has been an active participant in United Nations peacekeeping missions, including playing a major role in rescuing trapped US soldiers in Operation Gothic Serpent in 1993. Under Article 243 of the Constitution of Pakistan, the President is appointed the civilian Commander-in-Chief. The Chief of Army Staff (COAS), by statute a four-star general, is appointed by the

President with the consultation and confirmation needed from the Prime Minister. The Pakistan Army is currently commanded by General Raheel Sharif.

BACKGROUND OF PAKISTAN ARMY

Brian Cloughley's book on the Pakistan Army is a welcome addition to the extremely limited number of books on the Pakistan Army. The fact that such a book was not written by a Pakistani soldier or a civilian scholar does not paint a very bright picture about the state of history writing,or to be more specific military history writing in Pakistan. Brian Cloughley has the singular advantage of having served for a relatively long period in Pakistan as a UN Official and as a military attache. In addition he is also a soldier and thus his perception of military affairs is different from a scholar who is a civilian and thus suffers from certain limitations which can only be overcome by extraordinary analytical ability and painstaking hard research. Brian Cloughley has made an honest attempt to present things as they are or as he percieved them to be with whatever facts he could lay hands to and the result is a relatively significant work on Pakistani military history with reference to on ground military performance of the Pakistan Army in three Indo Pak wars.

On the whole Cloughley's account is fairly balanced and the layman reader can form a fairly continuous picture of the progress of the Pakistan Army from 1947 to date. The initial history of the Pakistan Army however is given a broad brush treatment and the British Indian Colonial social and military legacy is totally ignored. This leaves the reader with an impression that the Pakistan Army was an entity created in 1947 and all that it did from 1947 onwards had little connection with the pre 1947 British Colonial policy and the military experience of the Indian Army in the two world wars. The 1947-48 Kashmir War where the Pakistan Army got its baptism of fire as the independent army of a sovereign country is hardly discussed. Thus important military controversies like the Operation Venus Controversy etc are not discussed at all. The conduct of Kashmir War by the Pakistani civilian leadership and its resultant impact on the army's perception of the civilian leadership is not discussed. The British recruitment policy and their irrational advocacy of the "Martial Races Theory" is not discussed at all. The impact of the conservative British military heritage on the intellectual development of the post 1947 Pakistani military leadership is totally ignored. The Ayub period has been given a relatively more detailed treatment and the conduct of 1965 war is reasonably detailed and the analysis of military operations is objective, critical and thought provoking. No serious effort is however made to explain why the Pakistan Army failed to achieve any decisive breakthrough despite having technically superior equipment as well as numerical superiority in tanks. The 1971 war which was more of a one sided show and a war in which Indian victory in the Eastern Theatre in words of Field Marshal Mankekshaw was a "foregone conclusion" keeping in view the overwhelming Indian numerical superiority ,has been discussed in much greater detail than 1965 war. This is a serious draw back since 1965 deserved more space because it had more lessons keeping in view the fact that both sides employed their strategic reserves. The post 1971 history of the army has been given a better treatment and enables the layman reader to understand many aspects of the present state of confrontation in the Sub Continent.

There are many factual and analytical errors in the book which were entirely avoidable and were not beyond the author or the publishers control. The publisher shares a major responsibility in ensuring accuracy of facts while analytical errors or analytical drawbacks are more within an authors sphere of responsibility. Lancers was not raised in 1948-50 but in 1955. Iskandar Mirza was not from the ICS (Indian Civil Service) but the Indian Political Service. The author has asserted that Ayub Khan was "gallant in combat" but there is no record of it in terms of gallantry awards or mention in despatches.On the contrary Ayub was accused of tactical timidity in Burma. Akhnur has been mentioned as the only road link to Kashmir whereas Akhnur ,as a matter of fact was the only road link to Poonch Valley only. The Indian 50 Para Brigade was not moved on 7th September to relieve the 54 Brigade as asserted on page-87 but made its appearance in the 15 Division area only on 10th September and that too in the Hudiara Drain area. On page-96 the author states that 13 Dogra in 4 Indian Mountain Division area captured Bedian but was driven out by

7 Punjab's counter attack the next day. In reality 13 Dogra never attacked Bedian ,nor was Bedian defended by 7 Punjab. Bedian was defended by 7 Baluch and attacked by 17 Rajput. Further Bedian was not attacked by a unit from the 4 Mountain Division but by a unit of 7 Indian Division which failed to capture it in the first place. Jassar was not defended by a Pakistani Tank Troop as written on page-110 but by the whole 33 Tank Delivery Unit. The Jassar operation did not result in release of a whole Indian tank regiment but release of two infantry battalions and a squadron minus 10.4 FF was not part of 6 Armoured Division as stated on page-117. The whole "Order of Battle" of the Pakistan Army on the Western Front as given on page-225 is incorrect. Formations of the I Corps have thus been shown as formations of 11 Corps and vice versa. Armoured Brigade which was a part of 1 Corps has been shown as part of 4 Corps.

Rahimuddin Khan has been promoted to Zia's son in law on page-275 whereas Ejaz ul Haq was Rahim's son in law. Aziz Ahmad the famous civil servant has been described as Aziz Ali. The order of battle of the Pakistan Army on page-284 has also some factual errors;eg Pakistan Army does not have any mechanised infantry divisions whereas the author has shown two divisions as mechanised divisions. One tank unit allotted to Pakistan in 1947 ie the 19 Lancers has not been listed at all in the list of armoured units allotted to Pakistan.

The author rightly wonders why some military commanders guilty of timidity in Khem Karan were not immediately sacked! But he fails to mention that one of them was promoted to the rank of major general few years after the war. His analysis of the Khem Karan operations is considerably thought provoking. But the major reason for failure of the Khem Karan offensive ie poor initial planning which led to traffic congestion and poor engineers effort and delayed the concentration of the Pakistani 1st Armoured Division has not been discussed at all. The author however rightly points out that failure to carry out thorough reconnaissance was one of the major reasons of failure of the Pakistani armoured thrusts failure in Khem Karan. However his assertion that the Indians had considerable reserves to contain Pakistan Army even if it had achieved a breakthrough is not based on material facts. India did have its 23 Mountain Division, but this formation was nowhere near Khem Karan when the Pakistani offensive was launched. In any case a Mountain Infantry division could have been of little value against the Pakistani 1 Armoured Division.

The analysis of the tank battles in Sialkot is not comprehensive and lacks depth. The authors assertion on page-120 that the ad hoc force under direct command of the I Pakistani Corps forced the Indians back to the border is not correct. The 24 Brigade which did so was a part of the 15 Division and 25 Cavalry the tank unit which in the words of Indians stopped them acted on orders of its commanding officer alone and 1 Corps Headquarter had little idea of what 25 Cavalry did in stopping the Indians till the evening of 8th September. The author has not mentioned 25 Cavalry at all which in words of the Indian Armoured Corps's historian; was the unit whose " performance was certainly creditable because it alone stood between the Indian 1st Armoured Division and its objective, the MRL Canal 11a" and stopped the 1st Indian Armoured Division on 8th September, all by itself. The authors reproduction of the Indian writer Verghese's views that the Indian 1st Armoured Division dashed forward rashly is not based on facts. The Indian advance was fairly balanced and it was halted on 8th September not because the Indians had completely committed their armour but because the Commander 1st Armoured Brigade lost his nerve because of false and unsubstantiated reports of his flanks being under counter attack at a time when both the advancing Indian tank regiments had committed a total of only three squadrons with three squadrons uncommitted and the Indian 1st Armoured Division had a third tank regiment totally fresh and in a position to easily outflank the Pakistani armour in Gadgor area. The author has also not discussed at all the Indian armours total lack of activity on 9th and 10th September. This inactivity at a time when there was just one tank regiment to oppose five Indian tank regiments was the main reason for the Indian main attack's failure in Sialkot Sector.

The treatment of the 1971 war is far more detailed than 1965 war. All the emphasis is however on the Eastern Theatre where the Indian victory in words of the Indian Chief was a foregone conclusion. The author has highlighted actions of bravery at small unit level and has shown that the Pakistan Army put up a good show in East Pakistan as far as the junior leadership was concerned. The battles on the Western Theatre have however been largely ignored and the battle of Chhamb which was described by the Indians as "the most serious reverse suffered in the 1971 war 13" has not been discussed in much detail. Major General Eftikhar was the finest commander at the operational level as far as the Pakistan Army is conerned and any history of Pakistan Army is incomplete without discussing Eftikhar's brilliant opearational leadership in Chhamb. Eftikhar was one of the only two Pakistani senior commanders praised by the Indian military historians. One Indian military historian described him as one who "showed skill and determination in carrying out his mission".

The analysis of the Bhutto period is quite comprehensive and the personality of Mr Bhutto and his attitude towards the army has been described quite correctly. The sycophantic persoanlity of Zia has however been given a generous treatment and many of Zia's well known antics to please Mr Bhutto like orders to all officers of Multan Garrison to line up their wives to greet Mr Bhutto's cavalcade passing through the Fort Colony have not been discussed at all.

The intelligence and operational failure in Siachen on part of the ISI and the formation responsible for the defence of Siachen as a result of which the Indians were able to infiltrate 35 miles inside Pakistani territory have not been discussed at all. On the contary General Pirdad who was the formation commander during the Siachen debacle has been praised as an admirable officer. The authors assertion that English language was neglected during the Zia era is not based on facts. I was a cadet in Zia's tenure at the Pakistan Military Academy. Any cadet who failed in English was not promoted to the next term and English teaching and examination standards were very tough. The crux of the problem was the overall deteriorating English standards in Pakistan following Bhuttos nationalisation of educational institutuins and the relatively poor material joining the army in the post 1971 era.

The post Zia era has been covered in a very incisive manner. The authors assertion that the "Director infantry" was a post that any infantry officer would welcome is incorrect. Mahor General Zahir Ul Islam Abbasi was posted as Director Infantry following a diasastorous Charge of the light Brigade type attack in Siachen which he had ordered without prior approval of his next senior operational headquarter. in which one of the Pakistani units suffered unnecesarily high casualties including the death of a brigade commander. The authors criticism of the ISI is forthright, accurate and thought provoking. In this regard he has shown courage in criticising a top heavy agency whose much trumpeted reputaion is not matched by actual on ground performance and which suffers from a tendency to embark on private wars.

Brian Cloughley has done a remarkable job in writing a fairly critical history of the Pakistan Army. Most of the factual errors were avoidable but something which should have been taken care of by the publishers who knew that the author was a foreigner and did not have the time to cross check or recheck all the facts because of not permanently residing in Pakistan. The author appears to be too much of a gentleman to critically analyse many of the Quixotic blunders of Indo Pak military history. Nevertheless Brian Cloughley's book has filled a void in Indo Pak military history by at least constructing a continuous and fairly comprehensive picture of one of third worlds important armies. Regardless of the fact whether any one may agree or disagree with Cloghley's analysios, the book by and large retains the position of a book which is compulsory for any layman or foreigner doing research on the Pakistan Army.

MISSION

Chapter 2 of PART XII of the Constitution of Pakistan defines the purpose of the Army along with the other parts of the Armed Forces as:

"The Armed Forces shall, under the directions of the Federal Government, defend Pakistan against external aggression or threat of war, and, subject to law, act in aid of civil power when called upon to do so. "

HISTORY

1947–1958

The Pakistan Army was created on the 30th of June of the year 1947 from the division of the British Indian Army. The then soon to be created Dominion of Pakistan received six armoured, eight artillery and eight infantry regiments compared to the twelve armoured, fourty artillery and twenty one infantry regiments that went to India. Fearing that India would take over the state of Kashmir, irregulars, scouts and tribal groups entered the Muslim majority state of Kashmir to oppose the Maharaja of Kashmir 1947. In response to this, the Maharaja acceded to India. The Indian Armed Forces were then deployed to Kashmir. This led to the Indo-Pakistani War of 1947. Regular Army units joined the invasion later on but were stopped after the refusal of the Chief of Army Staff, British officer General Sir Frank Messervy, to obey Pakistani leader Muhammed Ali Jinnah's orders to move the Army into Kashmir. A ceasefire followed on UN intervention with Pakistan occupying the northwestern part of Kashmir and India occupying the rest. Later, during the 1950s, the Pakistan Army received large amounts of economic and military aid from the United States and Great Britain after signing two mutual defence treaties, the Baghdad Pact, which led to the formation of the Central Treaty Organization (CENTO), and the Southeast Asia Treaty Organization (SEATO) in 1954. This aid greatly expanded the Pakistan Army from its modest beginnings.

1958–1969

The Pakistan Army took over from politicians for the first time when General Ayub Khan came to power through a bloodless coup in 1958. He formed Convention Muslim League which included Zulfikar Ali Bhutto, who would later become Pakistan's first democratically elected Prime Minister. Tensions with India flared in the 1960s and a brief border skirmish was fought near the Rann of Kutch area during April 1965. The War began after the failure of Operation Gibraltar on 5 August 1965. On the night of 6 September 1965, the Indian Army opened the war front to the Province of Punjab of Pakistan, The Indian Army almost reached near the Pakistani city of Lahore, but the Pakistan Army eventually managed to halt the Indian military advance. The War eventually ended with a United Nations (UN) backed ceasefire and was followed by the Tashkent Declaration. According to the Library of Congress Country Studies conducted by the Federal Research Division of the United States, the War was mostly inconclusive militarily. Each side held prisoners and some territory belonging to the other.

The Pakistan Army considers itself to have achieved a victory because its main aim was to defend Lahore and its other territories against a surprise declaration of war by India in which it succeeded. Although, Pakistan failed in gaining all of Kashmir, there was highly effective support from the Pakistan Air Force (PAF) which was unexpected and often considered to have neutralized India's advantage in quantity of forces to a great extent. The accurate artillery fire provided by the Pakistan Army artillery units is also stated to have played a significant role.

An uprising against General Ayub Khan during 1968 and 1969 resulted in Ayub Khan relinquishing his office as President and Commander-in-Chief of the Army in favour of General Yahya Khan, who assumed power in 1969. The 16th Division, 18th Division and the 23rd Division were raised at some point between 1966 and 1969 and the 9th Division was also re-raised during this period.

1969–1971

During the rule of Yahya Khan, the people of East Pakistan protested against various political and economic disparities that had been imposed on them by West Pakistan and massive civil unrest broke out in East Pakistan. During operations against these rebels which was called Operation Searchlight, some factions of the Pakistan Army were responsible for the 1971 Bangladesh atrocities. Beginning with the start of Operation Searchlight on 25 March 1971 and due to the Bangladesh Liberation War, there were numerous human rights abuses in East Pakistan (now Bangladesh) perpetrated by the Pakistan Army, with support from local political and religious militias, especially against Hindus. *Time* reported a high ranking US official as saying "It is the most incredible, calculated thing since the days of the Nazis in Poland."

The original plan envisioned taking control of the major cities on 26 March 1971, and then eliminating all opposition, political or military, within one month. The prolonged Bengali resistance was not anticipated by Pakistani planners. The main phase of Operation Searchlight ended with the fall of the last major town in Bengali hands in the mid of May.

Soon heavy fighting broke out between the Pakistan Army and the Indian-backed Bengali rebels. In this period the Pakistan Army killed an estimate ranging from 26, 000 to as many 3 million people. In December 1971, Pakistan attacked India's western air bases, in an attempt to thwart Indian support for the rebels. This officially led to start of the Pakistan India War of 1971 (also called the Bangladesh Liberation War). In the eastern theatre, the Pakistan Army was decimated by the Indian Army and rebels, while in the western front the Pakistan Army was defeated in the battles of Basanter and Longewalla.

On 16 December 1971, Lt. General Amir Abdullah Khan Niazi, CO of Pakistan Army forces located in East Pakistan signed the Instrument of Surrender. Over 93,000 Pakistani personnel surrendered to the joint Indian and Bengali forces making it the largest surrender since World War II.

In 1997 R. J. Rummel published a book, available on the web, called "Statistics of Democide: Genocide and Mass Murder Since 1900", In Chapter 8 called "Statistics Of Pakistan's Democide Estimates, Calculations, And Sources" he looks at the 1971 Bangladesh Liberation War. Rummel wrote:

In East Pakistan (now Bangladesh) [the President of Pakistan, General Agha Mohammed Yahya Khan, and his top generals also planned to murder its Bengali intellectual, cultural, and political elite. They also planned to indiscriminately murder hundreds of thousands of its Hindus and drive the rest into India. And they planned to destroy its economic base to insure that it would be subordinate to West Pakistan for at least a generation to come. This plan may be perceived as genocide.

According to Maj. (Retd.) Agha Humayun Amin, the Pakistan Army commanders had not seriously considered an Indian invasion of East Pakistan until December 1971, because it was presumed that the Indian military would not risk intervention by China or the United States (US), who were generally close Pakistani allies. Maj Mazhar states that the Pakistan Army's senior command failed to realize that the Chinese would be unable to intervene during the winter months of November to December, due to snowbound Himalayan passes, and the US had not made any real effort to persuade India against attacking East Pakistan.

1971–1977

A Pakistan International Airlines (PIA) flight was sent to fetch Zulfikar Ali Bhutto from New York, who at that time was presenting Pakistan's case before the United Nations Security Council (UNSC) on the East Pakistan crisis. Bhutto returned home on 18 December 1971. On 20 December, he was taken to the President House in Rawalpindi where he took over two positions from Yahya Khan, one as President and the other as Chief Martial Law Administrator. Thus, he was the first civilian Chief Martial Law Administrator of Pakistan.

1977–1999

In 1977, a coup, Operation Fair Play, was staged by General Zia ul-Haq and the government was overthrown. This led to the hanging of Bhutto after he was tried and proclaimed guilty of conspiracy of murdering a political opponent by Zia's handpicked judges. Zia retracted on his promise of holding elections within 90 days and ruled as a military dictator until his death in an air crash in 1988. General Mohammad Iqbal Khan served as a joint chief from 1980 to 1984 and was the Chief Martial Law Officer during that time.

In mid-1970s, the Pakistan Army was involved in fighting an uprising in the Province of Balochistan. Various Baloch factions wanted independence or at least greater provincial rights. The rebellion was put down on the behest of the Bhutto government but the Army suffered heavy casualties. After Bhutto was deposed, the province returned to normalcy under General Rahimuddin.

In 1980s, the Pakistan Armed Forces co-operated with the United States to provide arms, ammunition and intelligence assistance to Afghan rebels who were fighting the Soviet invasion of Afghanistan. During 1st Gulf War, the Pakistan Army contributed troops for the defence of Saudi Arabia against a possible attack by Iraq. The 153 SP Air Defence Regiment deployed in Tabuk scored multiple hits on number of Iraqi Scuds and provided round the clock air defence protection to Saudi troops in the area.

1999–2008

In October 1999, after the Kargil Conflict ended with the unconditional withdrawal of the Pakistani forces from the Indian controlled peaks, the Pakistan Army overthrew a democratically elected government once more, resulting in additional sanctions being applied against Pakistan, leading to General Pervez Musharraf coming to power in a bloodless coup. However, this time Prime Minister Nawaz Sharif sacked Musharraf when he was on his way to Pakistan from Colombo. He dismissed him as Chief of Army Staff and appointed General Ziauddin Butt to that position instead, when Musharraf's plane was in the air. That was not enough, the plane was not allowed to land at the airport in Karachi and barricades were erected on the runway.

The corps commanders acted swiftly across Pakistan, particularly in Karachi and Islamabad. Brigadier Muzaffar Usmani took control of the airport in Karachi and arrested the then Inspector General of Sindh Police, Rana Maqbool Ahmed. Musharraf stepped down as President in August 2008. On 30 July 2009, the Supreme Court of Pakistan ruled that Musharraf's imposition of emergency rule was unconstitutional.

After the September 11 attacks in the United States, Pakistan joined the US-led War on Terror and helped the United States Armed Forces by severing ties with the Taliban and immediately deploying 72,000 troops along Pakistan's western border to capture or kill Taliban and Al-Qaeda militants fleeing from Afghanistan. On the north western front, Pakistan initially garrisoned its troops in military bases and forts in the tribal areas. In May 2004, clashes erupted between the Pakistani troops and Al-Qaeda's and other militants joined by local rebels and pro-Taliban forces. However, the offensive was poorly coordinated and the Army suffered heavy casualties, while public support for the attack quickly evaporated. After a two-year conflict from 2004 until 2006, the Pakistani military negotiated a ceasefire with the tribesmen from the region in which they pledged to hunt down Al-Qaeda members, stop the "Talibanization" of the region and stop attacks in Afghanistan and Pakistan. However, the militants did not hold up their end of the bargain and began to regroup and rebuild their strength from the previous two years of conflict.

Militants took over the Lal Masjid in Islamabad. After a six-month standoff fighting erupted again in July 2007 when the Pakistani military decided to use force to end the Lal Masjid threat. Once the operation ended, the then newly formed Tehrik-i-Taliban Pakistan (TTP), an umbrella group of militants based in the Federally Administered Tribal Areas (FATA), a semi-autonomous region of Pakistan, vowed revenge and launched a wave of attacks and suicide bombings which erupted all over North-West Pakistan and major Pakistani cities, including Karachi, throughout 2007.

The militants then expanded their base of operations and moved into the neighbouring Swat Valley, where they imposed Sharia law. The Pakistan Army launched an offensive to re-take the Swat Valley in 2007, but was unable to clear it of the militants who had fled into the mountains and waited for them to leave before taking over the valley again. The militants then launched another wave of terrorist attacks inside Pakistan. The Pakistani government and military tried another peace deal with the militants in Swat Valley in 2008. This was roundly criticized in the West as abdicating to the militants. After initially pledging to lay down their arms if Sharia law was implemented, the Pakistani Taliban subsequently used the Swat Valley as a springboard to launch further attacks into neighbouring regions, reaching to within 60 kilometres (37 mi) of Islamabad.

Public opinion then turned decisively against the Taliban terrorists. This opinion was highlighted following the release of a video showing the flogging of a girl by the Pakistani Taliban in the Swat Valley. Similar events and terrorist attacks finally forced the Pakistan Army to launch a decisive attack against the Taliban occupying Swat Valley in April 2009, after having orders received from the political leadership. After heavy fighting, the Swat Valley was largely pacified by July 2009, although isolated pockets of Taliban remained in the area.

The next phase of the Pakistan Army's offensive was the formidable Waziristan region. A US inmanned combat aerial vehicle (UCAV) bomb strike in FATA killed the leader of the Taliban, Baitullah Mehsud, in August. A power struggle engulfed the Taliban during September, but by October a new leader had emerged, Hakimullah Mehsud. Under his leadership, the Taliban launched another wave of terrorist attacks throughout Pakistan, killing hundreds of people. After a few weeks of air strikes, artillery and mortar attacks, 30,000 troops moved on into South Waziristan. The Army eventually re-took all of South Waziristan. In April 2012 an avalanche struck the 6th Northern Light Infantry Battalion headquarters in Ghyari sector of Siachen, entrapping 135 soldiers.

STRUCTURE OF THE PAKISTAN ARMY

The Structure of the Pakistan Army can be broken down two ways, administrative, and operational. Operationally the Pakistan Army is divided in 11 Corps having areas of responsibility (AOR) from mountainous regions of northern Pakistan to the desert and coastal regions of the south.

Administratively it is divided in different regiments. The General Headquarters (GHQ) of Pakistan Army is located in the garrison city of Rawalpindi in Punjab province. It is planned to be moved to the capital city of Islamabad.

ARMY HEADQUARTERS AND STAFF

The Chief of the Army Staff (COAS), formerly called the Commander in Chief (C in C), is challenged with the responsibility of commanding the Pakistani Army.

The COAS operates from army headquarters in Rawalpindi, near Islamabad. The Principal Staff Officers (PSO's) assisting him in his duties at the Lieutenant General level include:

- Chief of General Staff (CGS) — Lt. Gen. Ishfaq Nadeem Ahmad
- Chief of Logistics Staff (CLS) — Lt. Gen. Syed Tariq Nadeem Gilani

- Inspector General Arms (IGA) — Lt. Gen. Muhammad Ijaz Chaudhry
- Adjutant General (AG) — Lt. Gen. Zamir Ul Hassan Shah
- Quarter-Master General (QMG) — Lt. Gen. Najib Ullah Khan
- Inspector General Training and Evaluation (IGT&E) — Lt. Gen. Ikram Ul Haq
- Military Secretary (MS) — Lt. Gen. Mazhar Jamil
- Inspector General Communications and IT (IGC&IT) — Lt. Gen. Khalid Asghar

The Military Operations and Intelligence Directorates function under the Chief of General Staff (CGS).

A major reorganization in GHQ was done in September 2008 under General Ashfaq Parvez Kayani, when two new PSO positions were introduced: the Inspector General Arms and the Inspector General Communications and IT, thus raising the number of PSO's to eight.

The headquarters function also includes the Judge Advocate General (JAG), and the Comptroller of Civilian Personnel, the Chief of the Corps of Engineers (E-in-C) who is also head of Military Engineering Service (MES), all of them also report to the Chief of the Army Staff.

OPERATIONAL STRUCTURE

Hierarchy

- Corps: A Corps in the Pakistani Army usually consists of two or more Divisions and is commanded by a Lieutenant General. Currently the Pakistani Army has 11 Corps. The eleventh one is the recently raised Army Strategic Force Command (ASFC), responsible for bearing the national strategic and nuclear assets. Initially a Division, but then raised to the status of a Corps.
- Division: Each division is commanded by a Major General, and usually holds three Brigades including infantry, artillery, engineers and communications units in addition to logistics (supply and service) support to sustain

independent action. Except for the Divisions operating in the mountains, all the Divisions have at least one armoured unit, some have even more depending upon their functionality. The most major of all ground force combat formations is the infantry division. Such a division would primarily hold three infantry brigades. There are 19 Infantry divisions, two mechanised divisions, two Armoured Divisions and 2 Artillery Divisions in the Pakistani Army.

- Brigade: A Brigade is under the command of a Brigadier and comprises three or more Battalions of different units depending on its functionality. An independent brigade would be one that primarily consists of an artillery unit, an infantry unit, an armour unit and logistics to support its actions. Such a brigade is not part of any division and is under direct command of a corps.
- Battalion: Each battalion is commanded by a Lieutenant Colonel and has roughly 600 to 900 soldiers under his command. This number varies depending on the functionality of the battalion. A battalion comprises either three batteries (in case of artillery and air defence regiments - generally named Papa, Quebec, Romeo, and Headquarters Battery) or four companies (in case of infantry regiments - generally named Alpha, Bravo, Charlie, and Delta - and other arms excluding armoured units that are organized into squadrons) each under the command of a major and consisting of individual subunits called sections (which are further divisible into platoons and squads).

Corps

Independent Brigades

There are seven Independent Mechanized Infantry Brigades, eight Independent Armoured brigades, 4 Artillery Brigades, and nine Engineer brigades.

These include 105 Independent Brigade Group in XXXI Corps, 111 Independent Infantry Brigade at Rawalpindi with X Corps, 212 Infantry Brigade at Lahore with IV Corps and 105 Independent

Infantry Brigade under V Corps. Nine independent signal brigade groups are also present (one in each corps).

Former Formations

Eastern Command was a Corps level formation in the former East Pakistan consisting of 14th, 9th and 16th Infantry Divisions. All three were re-raised after the war and exist today. 14 ID pretty much did not fight, since it was heavily Bengali and 6 of its battalions deserted when the operation began. 36 ID and 39 ID were raised to command the Paramilitary troops and a few loyal battalions. Were later reinforced with a couple of other battalions each. They were not re-raised after the war.

PAKISTAN ARMY STRUCTURE 2013

Other Field Formations

- Division: An Army Division is an intermediate between a Corps and a Brigade. It is the largest striking force in the army. Each Division is headed by [General Officer Commanding] (GOC) in the rank of Major General. It usually consists of 15,000 combat troops and 8,000 support elements. Currently, the Pakistani Army has 29 Divisions including 20 Infantry Divisions, 2 Armoured Divisions, 2 Mechanized Divisions, 2 Air Defence Divisions, 2 Strategic Divisions and 1 Artillery Division. Each Division composes of several Brigades.
- Brigade: A Brigade generally consists of around 3,000 combat troops with supporting elements. An Infantry Brigade usually has 3 Infantry Battalions along with various Support Arms & Services. It is headed by a Brigadier, equivalent to a Brigadier General in some armies. In addition to the Brigades in various Army Divisions, the Pakistani Army also has 7 Independent Armoured Brigades, 5 Independent Artillery Brigades, 3 Independent Infantry Brigades, and 3 Anti-Tank Brigades. These Independent Brigades operate directly under the Corps Commander.
- Regiment: A regiment is commanded by a Colonel.
- Battalion: A Battalion is commanded by a Lieutenant-

Colonel and is the Infantry's main fighting unit. It consists of more than 900 combat personnel.

- Company: Headed by the Major/Captain, a Company comprises about 120–150 soldiers.
- Platoon: An intermediate between a Company and Section, a Platoon is headed by a Lieutenant or depending on the availability of Commissioned Officers, a Junior Commissioned Officer, with the rank of Subedar or Naib-Subedar. It has a total strength of about 30–36 troops.
- Section: Smallest military outfit with a strength of about 9–13 personnel. Commanded by a Non-commissioned officer of the rank of Havildar Major or Sergeant Major.

Regiments

There are several battalions or units associated together in an infantry regiment. The infantry regiment in the Pakistani Army is an administrative military organisation and not a field formation. All the battalions of a regiment do not fight together as one formation, but are dispersed over various formations, viz. brigades, divisions and corps. An infantry battalion serves for a period of time under a formation and then moves to another, usually in another sector or terrain when its tenure is over. Occasionally, battalions of the same regiment may serve together for a tenure.

Most of the infantry regiments of the Pakistani Army originate from the old British Indian Army and recruit troops from a region or of specific ethnicities. Regiments of the Pakistani Army include:

Special Forces

The Special Services Group (SSG) is an independent commando regiment/corps of the Pakistan Army. It is an elite special operations force similar to the United States Army Special Forces (Green Berets) and the British Army's SAS.

Personnel

According to the International Institute for Strategic Studies (IISS) the Pakistan Army has an active force of 725,000 personnel in 2013. In addition there were around 500,000 reserves bringing the total to 1,225,000.

Enlisted Ranks

Most enlisted personnel used to come from rural families, and many have only rudimentary literacy skills, but with the increase in the literacy level the requirements have been raised to Matriculate level (10th Grade). Recruits are processed gradually through a paternalistically run regimental training centre, taught the official language, Urdu, if necessary, and given a period of elementary education before their military training actually starts. In the thirty-six-week training period, they develop an attachment to the regiment they will remain with through much of their careers and begin to develop a sense of being a Pakistani rather than primarily a member of a tribe or a village. Enlisted men usually serve for eighteen years, during which they participate in regular training cycles and have the opportunity to take academic courses to help them advance.

Officer Ranks

Each year, about 320 men and women enter the Army bi-annually through the Pakistan Military Academy at Kakul in Abbottabad in the Khyber Pakhtunkhwa; a small number—like doctors and technical specialists—are directly recruited, and are part of the officer corps. The product of a highly competitive selection process, members of the officer corps have completed twelve years of education and spend two years at the Pakistan Military Academy, with their time divided about equally between military training and academic work to bring them up to a baccalaureate education level, which includes English-language skills.

Academic Institutions

The Army has twelve other training and educational establishments, including schools concentrating on specific skills such as infantry, artillery, intelligence, engineering, or mountain warfare. The National University of Sciences and Technology (NUST) has been established which has absorbed the existing colleges of engineering, signals, electrical engineering and medicine. At the apex of the army training system is the Command and Staff College at Quetta, one of the few institutions inherited from the colonial period. The college offers a ten-month course in tactics, staff duties, administration, and command functions through the division level. Students from foreign countries, including the United States, have attended the school but reportedly have been critical of its narrow focus and failure to encourage speculative thinking or to give adequate attention to less glamorous subjects, such as logistics.

The senior training institution for all service branches is the National Defence University, Islamabad. Originally established in 1971 at Rawalpindi, to provide training in higher military strategy for senior officers, the institution was relocated to Islamabad in 1995. It also offers courses that allow civilians to explore the broader aspects of national security. In a program begun in the 1980s to upgrade the intellectual standards of the officer corps and increase awareness of the wider world, a small group of officers, has been detailed to academic training, achieving master's degrees and even doctorates at universities in Pakistan and abroad.

Pakistani officers were sent abroad during the 1950s and into the 1960s for training in Britain and other Commonwealth countries, and the United States, where trainees numbering well in the hundreds attended a full range of institutions ranging from armoured and infantry schools to the higher staff and command institutions. After 1961 this training was coordinated under the International Military Education and Training (IMET) program, but numbers varied along with the vicissitudes of the United States-Pakistan military relationship. Of some 200 officers being sent abroad annually in the 1980s, over two-thirds went to the United States, but the cessation of United States aid in 1990 entailed suspension of the IMET program. In 1994 virtually all foreign training was in Commonwealth countries. However, after the 9/11 attacks, Pakistan again begun sending officers to US Army schools. Today there are more than 400 officers serving in foreign countries. Officers retire between the ages of fifty-two and sixty, depending on their rank.

Science and Technology

Apart from conducting military operations, exercises, and military ethics, the Pakistan Army maintains its own science and technology corps and organizations. Most notable science and engineering corps including Military Engineering Service (MES) Corps of Engineers, Corps of Electrical and Mechanical Engineering (EME), and Frontier Works Organisation. Its Army Strategic Forces Command served as the primary military organization in the matters of conducting and directing research on nuclear and space (such as military satellites). The cadets and officers of the Pakistan Army who wished to study science and technology are given admission at the College of Electrical and Mechanical Engineering (CEME) and the Military College of Engineering where the scientific and military education are taught. The admissions of engineering colleges are not restricted to civilians as they can also gain admission and graduate with engineering and science degrees.

Uniforms

Pakistan Army uniforms closely resemble those of the British Armed Forces. The principal colour is greenish brown. Dress uniforms were worn mostly on formal occasions. The service uniform was worn for daily duty. The service uniform for the ground forces was khaki (sand/tan) cotton. Officers purchased their uniforms, but enlisted personnel received a standard uniform issue, which consisted of service and field uniforms, fatigues, and in some cases, dress uniforms. The uniforms consisted of shirt, trousers, sweater, jacket or blouse, and boots. There is also a white dress uniform. The fatigues were the same for winter and summer. Heavy winter gear was issued as needed. Headgear included a service cap for dress and semi-dress and a field cap worn with fatigues. Army personnel also wear berets, usually worn in lieu of the service cap.

Brown and black and more recently former US BDU style camouflage fatigues are worn by army troop units. The uniform of a Pakistan army soldier exhibits much information i.e. Pakistan Army has introduced pixilated arid camouflage pattern in uniform and resized qualification badges which are now colourless and service ribbons are no longer worn along with the ranks are now embroidered and are on chest. The name is embroidered and is on right pocket and the left pocket displays embroidered Pak Army. Flag of Pakistan is placed over the black embroidered formation sign on the left arm and adventure course insignias are put up as per ADR for khaki uniform, decorations & awards and the ranks.

Ethnic Composition

Traditionally, the army was a predominantly Punjabi force because of its dominant Population (Punjab is the most populous province of Pakistan, with approximately 45% of the country's total population). In British India, three districts: Jhelum, Rawalpindi, and Campbellpur (now Attock) dominated the recruitment flows. By 2007 the percentage representation in the Pakistan Army as a whole was approximate as follows:

Punjabis: 53.19%

Pashtuns: 21%

Sindhis: 13.5%

Kashmiris: 9.11%

Baloch: 3.2%.

Extensive efforts have been made to bring the Baloch and Sindhis on par with other ethnicities, presently the Army recruitment system is enlisting personnel district-wise irrespective of provincial boundaries. This decision has given a fair chance to every citizen of Pakistan to be part of the Pakistan Army as each district possesses a fixed percentage of seats in all branches of the army, as per census records. Large numbers of men from Sindh and Balochistan have joined the ranks of the army and have proved their commitment and bravery to the national cause in Kargil and the ongoing global war on terrorism.

Women and non-Muslim Pakistanis

Women have served in the Pakistan Army since its foundation. Currently, there is a sizeable number of women serving in the Pakistan Army. Most women are recruited in the Army to perform medical and educational work. There is also a Women's Guard section of Pakistan's National Guard where women are trained in nursing, welfare and clerical work and there are also women recruited in very limited numbers for the Janbaz Force. Only recently has Pakistan began to recruit women for combat positions and the Elite Anti-Terrorist Force in 2007, several female graduates were nominated to be Sky Marshals for Pakistan based airlines. In addition recently eight of the 41 cadets from the Pakistan Military Academy at Kakul became the first women guards of honour. Pakistan is the only country in the Islamic world to have female *Major Generals* in the Army. Major General Shahida Badshah was Pakistan's first female two-star general.

Non Muslim Pakistanis are allowed to sit in all examinations and serve in any part of the Pakistan Army.

There have been numerous Christians who have risen to the rank of Brigadier; and in the 1990 the first Christian promoted to the rank of Major General was Julian Peter who commanded the 14th Div in Okara Cantt.

In 2009 brigadier Noel Israel Khokhar, was also promoted to rank of Major General. Capt. Hercharn Singh, the first Sikh as Commissioned Officer in Pakistan Army. He was commissioned in Baloch Regiment. Currently, he's serving as an ADC to a Corps Commander.

Recipients of Nishan-e-Haider

The Nishan-e-Haider (Sign of the Lion) is the highest military award given by Pakistan, ranking above the Hilal-i-Jur'at (Crescent of Courage). Nishan-e-Haider recipients receive an honorary title as a sign of respect: *Shaheed* meaning *martyr* for deceased recipients. As of 19 Sep 2013, all Nishan-e-Haider awards have thus far been given to the people engaged in battles with India.

PAKISTAN AIR FORCE - MODERNIZATION

The US security assistance relationship with Pakistan resumed subsequent to September 11. Given its geo-strategic location and partnership in the Global War on Terrorism (GWOT), Pakistan is a vital ally of the United States, as reflected in the June 2004 designation of Pakistan as a Major Non-North Atlantic Treaty Organization Ally. By 2008 the United States had delivered a variety of equipment to Pakistan, including refurbished C-130E transports, refurbished P-3C surveillance aircraft, refurbished Cobra helicopters, new Bell 412 helicopters and a number of Harpoon missiles, Harris radios, AN/TPS-77 surveillance radars, night vision goggles and AIM-9M Sidewinder missiles. On 16 July 2002, the Defense Security Cooperation Agency notified Congress of a possible Foreign Military Sale to Pakistan of C-130E Cargo Aircraft and associated equipment and services. The total value, if all options are exercised, could be as high as $75 Million. The Government of Pakistan has requested a possible sale of six used C-130E aircraft with engines, one C-130E operational capabilities upgrade aircraft for cannibalization with engines, upgrade of engines to Allison 56-A-15 engines, modification kits, spare and repair parts, devices, support equipment, publications and technical documentation, personnel training and training equipment, U.S. Government and contractor engineering and logistics personnel services and other related elements of logistics support.

The estimated cost is $75 million. This proposed sale will contribute to the foreign policy and national security of the United States by helping to improve the security of a friendly country which has been and continues to be an important force for economic progress in South Asia. Pakistan needs these aircraft to support a current and long-term airlift shortfall, both for Pakistan Air Force internal requirements, and as it seeks to support the U.S. Government with Operation Enduring Freedom. These C-130E aircraft will be used for the purpose of providing airlift support. Pakistan can easily absorb and utilize these within its existing structure.

In August 2003 Pakistan agreed to receive from the US six ex-Australian Air Force Lockheed C-130E Hercules aircraft. The seven aircraft had been in storage in the USA for three years awaiting re-sale. A contract was signed in September 2004, for Lockheed to upgrade the six aircrafts, while the seventh example will be used as spares. The first of the six Lockheed C-130 Hercules military cargo airplanes ordered by PAF in 2003, left US on 31 October 2005, heading for Islamabad. *The disposition of these aircraf is unclear - logically, they would replace the older L-100 and C-130B in the PAF inventory, but this point is unresolved in the open literature.*

PAF ordered four Mi-171 helicopters in 2002 from Ukraine for its Special Services Group, which were delivered in 2004. A follow-on order of further 12 examples was also placed. The helicopters were intended for search and rescue duties at various PAF bases. The delivery of the follow on order also commenced in 2004.

The first of four CN-235 transport aircraft ordered by PAF was delivered three months late, in February 2004, due to labour dispute at the aircraft factory. PAF ordered these planes in 2002 in a $52 million deal. The second example was delivered in September 2004. The delivery of the third was due in October and the final was due in December 2004. The final of the four CN-235 ordered by PAF from Indonesia, was delivered in Jun 2005. This is a VIP aircraft, the interior of which has been designed and fitted by Avion-interiors of Italy.

In July 2004 PAF finalised a deal with Libya to buy its fleet of 50 Mirage IIIs and Vs, 150 sealed pack engines and a huge quantity of Mirage spares. Libya had purchased the Mirage jets in the 1970s, and they had been grounded for the previous decade following sanctions imposed after the Boeing 747 was blown up over Lockerbie. With these airframes, Pakistan operated more Mirages than the French Air Force. It is believed that jets would be cannibalized for spare parts to provide spares for the PAF fleet of Mirages for the next seven to ten years. As of 2009 the Mirage Rebuild Factory, which is a part of PAC, had been rebuilding 35 year old version of the Mirage aircraft which were bought as scrap from various countries.

Following the delivery of two JF-17 aircraft from China in 2007, PAF received delivery of a further six which were undergoing tests & evaluation at PAC Kamra as of April 2008. The assembly of JF-17 aircrafts in Pakistan was formally launched on 22 January 2008 at PAC Kamra. In the first year (2008), eight to ten aircrafts will be assembled for the Pakistan Air Force. The assembly will gradually increase to 25 aircraft per year by 2011. It is reported that around 60% of the frame of the aircraft and 80% of the avionics to be fitted in the aircraft will be manufactured in Pakistan by 2010. PAF have a requirement of 150 aircraft in phase-I. The first 40 to 50 examples would have the Chinese avionics, thereafter the aircraft would be fitted will indigenously developed avionics.

In June 2006, the PAF had signed a deal for the supply of six Saab 2000s. However, because of shortage of funds, the number of aircraft was revised to five. Another report suggests that the Erieye airborne surveillance system deal involves up to eight Saab 2000 aircraft. The first Saab 2000 AEWC aircraft ordered for the PAF was rolled out on 3 April 2008 at the SAAB factory in Sweden. The ERIEYE, developed by the Ericsson Microwave Systems, comprises fixed, dual-sided and electronically scanned phased-array pulse-Doppler radar mounted on top of the fuselage.

Pakistan Air Force received the delivery of a second Gulfstream 450 aircraft in November 2007. The first aircraft was delivered in December 2005.

In September 2008 it was reported that Pakistan was to receive 20 refurbished T-37 training aircrafts from the USA. The aircraft will be supplied to Pakistan free of charge, however Pakistan will bear the cost of shipment only. The delivery of the aircraft was due in two months time.

On 25 January 2009 Pakistan's defence minister informed the parliament that Pakistan has placed a $278 million order for the Chinese AWACS system ZDK-03 based on Chinese Y-8 aircraft.

In January 2009 PAF received delivery of two IL-78 tanker aircraft from Ukraine, out of the four ordered. Once the IL-78 tanker aircraft have been commissioned into service, it will enhance the long range capability of Pakistan air force.

Pakistan Air Force (PAF) Chief of Staff Tanveer Mehmud Ahmad gave an interview to AFM and was published in the September 2008 issue.

- By 2015, PAF would comprise 240 JF-17, 60 F-16's, 40 FC-20's (PAF version of J-10), 50 F-7PG's [for a total of 390 combat aircraft, versus 335 in 2008], along with 4 SAAB Erieye, 4 ZDK-03 (PAF version of Y-8), 4 IL-78 Midas. In 2015 the PAF will remain at its current strength of 15 Squadrons.
- The current order status comprised 150 JF-17's, 32 F-16's (variant unspecified), 4 Erieye's, and 4 IL-78.
- The Block 52 F-16's will be based at PAF Shahbaz to replace Mirage air defense aircraft.
- The Peshawar based 26 & 16 Squadrons will be the first to convert from A-5 to JF-17 in 2009. Delivery of JF-17 had

started and once the assembly facility had been completed at AMF, the induction pace will pick-up to eventually allow delivery of 25-30 aircraft per year to achieve the final numbers by 2015 [this makes no sense, with a 30/year production rate only yielding about 150 aircraft by 2015, not the stated 240]. The 150 JF-17's are expected to equip 7 or 8 squadrons.

- The FC-20 order would be confirmed in 2009. The current J-10 technology was not up to PAF requirements, and PAF hoped to include western equipment in the J-10. This would create a different version than the PLAAF J-10, which would be known as FC-20 in PAF service. The FC-20 would not be required to have conformal fuel tanks, since it had sufficient internal fuel capacity as well as AAR by Il-78 Midas tankers. The FC-20 requirement was 2 squadrons of 36-40 single and dual seater aircraft.
- The IL-78 Midas tankers would provide aerial refueling for all PAF fighter aircraft excepttf the US manufactured F-16s. The F-16s can only refuel with a boom system, and the Midas will be equipped with a probe and drogue underwing pods system. First Midas delivery will commence early 2009. PAF is holding out hope that a KC-135 could be acquired from the US in the near future.
- While the Erieye's will datalink the F-16's, they will not be able to do so with the Mirage fleet. The first Erieye will be delivered in 2009, followed by the remainder by 2011. The Chinese origin fighter aircraft will have AEW&C support from the planned acquisition of 4 ZDK-03 (Chinese Y-8 AWACS). The ZDK-03 contract was close to be being finalised for the required 4 aircraft.
- The PAF is acquiring 2 Squadrons of the Italian Falco UAV with coversion taking place for operations from PAF Mushaf and PAF Peshawar. Eventually, the PAF plans to field 5-6 UAV Sqn's.

On November 20, 2008 Air Chief Marshal Tanvir Mahmood Ahmad said 36 high-tech combat aircraft (CF-20) would be inducted into the PAF fleet by 2010. He said that modalities were being discussed to acquire two squadrons of the aircraft for the PAF. He said the FC-20 aircraft had been selected after hectic and lengthy deliberations besides considering a long list of the similar category aircraft of various origins. In December 2010 Pakistan Air Force received the final batch of the F-16 fighter jets from the United States. These new F-16 C/D Block 52+ fighter jets were part of the 18 aircrafts ordered by the Pakistan Air Force. These new F-16 C/D Block 52+ fighter jets are stationed at the Pakistan Air Force's Shahbaz airbase. Pakistani defense minister said that PAF is interested in purchasing the F-16 fighter jets from the Royal Norwegian Air Force which was looking to replace them with the low observable stealthy F-35 fighter jets.

The deliveries of the Block II JF-17 Thunder to Pakistan Air Force were scheduled to start from the second half of the 2012 and will continue till 2015. From 2016, JF-17 Thunder Block III would enter into production.

In August 2011 it was reported that the Chinese government had offered to provide its advance fourth generation J-10B fighter jets to the Pakistan air force to meet its requirements of high tech fourth generation frontline fighter aircraft.The J-10B is an improved version of the basic J-10A powered by the Chinese WS-10 engine. Pakistan has total requirement of 150 front line fourth generation aircrafts which will be met with the induction of Chinese J-10B/ FC-20, F-16AM/BM and F-16 C/D Block 52+ fighter aircraft. In September 2013 it was reported that Pakistan air force (PAF) would receive its first FC-20 / J-10B fighter jet in 2014.

In February 2014 the Pakistan Air Force acquired 13 F-16A/ B block 15 aircraft Fighter jets from Royal Jordanian Air Force (RJAF). Pakistan was to take the delivery of 12 F-16A and 1 F-16B fighter jets starting in March 2014. The Jordanian fighter jets would increase the F-16 total to 76. These fighter jets will serve PAF for another 20 years with almost 3,000 hours on average available to them for flying.

Pakistan Air Force achieved another significant milestone in its quest for modernization and expansion of fighter aircraft fleet, as the first batch of F-16s from Jordan landed at an operational Air Base 27 April 2014. The aircraft were purchased from Royal

Jordanian Air Force after series of negotiations held between concerned Ministries and the concerted efforts of Air Chief Marshal Tahir Rafique Butt, Chief of the Air Staff Pakistan Air Force. To avoid extra burden on the national exchequer, PAF opted for the used planes as they were acquired at nominal cost per bird and could serve for longer duration.

The Pakistan Air Force (PAF) showed interest in buying fourth generation stealth fighter aircraft FC-31 from China. Janes reported 12 November 2014 that the Pakistan Air Force (PAF) was in talks with China to buy 30 to 40 of the Shenyang FC-31 twin-engined stealth fighter displayed at Airshow China 2014 in Zhuhai. Pakistani Defence Production minister Rana Tanveer Hussain said in late Novembe 2014 that the matter was being discussed with Chinese authorities. According to Dawn, it was for the first time that a senior government functionary had confirmed talks with China over purchase of the longer-range stealth aircraft.

4

Pakistan Armed Forces Deployments

Pakistan Armed Forces deployments include all Pakistani military deployments that are stationed outside Pakistan and serving in other countries. The seventh largest military power in terms of active troops, Pakistan has an extensive history of overseas military presence, especially in the Middle East, where it has maintained military contingents, missions and battalions in several states. As part of its foreign policy efforts to expand its military relations and influence in the region, Pakistan signed defence protocols during the 1970s with several Arab countries including Saudi Arabia, Libya, Jordan, Iraq, Oman, the United Arab Emirates and Kuwait, under which members of the armed forces of these countries were imparted professional training by Pakistani advisers and military trainers. Saudi Arabia signed a bilateral agreement with Pakistan on defense cooperation; during that time, there were 40,000 to 50,000 Pakistani military personnel serving abroad with the largest number of these, about 20,000, deployed in Saudi Arabia. By the 1980s, Pakistan maintained military missions in 22 countries, becoming the largest military manpower deployer in the Third World.

BACKGROUND

The oil boom in the Persian Gulf during the 1970s and 1980s brought rapid economic growth and geostrategic importance to the region. During this period, many Gulf states sought regional neighbour Pakistan's assistance in the formation of their military capabilities. A number of Pakistan Air Force, Army and Navy personnel were deputed to Saudi Arabia, the United Arab Emirates, Qatar, Bahrain, Jordan, Iraq and Syria, primarily to train and establish local security forces, as well as provide technical assistance.

Defense attachés from Russia and Pakistan visit the communications center at a Nigerian Air Force base in 2008.

HISTORY OF DEPLOYMENTS

Africa

The Air Force of Zimbabwe (AFZ) underwent a series of restructuring in the early 1980s, followings its reconstitution from the previously-existing Rhodesian Air Force. During this period, the AFZ sought Pakistani and foreign assistance to remain operational. Zimbabwean President Robert Mugabe requested Pakistan to detach an officer to head the AFZ and serve as its commander. Subsequently, Air Vice-Marshal Azim Daudpota was appointed Commander of the Air Force of Zimbabwe, serving in the position from July 1983 to January 1986. He remains the first and only non-local commander of the AFZ. A large number of other PAF officers were deployed in Zimbabwe as well, along with Daudpota.

Kuwait

Defence cooperation between Pakistan and Kuwait dates back to the late 1960s. Officers from the Pakistani army, air force and navy have been deployed in Kuwait to provide training and instruction to Kuwaiti forces. In 1990, up to 700 personnel of the Pakistan Armed Forces were stationed in Kuwait. Pakistani officers served in technical and advisory roles in the Kuwaiti Army during the Gulf War. Pakistan was a member of the coalition forces against the 1990 invasion of Kuwait, and Pakistani personnel took part in UN mine hunting operations in Kuwait.

Saudi Arabia

Saudi Arabia has historically remained Pakistan's closest defense partner in the Middle East, with both countries sharing extensive military and intelligence cooperation. Military relations between the two were expanded in 1967. Former Saudi intelligence chief Prince Turki bin Sultan described the level of cooperation as "probably one of the closest relationships in the world between any two countries" while Pakistan's ambassador to Saudi Arabia, Naeem Khan, stated that Pakistan considered Saudi Arabia's security as a "personal matter". The Pakistan Air Force has been in contact with the Royal Saudi Air Force (RSAF) since the early 1960s. Following grievances over British military cooperation in the 1960s, King Faisal turned to Pakistan's assistance for air force training and maintenance. In the 1960s, Pakistan helped the RSAF build and pilot its first jet fighters. Pakistan Air Force pilots flew RSAF Lightnings in 1969 to repel South Yemeni incursions on Saudi Arabia's southern border.

Pakistani troops participated alongside Saudi forces in quelling insurgents during the 1979 Grand Mosque Seizure at Islam's holiest site in Mecca. A protocol was signed between Pakistan and Saudi Arabia on 14 December 1982 following the latter's request for military manpower assistance. Throughout the 1970s and 1980s, up to 15,000 Pakistani troops were stationed in Saudi Arabia, to provide defense to the country. Some of them were part of a brigade combat force positioned near the Israeli-Jordanian-Saudi border. As of the Gulf War in 1991, up to 13,000 troops and 6,000 advisers from Pakistan were posted in Saudi Arabia. Under the 1982 protocol, cooperation was widened to include military training, defense production and sharing, and joint exercises. Contingents of the Pakistani Armed Forces have frequently participated in joint military exercises inside Saudi Arabia in conjunction with the Saudi Armed Forces. Pakistani military presence in the kingdom continues presently, providing Riyadh support against internal and external regional threats.

The Pakistan Navy and Royal Saudi Navy also share wide-ranging maritime cooperation, having conducted a series of joint naval exercises. Officers of the Royal Saudi Navy were provided training by the Pakistan Navy during the RSN's formative years.

United Arab Emirates

Defence relations between Pakistan and the UAE began shortly before the UAE's formation in 1971. Pakistani troops imparted training to members of the Abu Dhabi defence forces as far back as 1968, upon the request of the founder of the UAE Sheikh Zayed, as the British were about to hand over command of the Gulf Trucial States. A protocol was signed in the mid 1970s, and defence cooperation continued for the succeeding decades. Both countries share geographical proximity and a longstanding history of bilateral relations.

The Pakistan Army established an armour training school in the UAE, and provided training to UAE commando battalions, as well as all armed and artillery corps officers. Pakistani personnel also held prominent positions as advisers and trainers in the UAE Air Force (UAEAF). The UAEAF is dubbed to have been "an extension of the Pakistan Air Force" at one point. The first Chief of Air Staff of the UAE, appointed by Sheikh Zayed, was Air Cdre Ayaz Ahmed Khan, followed by Ghulam Haider, Jamal A. Khan and Feroz A. Khan, all of whom were Pakistan Air Force (PAF) officers. The succeeding commanders were native officers, although group captain ranked officers of the PAF continued serving as Deputy Chief of Air Staff. As of 2004, the UAEAF had around 55 Pakistani flying instructors, and there were a few number of Pakistani personnel serving in the UAE Army and Navy. Officers of the Pakistan Navy have served in the UAE while training the local naval force.

During active conflicts

- Six-Day War: During the Six-Day War, Pakistani flying ace Saiful Azam shot down two Israeli aircraft and was awarded Jordan's Order of Istiqlal and Iraq's medal of bravery, the Nut al-Shujat as well as becoming the only Pilot with kills against two airforces (India and Israel) and highest shooter of Israeli aircraft to date.
- Battle of Mogadishu (1993): More commonly known as *Black Hawk Down*, a Pakistani soldier was killed and two Pakistanis were wounded in support of United States.
- Black September in Jordan: Then Brigadier Muhammad Zia-ul-Haq (later Chief of Army Staff and President of Pakistan), played a key role in planning the offensives in this conflict in support of Jordan.

- Operation Gothic Serpent: One of the deadliest attack and encirclement of UN forces (also comprising Pakistan Army troops), later relieved by a heavy rescue convoy of US, Pakistani and Malaysian troops.
- Grand Mosque Seizure: Pakistani Special Services Group lead the charge to free the Mosque of the militants, by flooding the mosque and using electrical charges.
- Unified Task Force: After killing of several Pakistani peace keepers in the task force, the task force's mandate was changed to using 'all necessary measures' to deliver humanitarian aid resulting in mission success. and is regarded as a success.

CURRENT DEPLOYMENTS

Anti-piracy operations

Pakistan Navy has been a major participant of Combined Task Force 150, based in Bahrain, established to monitor, inspect, board, and stop suspect shipping associated with terrorism in the Horn of Africa. This task force comprising warships of Italy, France, Germany, Pakistan, Canada, the United Kingdom and United States has also been commanded by a Pakistani Admiral.

On the announcement of Pakistan taking the command, several other nations have also expressed their interests in participating in Combined Task Force 150 in some way.

PAKISTAN ARMY WARNS OF 'DISPROPORTIONATE RESPONSE' IN FUTURE WARS

Pakistan's official Army Doctrine calls on the country to "invoke disproportionate responses" in future wars with India, a copy of the document obtained by *TheHindu* has revealed. "The causes of conflict with the potential to escalate to the use of violence," the classified internal document states, "emanate from the unresolved issue of Kashmir, the violation of treaty arrangements on sharing of natural resources, and the organised and deliberate support by external powers to militant organisations."

The December, 2011, Doctrine does not name any country as a threat, but Pakistan has accused India of seeking to block its access to Indus waters, and backing terrorism. The Doctrine describes itself as the "army's mother document" and "the fountainhead for all subordinate doctrines."

Indian military sources told *TheHindu* the study was commissioned in the summer of 2008, soon after former chief of army staff General Pervez Kayani took office. It evolved through intensive discussions of the Kargil war of 1999 and the near-war that followed the December, 2001, terrorist attack on Parliament House

Georgetown University scholar Dr. C. Christine, author of a forthcoming book, *Fighting to the End*, says the Doctrine confirms what scholars have long known. "It tells us several interesting things," she says, "among them that the Pakistan army sees Indian military modernisation as a threat, but that they also think nuclear weapons will insulate them from the consequences of pursuing high-risk strategies, like backing jihadist clients."

Future wars, the Doctrine states, "will be characterised by high-intensity, high-tempo operations under a relatively transparent battle-space environment." This, it states, is because of the "incremental increase in asymmetry of conventional forces and [the] nuclear overhang" — evident references to the programme of rapid modernisation India put into place after the 2001-2002 crisis, and both countries' efforts to expand their nuclear weapons capabilities.

In the view of the Doctrine's authors, de-facto parity between the two countries induced "through a combination of conventional and nuclear deterrence, has obviated the [likelihood of] conventional war."

However, the Doctrine argues, "a disparity at the conventional plane continues to grow disproportionately, which too disturbs the strategic equilibrium of the region." This, it states, "depletes peaceful diplomacy and dialogue, replacing it with coercion on the upper planes and violence across the lower-ends of the spectrum."

"What worries Pakistan's army," says the former Indian Army vice-chief, Arvinder Lamba, "is their inability to organise offensive or defensive responses to our growing rapid mobilisation capacity.

Their challenge is to deter us from striking by threatening nuclear weapons use in the face of the least provocation.

"India's government and military must seek perceptual clarity on exactly what we intend to do in the face of such threats," he said.

The Doctrine states that Pakistan will use nuclear weapons "only as a last resort, given its scale and scope of destruction." Nuclear parity between India and Pakistan, it argues, "does not accrue any substantial military advantage to either side, other than maintaining the status quo."

"In a nuclear deterrent environment," it adds, "war is unlikely to create decisive military or political advantage." However, it argues that "integration and synergy between conventional and nuclear forces, maintaining both at an appropriate level... [will avoid] an open-ended arms race."

It does not state what the red lines compelling nuclear weapons use might be, but says future strategic "force development centres around developing and maintaining credible minimum deterrence, based on a [land, sea and air] triad, including an assured second-strike capability [to an Indian nuclear first-strike]."

"Lots of this thinking has been operationalised in Pakistan's military," says Rana Banerjee, a New Delhi-based expert on the Pakistan army, and former Research and Analysis Wing official. "Basically, this document signals they intend to react to even limited Indian military operations with disproportionate force, and hope fear of escalation deters New Delhi from reacting to events like 26/11."

CIVIL MILITARY RELATIONS IN CONTEMPORARY PAKISTAN

Governance in Pakistan is a delicate balancing act between the military chiefs and the elected civilian government. It is a power-sharing arrangement whereby the military has important influence over foreign, security and key domestic issues, and mediates confrontations among feuding political leaders, parties or state institutions- if such confrontations are deemed threatening to political order and stability. Although the civilian government enjoys considerable autonomy for political and economic management and exercise of state authority, it is expected always to consider the military's sensibilities. The military has repeatedly demonstrated that it can and will influence the nature and direction of political change without necessarily assuming power.

How to cope with this kind of 'soft' military intervention is a common dilemma for civilian leaders of states that have experienced prolonged military rule. The civilian regimes that succeed military rule face serious identity crises. On the one hand, these governments want to prove that they are not under the tutelage of the military and can act autonomously. On the other hand, they cannot afford to alienate the military leadership, whose support is crucial to their survival. Their task is complicated by the fact that the top brass are loath to surrender the power and privileges that they enjoyed during the years of military rule. The military ensures that there are sufficient constitutional and political safeguards to sustain their entrenched position in the period after their withdrawal from direct rule. Extended military rule in a multi-ethnic and diversified society also increases political fragmentation and creates vested interests supporting authoritarian and non-democratic political arrangements. These conditions make the task of political management difficult for any post-martial law civilian regime aiming to establish its credentials as a genuine democratic government while not alienating the senior commanders.

Civilian Rule

The ascendancy of Pakistan's military began shortly after the country achieved independence in 1947. The rapid degeneration of the political process enabled the military to become an important decision-maker at the national level, culminating in the direct assumption of power by the Army Chief, General (later Field Marshal) Ayub Khan, through a coup in October 1958. He ruled under martial law until June 1962, when he civilianised his regime by co-opting some politicians and establishing a constitution which legitimised the continuation of his rule after the withdrawal of martial law. A second coup was staged in March 1969' by General Yahya Khan, who surrendered power to an elected civilian leader in December 1971' after the military debacle in the 1971 Indo-Pakistan war. The military overcame the trauma of defeat within a few years, and General Zia ul-Haq reasserted military dominance by overthrowing the civilian government in July 1977. He presided over the longest period of martial law in Pakistan's history (July 1977 December 1985) and handed power over to a civilian government through a carefully managed disengagement.

The civilian system that replaced Zia's military rule in 1985 enabled the military to shift its emphasis from overt 'rule' to a more subtle, but still ubiquitous 'role'. Instead of exercising power directly (although the coup option is still available), the military has become a formidable political actor, influencing the nature and direction of political change. This planned transition began when Zia introduced far-reaching changes in the 1973 Constitution, emphasising an all-powerful President (Zia himself) and a weak Prime Minister.

Zia saw his relationship with the Army as crucial to his survival and thus guarded its professional and corporate interests. He underlined his primacy in the political process, not merely through his enhanced presidential powers, but also by projecting his position of Army Chief as a 'bridge' between the newly established civilian government and the powerful armed forces. He periodically lashed out at the civilian government to keep it in line. When the Prime Minister tried to assert his autonomy, Zia sacked him in May 1988, thereby demolishing the civilianised system he had created. He was trying to co-opt another set of civilian leaders who could serve as 'adjuncts to military supremacy' when he was killed in an air crash in August.

The military's decision not to assume power after Zia's death led to the holding of multi-party elections and subsequent transfer of power to a civilian government in December 1988. Since then, the Army Chiefs have emphasised professionalism and no direct involvement of soldiers in politics; they have generally supported the democratic process and civilian governance. This support is tactical, however, based on a realistic assessment of the political situation. It does not change the fact that they are central to the political process.

A Pivot in the Power Structure

The Army Chief is a pivot in Pakistan's post-1988 power structure. Together with the President and the Prime Minister, he constitutes one-third of the 'Troika' -an extra-constitutional arrangement for civilian-military consensus-building on key domestic, foreign policy and security issues. The Troika meets periodically; senior military and civilian officials are summoned to give briefings relating to the issues under discussion. The Army Chief also holds meetings separately with the President and Prime Minister on political and security affairs. Another institution that has gained prominence is the Corps Commanders' meeting. Presided over by the Army chief, this conference includes top commanders, Principal Staff Officers at the Army Headquarters and other senior officers holding strategic appointments. Its members not only discuss security and organisational and professional matters, but also deliberate on domestic issues such as law and order, and general political conditions-especially when the government and the opposition are engaged in intense confrontation. These discussions are intended both to underline senior officers' political concerns and to develop a broad-based military consensus. Executing the consensus decisions is left to the Army Chief, thereby strengthening his position when he interacts with the President and the Prime Minister.

A smooth interaction among the Troika members ensures the military's support for the Prime Minister, which contributes to general political stability. If serious differences develop among these key players, political uncertainty and instability are likely. The Prime Minister - the civilian side of the power equation - can find him or herself in a difficult situation. The military is well placed to exert pressure on him. Furthermore, the 1973 Constitution, as amended by Zia in 1985, greatly strengthened the position of the President vis-a-vis the Prime Minister, making it difficult for the latter to emerge as an autonomous power.

The Prime Minster's position was boosted somewhat by an April 1997' Constitutional amendment curtailing the President's powers so that he cannot dismiss the Prime Minister. However, so long as the Prime Minister presides over divided and mutually hostile political forces, he will have to work in harmony with the President - and the Army.

The military's primary consideration is not direct exercise of power, but protection and advancement of its professional and corporate interests. If these interests can be protected, it would prefer to stay on the sidelines. Given military's political experience, organisational resources and institutional strengths, its senior commanders are reasonably confident that they can pursue such a strategy. The senior commanders are willing to negotiate their interests and accommodate the civilian leaders. What is not acceptable to them, however, is a frontal attack on their institutional and corporate interests as they define them, a deliberate campaign to malign the military, or unilateral decision-making by the civilian leaders on matters which directly concern them. They will not support a discredited civilian government nor allow the military's name to be used by civilian leaders, whether in government or in opposition, in their power struggle. The scope for manoeuvre for the civilian leaders can thus expand if they establish a relationship of trust and confidence with the military.

The Military's Interests

National security is obviously paramount. During the Zia era, the military directly controlled nuclear policy and the conduct of the Afghan War. Nuclear policy has remained their close preserve, even under civilian rule. Benazir Bhutto complained in September 1991 that she was denied information about highly sensitive aspects of the country's nuclear programme during her first term as Prime Minister. The role of the Foreign Office and the civilian leadership in formulating and implementing the Afghanistan policy increased after the 1989 withdrawal of Soviet troops, but senior Army commanders and the Inter-Service Intelligence (ISI) continue to have a significant input. Similarly, the Army maintains deep interest in policy towards India, including Kashmir. The military elite are not opposed in principle to Indo-Pakistani rapprochement, but they are concerned that the civilian government not ignore what they see as New Delhi's 'hegemonic' agenda. Strong and credible conventional defence and nuclear-weapons capabilities are considered vital to ward off Indian pressures and to enable Pakistan to conduct independent foreign and domestic policies. Unless the military is satisfied that there are credible guarantees against India's efforts to interfere, it will resist surrendering its nuclear-weapon option and advise caution on normalising relations. Furthermore, the military-like most civilian policy-makers-will not want to improve bilateral relations unless India addresses the issue of Kashmir.

Overseas weapons and equipment procurement is another military interest with foreign-policy implications. The three military services thus press the civilian government to pursue foreign policy to facilitate this objective.

Military autonomy and civilian non-interference in internal organisational matters and service affairs is jealously guarded by senior commanders. The service chiefs generally resist any Ministry of Defence tampering with their personnel recommendations, including promotions, transfers and postings. Military leaders view their autonomy and civilian non-interference as crucial in maintaining service discipline and professionalism. If the political leaders are able to make in-roads into the military and establish their lobbies, the senior commanders think, the military's overall discipline, organisational coherence and institutional capacity to cope with the political environment will be compromised.

The military is opposed to any unilateral cut in defence expenditure by civilian leaders. Its senior commanders are prepared to discuss budgetary issues with their non-military leaders, but they are opposed to critical public statements by government leaders or to any reduction that has not previously been cleared with them.

The repeated exercise of power under martial law has enabled officers to accumulate considerable perks and privileges, which the military inevitably wants protected - along with generally improving service conditions.

The military also expects a civilian government to ensure socio-political stability. The senior commanders therefore constantly review the government's political and economic management, especially its interaction with the political adversaries, the handling of law and order, and such issues as corruption, use of state machinery and patronage.

Army Chiefs have not hesitated to comment publicly on the political situation, advising political leaders to put their house in order, not to crush their opposition, to settle contentious issues through political means and negotiations, and on the need to establish a corruption-free, transparent and effective administration. Their interest in these matters stems from the assumption that a polity in turmoil cannot sustain a professional military. Furthermore, with the military's industrial and commercial activities expanding through its four welfare foundations, the government's economic and industrial policies have also acquired direct relevance.

On a number of occasions, top Army commanders have used their influence to moderate a conflict among the politicians and/or forced them into a settlement when they felt that a confrontation would cause a major constitutional or political breakdown. They supported the President in removing civilian governments in August 1990, April 1993 and November 1996, having concluded that these governments could no longer ensure domestic peace, stability and order. In December 1997, on the other hand, the Army ultimately supported the Prime Minister in his bitter confrontation with the President and the judiciary.

PAKISTAN ARMY STEPS INTO GOVERNMENT ROLE AMID POLITICAL CRISIS

Pakistan's army stepped into a political struggle between the country's embattled prime minister and the opposition on Thursday, signaling a possible end to a crisis that has destabilized the coup-prone nation.

Pakistan has been gripped by mass rallies for more than two weeks, with protesters led by cricketer-turned-politician Imran Khan and firebrand cleric Tahir ul-Qadri camped outside parliament demanding Prime Minister Nawaz Sharif resign.

Attempts to resolve the crisis through talks have failed, creating a deadlock and raising the specter of violence as thousands of increasingly impatient activists, some armed with sticks, massed in the heart of Islamabad despite intense heat.

Addressing the roaring crowd late at night, Qadri said the army had offered to mediate in the stand-off, a proposal he immediately endorsed.

"The army chief has asked us to give him 24 hours to solve the crisis," he told thousands of flag-waving supporters. Khan, speaking shortly after him, echoed his remarks.

"The army will compile and put together a package of our demands and make sure they are implemented," Qadri added.

The army's press wing tweeted that army chief General Raheel Sharif would meet both opposition leaders late on Thursday. No other official comment was immediately available.

Some officials in Sharif's administration have accused the army itself of orchestrating the protests as a way to weaken the prime minister, and many believe that the fate of the anti-government movement ultimately lies in the military's hands.

Pakistan, a nuclear-armed nation of 180 million, has been ruled by the military for half of its entire history and has repeatedly swung between democracy and military. Sharif himself was toppled in a coup in 1999 during his previous tenure.

PAKISTAN ARMY MOVED INTO THE POLITICAL ARENA

Pakistan Army, throughout its 54 years of existence, has been involved in the administration of the country — often in augmentation of bureaucracy in purely civil jobs, occasionally in aid of civil power for maintenance of law and order and off and on in governing the country under Martial Law regimes. It has earned kudos and criticism depending on its aims and achievements in the assigned or assumed tasks. Escorting caravans of refugees, fighting floods, checking illegal trade, running steamers and trains, building roads or killing wild boars were all people friendly activities. Number of times troops were called out in aid of civil power for maintenance of public peace and imposition of the will of the government. Lahore (1953), Kalat (1958), Dir-Bajaur (1961), Balochistan (1974) are examples that fall in this category. These operations were constitutional and executed with efficiency and elan.

Three times 1958, 1969 and 1977 the whole country was placed under Martial Law. In 1999 when the mismanagement of a ruthless dictator had reached a new zenith the Army moved in and replaced the civilian government. Martial Law was not declared. The regime received its legitimacy from the Supreme Court. In all these cases, the purists have vehemently argued against assumption of civil power by the army.

According to them, problems of political adjustment and consensus could have been sorted out through the political process had it been allowed the time. Others make vigorous case in favour of the army leaders' actions and credit them with having saved the country at relevant times.

However, even by the standards of pro-military elements the glaring failure of army leadership to keep the country together in 1971, prevent estrangement of Balochistan in the wake of 1974 Marri-Bugti operations and thwart understated hostility in Sindh during the MRD movement (1983) are exceptions that cannot be glossed over lightly.

It must also be admitted that differences did exist in the perceptions of junior ranks and the leadership component on the role of the army in situations that were purely political. It goes to the credit of the institution and its leadership that the essential unity of the force has remained rock solid.

For this compliments are due to the moral and mental prowess of the army commanders who at relevant times were able to convince the rank and file and indeed the whole country that army's actions were indeed in the defence and extension of supreme national interest. Part of credit must go to army's recruitment and training policies that emphasise loyalty under stress and willing subordination of the individual to the collective will of the institution.

Now back to history. The departing British rulers had initially not contemplated the division of the Indian Army. The Chiefs of Staff in London had 'hoped for a political settlement'. When the Quaid made it clear that he meant to see Pakistan a fully independent country with no binds on its sovereignty, the directive for the bifurcation of the Indian Army was issued. Liaquat Ali

Khan echoed the Quaid and said that Pakistan without an army would collapse like a 'house of cards'. Muslim League was resolved to take over only when the incipient government of Pakistan had its army and under its own control.

A degree of emphasis is detectable. Why such a stance? Was it solely due to the external dangers that undoubtedly loomed large? Or did their concerns have an internal dimension also? Wasn't there an element of doubt in the mind of the two leaders about the capability of political institutions to control and ensure cohesion in the newly acquired state?

'Moth-eaten,' lamented the Quaid-e-Azam when he first saw the map of Pakistan. Implied was a cause to worry and a reason for speedy acquisition of strength to offset the diminished capability. Machinations of the Hindu bureaucracy in the Ministry of Defence ensured that Pakistan's Armed Forces are denied their rightful share of defence equipment.

The new state with no government machinery and infrastructure faced danger from two sides. An influx of refugees and a war in Kashmir in the east and claims to the Frontier province by Afghanistan in the west put Pakistan in a bind. However, despite meagreness in men and material, the Army proved to be the most effective, reliable and stable among the instruments of state power.

Colossal problems and chaos on one hand and proven effectiveness of the army on the other persuaded the early rulers to quickly 'starch the limp security apparatus' they had inherited. The Army claimed and received special patronage from the government. In view of what it could be asked to do in a situation of extreme uncertainty allocation of resources was perfectly justified.

Says Stephen Cohen in his treatise on Pakistan Army, 'There are armies that guard the nation's borders, there are those that are concerned with protecting their own position in the society, and there are those that defend a cause or an idea. The Pakistan Army does all three.' This is a tall order. Its successful fulfilment demands equal in size resources implying a position of pre-eminence in the financial and hence political scheme of things.

The task of maintenance of national unity and cohesion also fell to the lot of the army by default. Pakistan's political leadership was land based and parochial in make-up, approach and outlook. The top rung was always prone to suggestions, allurements and intimidation. In the absence of strong political programmes, parties aspiring for power made no appeal to the people. National politics was confined to the drawing rooms of the elite. Inevitably a permanent climate of instability, like that of monsoon weather alternating regularly between the fair and the cloudy was created.

Pakistan Peoples Party of 1967-71 was an exception but soon after its assumption of power it also became like any other grouping of the established classes. In good time the PPP became to be identified more as a disturber of social harmony and tranquillity than a proponent of a new social order.

Now go back in time again and witness displacements and degradations of governments. At provincial level changes started from the first day of independence. Dismissal of Dr. Khan Sahib ministry in the Frontier on the morrow of independence was followed sometime later by Khurro in Sindh and Mamdot in the Punjab. This points out to early fissures between the centres of power. In East Pakistan Mr. Nur ul Amin was defeated in elections by a student that went to highlight the gulf between the ruling party and popular sentiment.

At the centre a game of musical chairs started after the assassination of Liaquat Ali Khan in 1951. In such a scenario everything had to come to a stand still. After 9 years of impasse, a constitution was finally promulgated only to be abrogated two years later. By then, the politics of Pakistan had entered a dark phase. Sectarianism and parochialism had taken root. Occasionally riots were choreographed for show of force and intimidation. Leaders of political establishment, instead of focussing on the national level crises concentrated on games of power and pelf. The main political party, the Muslim League split up under such pressures.

The vacuum had to be filled in consonance with the laws of nature. The Army moved in on a very good logic. Political instability was affecting the integrity of the Army and hence the defence of the nation was jeopardised. The situation had to be put right. General Ayub Khan, first the Chief Martial Law Administrator, a little later the President, eagerly and competently filled the top leadership slot. He was a military man and had a clear mind but an authoritarian style. He had the Constitution of 1962 tailor made to his requirements. However, he ruled well and laid the foundations for the industrialisation of the country. He also laid the foundations of break up of Quaid-e-Azam's Pakistan.

He authorised a war over Kashmir soon after his victory against Miss Fatima Jinnah in the presidential election. Pakistan Army failed in its objectives in Kashmir (1965) but did succeed in defending the country against Indian invasion across international borders. The pointless war disillusioned people particularly in East Pakistan where they felt insecure, unprotected and exploited. By 1968 movement against Ayub government gathered tremendous momentum and in March 1969 he stepped aside handing over power to the Commander-in-Chief of the Army. Some observers point out that around that time the establishment led by Ayub Khan took the decision to let East Pakistan go its separate way. They point out that it was in conformity with that bias that General Ayub Khan handed over power to the Commander-in-Chief rather than to the Speaker of the National Assembly as was laid down in his own constitution. Theories that General Yahya Khan forced Ayub out are not convincing and are certainly not held out either by the character of Yahya Khan or by the events that followed.

Under General Yahya Khan came the East Pakistan tragedy. Thousands of innocent citizens were killed and the ensuing war resulted in the break of Quaid-e-Azam's Pakistan and emergence of Bangladesh. But was the Army as an institution to blame? Had not the political establishment coaxed, cajoled and encouraged the Army in its actions. Read again the first comment on the army action in Dacca on 26th March 1971 'Thank God, Pakistan has been saved'. It came from a political leader, Mr. Bhutto.

Mr. Bhutto, became the CMLA and the President before he became the first elected Prime Minister of Pakistan. Such was the influence of the military on a 'champion of democracy'. To remove a counterpoise, he quickly forced out General Gul Hassan Khan the incumbent C-in-C who according to many was instrumental in Mr. Bhutto's accession to power.

General Tikka Khan served loyally for four years. Then Mr. Bhutto in preference to a number of other equally competent officers selected General Zia-ul-Haq as the next Chief of Army Staff mainly because he believed the latter to be more reliable.

Events following the 1977 elections, created a crisis of huge proportions. The whole nation was in turmoil and the Army once again took over the administration of the country. True that the Army had intervened only when the country was on the verge of a civil war but equally true is the fact that there was a presence of highly ambitious officers among the top brass. Stephen Cohen mentions that Bhutto had been warned of the dangerous consequences of military crackdown in Balochistan as the middle ranks of Officer Corps were acquiring a taste for political power. Obviously, Mr. Bhutto ignored the warnings.

General Zia proceeded cautiously and read the whole situation carefully. He came up with a perfect solution. He realised that the Pakistani people could be easily rallied under the slogans of Islamisation. He promised Nizam-e-Mustafa leaving its definition in contemporary economic and political terms as vague. Under this scheme Zia acquired the brawn of the street in addition to the power of the state. With this intermixture of formal and informal power came a deeper penetration of the Army into politics. The army also assumed the role of the defender of the ideological borders of the state to the joy of a certain group.

Then in 1979 Soviet Union intervened in Afghanistan. Here the interests of Afghan Mujahideen, Pakistan, United States, China and other Muslim countries came to coincide. Pakistan supported Afghans and the Army trained Mujahideen guerrillas with American weapons. Mujahideen's success was a great plume in the hat of Pakistan Army but the country was left plagued with the fallout.

Zia's era ended in 1988. Some people draw a comparison between the regimes of Ayub and Zia. Although the two regimes lasted about the same number of years but Zia would have continued, had he not been killed in the air crash. Ayub Khan was a reformer who treaded on a number of toes in pursuit of a social agenda. Zia didn't commit that mistake. He brought about no reforms but preserved the status quo in the name of piety. As leader of the army also he was no patch on Ayub. Ayub's army was spick and span; straight, professional and exclusive. Zia transformed it beyond recognition to some of its old souls. It became 'awami' in culture, threw away its exclusivity, acquired hypocrisy, cultivated the art of compromise on standards and learnt the many unsavoury ways that were considered essential to ruling Pakistan.

After General Zia, came General Aslam Beg who now runs an NGO and a political party. He exercised political power through proxy. General Asif Nawaz, who was a little more forthright, created waves when he took on the MQM in Karachi although the party was a partner in the coalition at the centre. General Abdul Wahid was unobtrusive. However, when the occasion called, he exercised the power of his office in a most decisive manner and saw his constitutional bosses President Ghulam Ishaq Khan and Prime Minister Nawaz Sharif out of office. General Karamat was tolerable but towards the fag end of his tenure he was asked to resign over a non-issue. This highhandedness did not go well with the Army.

This was a period when a naval chief also had to go due to a corruption scandal. The overall image of the forces was badly smeared. Their former sheen and prestige had suffered. Their confidence and sharpness was reduced. They came to be treated like any other department of the Government of Pakistan and often assigned duties far removed from the business of warfare. Somewhere along the line they also picked up some of the tasteless peculiarities of their civilian counterparts and became poorer in self-regard.

In such a season of despair, General Pervez Musharraf took over as Chief of Army Staff. His first concern was restoration of the morale of the command. Kargil was an opportunity and he made the best of it. The soldiers found their mettle and were well on their way when the Prime Minister bungled. Victory won in the field was thrown away. Showing complete ignorance of the military system he began to conspire against his own Army Chief. A badly choreographed drama to sack the COAS rebounded with a force that knocked the Prime Minister from his perch.

Having taken over the country as a result of the consensual action by the army, General Pervez Musharraf is now striving for continuity. People have tentatively put their faith in the General and are hoping for results.

Mr.Nawaz Sharif like some of his predecessors had badly underestimated General Pervez Musharraf both as a leader of the army and leader of the country.

5

Time for Pakistan to Modernize its Military

It is necessary for Pakistan to monitor Indian military's modernisation and come up with adequate response. Pakistan is a democratic country with an effectual military force. Its military and political leadership can play a viable role to allay threats to the national security. Political leadership must show a clear direction to the armed forces. The political parties must support the ruling government and military in any crisis situation. Inter services harmony and coordination is necessary in the modern warfare. After the induction of nuclear weapons, wars have become limited, lethal and destructive. In such warfare, it is necessary to have Inter services synergy and better coordination. Therefore, keeping in mind the changing strategic environment and India's technological advancement, Pakistan has to develop and equip its military with latest weapons and equipment. It has to rely on its indigenous defense industry for the maintenance and development of its military machine

An assessment of the enemy's capabilities helps to analyze the intentions of the adversary and its future plans. Without knowing enemy's capabilities, it is difficult to meet future challenges. India is on course to revamping its military machine in next few years to compete with China and browbeat Pakistan. It is squandering about 2.5 percent of its GDP on defense which is a huge amount compared to the other South Asian states. India's defence budget for the year 2010-11 is $32 billion which shows its ambitious designs in the region. This article would assess some of the Indian military's modernization programmes and their implications for the region.

According to a report, India may spend about $120 billion in the next five years to refurbish its military. It has floated a tender to add almost 126 combat aircraft; it's the first time in its history that it has concluded a contract of this magnitude. Many international companies including Dassault Aviation SA, Chicago-based Boeing Co, Lockheed Martin Corp. Saab AB, Russia's United Aircraft Corp. and the European Aeronautic, Defense & Space Co are competing to get the contract. Moreover, India will spend approximately $48 billion through 2017 on purchase of combat jets, helicopters, transport and trainer aircraft. Indian Navy may also buy fighter jets and helicopters worth $7.5 billion through 2022. So it could be analyzed that the next decade would seemingly bring revolutionary change in the Indian military.

Europe's largest defense contractor – BAE Systems Plc – expects that India will become their second-biggest market after the US in the next decade. This company has already won $803 million contract with Hindustan Aeronautics Ltd. for 57 Hawk jet trainers. Such collaboration would improve Indian defense industry. India is also modernizing its fleet of helicopters; the Indian Air Force recently announced that it would acquire more than 230 choppers in the near future. Lockheed is also in talks with the Indian government to sell its Sniper advanced targeting pods for fixed-wing aircraft. All these contracts involve the transfer of technology to India. Such development will give boost to India's fading defense industry.

Indian military is also in negotiations with the US company to supply Hellfire Romeo missile and Longbow radar as part of a bid by Boeing to sell 22 Apache AH-64 helicopters to India. Lockheed is already implementing an order for supplying six Super Hercules planes in a deal worth about $1 billion. The company sealed the order in February 2008. The first plane was delivered to the Indian Air Force late last year and was inducted into the Indian Air Force on Feb. 7; the remaining planes will also be inducted in the IAF in coming years. India is also heading towards induction of Ballistic Missile Defence system. Such system would destabilise the region and may provoke an arms race in South Asia. The Indian government is in dialogue with Lockheed Martin Corp for sale of Patriot Advanced Capability-3 missile systems.

Indian navy will induct few Scorpene submarines with the help of France's state-owned DCNS for an estimated total cost of $4.6 billion. These subs can stay submerged for about a week, making difficult for enemy radars to track and giving more room to Indian navy in the Indian Ocean. India has also purchased eight maritime reconnaissance and anti-submarine aircraft from Boeing Co. for $2.1 billion in 2009 and government recently approved an order for another four. Such inductions would upgrade India's prying capabilities; it would also give Indian Navy strategic outreach in the Indian Ocean. In order to add more teeth to its amphibious warfare capabilities, the navy is planning to induct four Landing Platform Docks to join the fleet alongside INS Jalashwa. These ships will be of 200 meters long and to be able to transport main battle tanks, heavy trucks, Armoured Personnel Vehicles and other heavy machinery. It would also be able to carry out operations of heavy-lift helicopters of the navy. The four LPDs will also have a point missile defence system and a close-in weapon system to protect itself from enemy firing and aircraft.

Indian Army is making strides in modernization and introducing high-tech and all-terrain infantrymen. They will be the Futuristic Infantry Solider as a System (F-INSAS). These soldiers will have the capability to fight in network centric warfare and electronic warfare environment. Indian Army has recently floated a global tender for acquiring an integrated computer and communications system for its infantrymen. The systems included mini-computers or laptops along with GPS and radio systems, which will be part of the F-INSAS programme. The entire process is likely to cost more than $3 billion. The F-INSAS programme was first announced in 2007. The first phase of acquiring and training infantrymen is likely to be over by the end of 2011. These futuristic soldiers will have a more lethal but lighter rifle, lighter but stronger bulletproof jacket and lighter boots, besides ultra modern gadgets to increase his efficiency in the modern warfare. Latest technologies like GPS, radio systems and computers in the form of mini-laptops, helmet-mounted pads or wristbands will enable soldiers to exchange important information with the chain of command under all conditions. The main idea of the F-INSAS programme is to augment the soldier's lethality, survival capacity and mobility.

Indian Army has also inducted first indigenously designed and developed Nishant unmanned aerial vehicles. The 15-foot-long Nishant has a wingspan of nearly 22 feet and a ceiling of around 11,800 feet. Maximum speed is around 115 mph and turnaround launches can be done within 20 minutes. Niashant is also joined with Lakshya, which has a range of 370 miles, a flight ceiling of 29,504 feet and a maximum speed of about 600 mph. Such UAVs would enhance Indian Army's surveillance and reconnaissance capabilities, making things worse for Pakistan military. The army has recently issued a global tender for procurement of 400 towed artillery howitzers. It was recently revealed that trials on various kinds of guns would take place this summer, leading to their induction by end of 2012. India is already in an advanced stage of negotiations with the US for procuring over 145 ultra-light howitzers for their deployment in mountainous regions. Such induction is to deter Kargil type situation in future and also to meet any threat from China. In addition to that Lockheed Martin is also in talks with the Indian government to sell the Javelin shoulder fire missile system to the Indian Army. The potential contract for supplying 8,000 missiles and 300 command launchers could be valued at more than $1 billion.

India has also acquired an Israeli RISAT-2 satellite that has day and night viewing capability. This satellite will keep a 24/7 watch over Pakistan even when the landmass is covered by a thick cloud cover. This capability puts the satellite in the class of what are often called spy satellites. Indian Space Research Organisation (ISRO) has been developing its very own RadarSat at the cost of almost 400 million Indian rupees that would be operational in few years and it would give India an edge in the space.

The level of funds India allocated for the revitalization of its military's capabilities reveals that Indian military is on route to achieving the potential to establish its hegemony in South Asia and also to operationalise its aggressive doctrine against its neighbors. Induction of latest aircraft and Air-borne early warning systems will enhance its air mobility, firepower, reconnaissance and surveillance capabilities. Such a capability is essential for quick and swift operations. India has also brought changes in its military's night time operations' capabilities; such a shift would shore up Indian Military's capacity to carry out day and night operations without any time impediment.

It is necessary for Pakistan to monitor Indian military's modernisation and come up with adequate response. Pakistan is a democratic country with an effectual military force. Its military and political leadership can play a viable role to allay threats to the national security. Political leadership must show a clear direction to the armed forces. The political parties must support the ruling government and military in any crisis situation.

Inter services harmony and coordination is necessary in the modern warfare. After the induction of nuclear weapons, wars have become limited, lethal and destructive. In such warfare, it is necessary to have Inter services synergy and better coordination. Therefore, keeping in mind the changing strategic environment and India's technological advancement, Pakistan has to develop and equip its military with latest weapons and equipment. It has to rely on its indigenous defense industry for the maintenance and development of its military machine.

PAKISTAN'S MILITARY

Analysts today are skeptical about the possibility that Pakistani political parties – which have done little to promote a democratic culture internally, have pursued power with little regard for the public good and whose leaders are unable to communicate with each other without an "international broker" – can provide an alternative to the military. And yet, despite such political uncertainty, the restoration of party-based representative government is a positive development as it aids nation-building and helps facilitate agreement on issues of national significance. After the 2008 elections, for example, the leadership of the Pakistan

Peoples Party (PPP), Pakistan Muslim League-Nawaz (PML-N) and the Awami National Party (ANP) have conducted politics by consultation and consensus building, which has created an expectation that they will be able to sustain a coalition government and stable government-opposition relations. Yet this fragile consensus could rupture if the "international brokers" (mainly the United States) withdraw support, change direction or lose interest in "managing" Pakistan's internal politics.

The PPP-led coalition government is in its third year of rule, but corruption, violence and sectarian strife continue to deepen the crisis of governance. Despite significant political achievements – including the passage of the 18th Amendment, the seventh National Finance Commission Award (which governs the distribution of resources between the four provinces) and a Balochistan package (economic and other measures to address provincial sentiment after former President Pervez Musharraf 's use of force there) – the political government's public stock has been low on account of its weak governance and inability to solve the deepening energy crisis, rising inflation and joblessness. All this has eroded public confidence in party government and democracy. Furthermore, its poor and insensitive handling of the worst floods in Pakistan's history could turn out to be a watershed for the resurgence of the military and even the demise of party rule.

Two contradictory trends are evident in Pakistan's post February 2008 election era. The first is political continuity – the third and fourth generations of the traditional feudal, tribal, religious and business families are entering the political arena. Middle class representation in elite structures remains marginal. Political parties remain personality- centric and are in decay: they are organizationally weak, lack vision and a clear program, and have no leadership succession plan. The ruling coalition led by the Peoples Party has banded together not on the basis of any principle but of expediency and a desire for power.

Second, the social class origins of the dominant institutions, namely the military, is undergoing transformation – the recruitment pattern is shifting from the uppermiddle class to the lower-middle class. The emerging military elites are increasingly from an urban background and not rural. This means that the social composition of Pakistani elites is undergoing change. The emerging elite has humbler origins, hold conservative social and political views and reflect authoritarian tendencies rather than democratic values. Some elite circulation appears to be taking place but the implications for strengthening democracy and a party system remain uncertain.

Given these changing dynamics, the critical question is how is the military adopting to a party-led government? There are several indications that, despite serious crises, civil-military relations are undergoing an important transformation. This is borne out by several developments. In July 2010, Prime Minister Syed Yousuf Raza Gilani ended rising speculation about Gen. Ashfaq Parvez Kayani, chief of army staff, by granting him a three-year extension. This suggests an improved level of trust between the civil and military leadership that is helping to define the parameters of their evolving relationship. In theory and constitutionally, this establishes the norm of the supremacy of civilian leadership.

However, once the chief of army staff is selected, he assumes the role of an arbiter, sometimes broker, and of course, a potential intervener in the country's political process. What role the chief of army staff chooses to play depends on three factors: his personal orientation, political circumstances and the corporate interests of the military.

Seen from this perspective, Kayani has been careful and discrete, revealing little about his political or ideological beliefs except on national security issues. He went public in stating that the Pakistani military is "India centric" in its orientation and approach. Nationally and internationally, he is recognized as a "professional soldier." In 2009, Time magazine declared Kayani the "most influential general in the world." Officials who have worked with Kayani convey that he is calm, calculating and prudent, and keeps his cards close to his chest. While Kayani is trying to extricate the military from politics, a small number of vocal retired generals want to see greater involvement of the military in the governing of the country. On the subject of Kayani's three-year extension, political parties showed considerable restraint and in a muted way welcomed the decision, whereas some retired generals were vociferous in arguing that Kayani should not have accepted the extension. By and large, the decision has been welcomed and seen as the right of an elected government to make.

THE CHANGING CHARACTER AND COMPOSITION OF MILITARY ELITES

During the 1970s, particularly since 1979, the social origins of the military elite have undergone significant changes. Gens. Jehangir Karamat and Pervez Musharraf and their cohorts were the last of the pre-Independence generation. The year 2007 marked the ascendancy of an indigenous post-Independence generation at the helm of military decision making. Until 1971, the base of military elites (brigadiers to general) was relatively small, around 120 officers. Today, there has been a five-fold increase to more than 600 officers.

During the 1960s and until the mid-70s, the generals from a rural background and the Potohar – the so called martial races – were dominant. But the new breed is more urban and comes from more modest social backgrounds. There is a noticeable shift from the "Huntingtonian model of military professionalism" to the "Janowitzian model" – moving beyond a soldierly profession and assuming constabulary functions.

The first noticeable trend is that the military's role in Pakistani society has undergone transformation – it has acquired a new sense of confidence, and is tentative and cautious in showing "deference" to the political leadership. Second, the military elites have been vigorous and aggressive in consolidating control over the security, defense and foreign policy arenas. In relations with the U.S., the global war on terrorism, Afghan policy and relations with India, the military has shown tenacity and craftiness in conveying to the political leadership that in this policy arena, the military will set the direction. The political leadership has shown little resistance and has covered its incompetence by accepting the military's role as a senior partner in this domain. This could also mean the beginning of a new power-sharing mechanism between civil and military relations.

Is there any noticeable shift in this trend in the post February 2008 period? The indications are that the military has made a tactical withdrawal; under Musharraf (1999-2007), particularly after 2001, its policies had become too closely identified with the U.S.-led global war on terrorism. The operations that the military launched in 2005-06 in the Federally Administered Tribal Areas and in Khyber Pakhtunkhwa, formerly known as the North-West Frontier Province, for example, did not secure adequate political or public support, which had a de-moralizing effect on the troops. As political and professional costs mounted, the military leadership sought to regain the trust and confidence of the people.

In the post-Musharraf era, the military elites reassessed and re-strategized their role and relationship with the civilian leadership. They have shown "deference" to the political leadership, which in return has galvanized public support for military operations against the Taliban in Khyber Pakhtunkhwa and the tribal areas. This political support has helped the military refurbish its professional image. Occasionally the military high command has also shown measured resistance to American policy. Examples include the opposition to the Kerry-Lugar Bill (which sets out conditions for U.S. assistance) and pursuing nuclear cooperation with China. There is considerable debate about the ideological orientation of military elites. On that count, three types of groups are discernible: the Ideologicals, Professionals and Democracy Busters. Yet an outstanding feature of Pakistan's military is that having a large army, it has been able to maintain unity of command and considerable degree of coherence in its top echelons. That lends credibility to military professionalism at the global level. There have been coup attempts (1973, 1995, 2003) but none succeeded – the army top commanders gave total support to the army chief.

MILITARY: PUBLIC IMAGE AND TRUST

Has the army been able to restore its public image and rebuild trust? Under Musharraf, the military's professional reputation was damaged on three counts. First was the case of "missing persons" – allegations of abductions of suspected militants by intelligence agencies (ISI, MI) and illegally handing them over to the U.S. Second, during operations in FATA and NWFP (2004-07), allegations that the army violated the ethical principles and practice of warfare tarnished its image and reputation among citizens. Third, the allegations that the military cultivates, protects and supports the "Jihadi networks" implied that a military that relies on a dubious civilian force to pursue its professional objectives is tolerating mercenaries in the battlefield – the very antithesis of professionalism.

Indications are that the return to normalcy in Swat, where the military operation in 2009 drove out the Pakistani Taliban, has helped restore public trust. The July-August 2010 floods – which claimed 1,600 lives, displaced 10 million people in the country and caused extensive infrastructure and crop damage – saw the military take a lead role in relief, rescue operations and reconstruction. This contrasted with the weak response from political leaders and parties in managing the catastrophe. This means that it is too soon to tell whether the "deference" the military has shown for the political leadership is a tactical shift or more deeply rooted. It is visible that both are showing forbearance and caution not to violate the trust. At the highest level, the military leadership appears to be giving advice to civilian leaders privately and firmly. Yet another less recognized trait of Pakistani military elites is that, for almost two decades, they have been deeply involved in insurgency, counterterrorism and clandestine warfare along with the U.S. Therefore there is a segment of Pakistani military officers who are seasoned, proficient and have acquired skills to confidently communicate with domestic and international political leaders. The war in Afghanistan, tensions with India, deepening involvement in the strategic dialogue with the U.S. and military operations in Khyber Pakhtunkhwa and FATA, have given a new professional set skills of combat and negotiations to the top echelons of Pakistan's military.

Thus the current generation of military leaders seems to be showing greater forbearance toward political leadership as compared with their predecessors, yet it is still too soon to tell what the future holds. However, if Kayani stays on the course he has shown in his first tenure (November 2007-10) as chief of army staff into his second term (until November 2013), the direction of civil-military relations in Pakistan may see a new turn and sustainable democracy may become an achievable goal. By December 2010, six lieutenant generals were due to retire and allow Kayani to choose his new team for the next three years. In all probability, none will be given an extension, paving the way for next in succession. Khalid Shamim Wayne, the senior-most among the existing lot, was promoted in September as General and Chairman Joint Chief of Staff Committee. Three already on extension will retire in March 2011 and eight others will retire by the end of 2011; therefore, Kayani will really be designing the higher command of Pakistan for the coming decade. Will he strengthen and consolidate the Professionals and contain the Ideological and Democracy Busters?

The placing and position of a new set of commanders in the next six months will shape the orientation and outlook of the Pakistani army in the coming decade, and the Professionals are likely to retain their dominance. It is pertinent to recognize that the army is the largest among three services and army chief does have an impact in facilitating the selection of air force and naval chiefs. Kayani's second term implies not only continuity and stability among the armed forces but also that he will see the end of Prime Minister Gilani's five-year term in March 2013 and President Zardari's in September 2013.

SUMMARY CONCLUSION

Suffice it to say that the contestation among these groups of officers continues and the command structure allows debate, but at the highest level, shared decision making and collective responsibility prevails and preserves the unity of command. That conveys the strength and resilience of the military as an institution in Pakistan's political setting. There are two overarching factors on which there is broad consensus among all three groups. The first is that India is a serious and potent threat and that Pakistan's military must be ready to counter this threat on any and all forums. The second is that Pakistan's nuclear assets and nuclear power status must be preserved and protected. On both these points, there is a broad national consensus and popular support. What worries international observers and domestic policy analysts is whether the Ideological and the Democracy Busters can band together. Are these two groups a potent force to capture the military? They could become a serious threat if the disconnect between the state and civil society continues to widen. Already the devastating floods have bolstered the credibility of the military as a resilient and professionally competent institution. This could help the military to continue supporting the democratic process in the country or it could also encourage the military to rollback democratic transition. Which path the military chooses will reflect its professionalism or lack thereof.

Saeed Shafqat is an Adjunct Professor at the School of International and Public Affairs, Columbia University in the City of New York. He is also the Director and Professor at the Centre for Public Policy and Governance at FC College, Lahore.

The current generation of military leaders seems to be showing greater forbearance toward political leadership as compared with their predecessors, yet it is still too soon to tell what the future holds... the direction of civil-military relations in Pakistan may see a new turn and sustainable democracy may become an achievable goal.

PAKISTAN MODERNISATION FEEDS CHINA'S EXPORT GROWTH

China has replaced the United Kingdom in fifth position behind the United States, Russia, Germany and France as the world's largest exporters of weapons, according to the annual report on the global arms trade by the Stockholm International Peace Research Institute (SIPRI), released in March. The rise is largely due to growing arms exports to Pakistan, which according to SIPRI, are likely to continue.

"Pakistan – which accounted for 55% of Chinese arms exports – is likely to remain the largest recipient of Chinese arms in the coming years due to large outstanding and planned orders for combat aircraft, submarines and frigates," the SIPRI report said.

Defence ties between the two countries have combined materiel sales and shared geopolitical interests – not least a common enemy in India and a mutual suspicion of the United States. The latter is of particular interest as it was a US embargo in 1966 that first led China to become a materiel supplier to Pakistan in the form of MiG fighter aircraft.

The 1966 MiG sale followed the US decision to withhold further arms sales and spare parts in response to Pakistan's use of US weapons in its 1965 war with India. "The historical moment of 1966 has created the vital and indispensable relationship between Pakistan and China," a senior Pakistan military officer toldIHS Jane's .

CHINESE GREEN LIGHT

More recently, Pakistan's military officers point to the United States' 1990 decision to impose sanctions over its violation of the Pressler Amendment – a US law put in place to guard against Islamabad's development of nuclear weapons.

The most visible and high-profile consequence of the sanctions triggered by the amendment was a US decision to withhold the delivery of 28 Lockheed Martin F-16 fighter aircraft, for which Pakistan had made a partial payment.

In an act of further defiance, Pakistan conducted its first nuclear tests in May 1998 – just three weeks after a series of similar tests were carried out by India.

Within months of the US decision on the F-16s, Pakistani nationalists began denouncing Washington for its "broken promises"."We had people paint crude images of F-16s on the back of trucks alongside anti-US slogans," recalled a senior Pakistani diplomat.

Behind the scenes, discussions between the Pakistan Air Force (PAF) and China's People's Liberation Army Air Force (PLAAF) to jointly manufacture a new fighter aircraft were under way. On the drawing board was an upgraded version of the F-7: a Chinese variant of the Soviet MiG-21. Those discussions eventually bore fruit when the idea of a jointly manufactured aircraft became a reality in the form of the JF-17 Thunder.

A single-engined light fighter aircraft designed by Chengdu with assistance from MiG, the JF-17 was Pakistan's first experience of manufacturing fighter aircraft. So far, the PAF has produced about 40 JF-17s at the Pakistan Aeronautical Complex (PAC) north of Islamabad, but there are plans to eventually manufacture up to 150 aircraft. While it was originally mainly an assembly and test-flight facility, PAC is now manufacturing 60% of the airframe and 80% of the avionics.

Although the JF-17 was initially visualised as a second line of defence to fly alongside the US-manufactured F-16, senior PAF officers said they do not discount the possibility of the PAF one day relying almost exclusively on China for its frontline fighters.

The PAF has previously revealed discussions with China of the purchase of up to 36 Chengdu J-10 fighter aircraft, although IHS Jane's understands that a final agreement has been on hold since early 2012 due to Pakistan's fraught finances. One way to finance the J-10 purchase could be to export the JF-17s in partnership with China to third countries.

In early 2012 IHS Jane's reported that China and Pakistan expect to sell 300 JF-17s to markets across Africa, Asia and the Middle East by 2017, marketing the aircraft as a cost-effective alternative to surplus US Air Force or other second-hand F-16s that they might otherwise consider.

In mid-2012 Pakistan's ambassador to Indonesia was quoted by Indonesian media confirming that Islamabad had made an offer to sell a batch of JF-17s to the Indonesian Air Force, which faces this situation.

While the JF-17's development is one outcome of closer strategic ties, Western defence officials say the largest single defence contract between China and Pakistan is yet to come. The Pakistan Navy and China have been in discussions for the past two years over the potential purchase of up to six new Chinese submarines, although neither country has confirmed the types of boats under consideration.

In February IHS Jane's reported that the China Shipbuilding and Offshore International Corporation (CSOC) had offered rare information on the export version of China's latest conventionally powered submarine, the S20 or Yuan class. Western defence officials say the Pakistan Navy's previous experience of operating Khalid-class (Agosta 90B) submarines purchased from France in the 1990s gives it the ability to add modern systems that are currently not standard features on the S20.

The systems mentioned include the air independent propulsion (AIP) system installed on the Agosta 90B boats.

TRI-SERVICE ARMS PROVIDER

The PN has also received Azmat-class fast-attack craft, 63 m-long, 560-tonne vessels based on Houjian-class (Type 037/2) missile craft in service with the People's Liberation Army Navy.

Designed to carry eight C-802A (YJ-83/CSS-N-8 'Saccade') surface-to-surface missiles, two 25 mm guns and two 12.7 mm machine guns, two have been built – one in China and the second by Karachi Shipyard and Engineering Works (KSEW) under a technology transfer agreement.

China also previously agreed to sell four Sword-class (F-22P) frigates – a modification of the Jiangwei II (Type 053H3) design – to the Pakistan Navy in a similar deal involving collaboration between KSEW and Chinese shipbuilders.

China has either jointly produced or provided the Pakistan Army with main battle tanks in the form of Al Khalid (MBT 2000), Al Zarrar (Type 59/59M), Type 69 and Type 85-IIAP, artillery, including Norinco 122 mm Type 83/D-30 howitzers, and indigenously produced Anza Mk II air-defence systems based on the China Precision Machinery Import and Export Corporation (CPMIEC) Qian Wei 1 (QW-1) Vanguard surface-to-air missile and the Anza Mk III based on the QW-2.

East looks west

In addition to meeting the defence hardware needs of Pakistan's armed forces, Beijing also appears to be working to further solidify its strategic ties with Islamabad.

In February the Pakistan government formally handed over the management of the Gwadar deep sea port in southwestern Pakistan to a Chinese operator.

The move followed a decision to revoke an earlier contract with Port of Singapore Authority (PSA), which signed a 40-year management contract for Gwadar in 2007 but had been criticised by Pakistani officials for failing to fulfil promises to develop the facility. The facility is about 700 km west of Karachi but only 80 km east of the Iranian border and close to the Gulf.

Other sources said that Pakistan Navy intransigence over its development of a nearby base, PNS Akram, had blocked PSA's development opportunities at the site. Pakistan Navy senior navy officers who have spoken toIHS Jane's have denied these claims.

Senior Pakistani government officials told IHS Jane's that the contract for Gwadar was a significant attempt by Pakistan to lure Beijing into establishing a larger presence in the Indian Ocean Region (IOR).

Some reports seen by IHS Jane's have suggested that China has promised Pakistan that it will spend USD1 billion to develop a road and train network linking Gwadar to western China.

This will radically reduce the travel time between China and the Gulf region and reduce China's dependence on the energy supplies travelling through the South China Sea, through which 80% of its gas and oil currently passes.

China has so far resisted Pakistan's overtures to establish a naval presence at Gwadar, but the strategic advantages of diversifying its energy lines of communication will not be lost on Beijing.

That closer ties with Pakistan also complicate India's plans to develop strategic dominance of the IOR is a definite bonus for China, while Pakistan's decision to pursue Chinese co-operation rather than rely on US technology offers a potential path for other developing nations that are leery of the threat of Western embargoes.

PAKISTAN NAVY MODERNIZATION PROGRAM

Traditionally the Pakistan Navy was seen as Pakistan's coastal guardian, the regulator of the country's maritime trade routes and the sea based counter to Pakistan's historical rival India. However since the advent of the September 11th attacks, the Pakistan Navy's roles and expectations have greatly been revised and expanded. Besides India, the threat of sea-based global terrorism, drug smuggling and trafficking has become critical. As a result the Pakistan Navy (PN) has been given greater national and international responsibility in countering these issues. For example the PN became a member of the primarily NATO (North Atlantic Treaty Organization) Combined Task Force – 150 (CTF-150). Next to war and terrorism, Pakistan's economic growth, reliance on sea-based trade as well as new economic assets such as Gwader Port have expanded the Navy's responsibility in its traditional roles. Thus the Pakistan Government and Navy have set out in not only modernizing, but also expanding the current surface, sub-surface and aviation fleets – as well as land based and electronic assets.

Surface Fleet

Presently the mainstay of the Pakistani surface fleet consists of six Type-21 frigates. Bought in the early 1990s and extensively upgraded, these frigates form the core of the PN's defensive and offensive forces. However new global and economic responsibility pushed the Pakistani government to revise the role of the Navy. Historically the Navy was and to an extent still is the weakest branch of the Pakistan Armed Forces. It is not only inferior in the sense that its budget is not as high as the Army or Air Force – but also neglected in modernization. The neglect was mainly due to economic and military sanctions on Pakistan during the 1990s – heavily impairing the military's modernization. However since the 21st century the Pakistan Navy has entered a phase of massive modernization and expansion, notably its surface combatant fleet.

In 2006 the Pakistan Navy ordered four F-22P type frigates from China in a deal valued $600mn U.S. The F-22P is based off the successive Type-053H3 design, however adopts the Radar Cross Section (RCS) reduction techniques of the 053H3's successor the Type-054 – and boasts a greater displacement of 2500 tons. The frigate is armed with eight C-802 anti-ship warfare (AShW) missiles; eight FM-90 surface-to-air missiles (SAM); one AK-176M main gun and two Chinese 30mm close in weapon systems (CIWS) – and can be loaded with one Z-9EC helicopter. Named the Zulfiqar Class by the Navy, the PNS Zulfiqar is expected to be delivered.

in 2009, and the remaining three by 2013. The fourth F-22P will be built in Pakistan.

The Pakistan Naval Chief of Staff, Admiral Muhammad Afzal Tahir said that the Navy would request for six Oliver Hazard Perry Class frigates from the United States. However the U.S Chief of Naval Operations Admiral Mullen said that the frigates the PN requested would not be available for transfer for at least two years – however once they are available, high priority would be given to Pakistan. It is unclear what role the Perry Class frigates would play in the PN.

It is possible that they will replace the aging Type-21 frigates in the short or medium term. What the PN Perry Class will be equipped with is also uncertain, however potent upgrades do exist and have been carried out on the Perry Class. For instance the Perry Class can be upgraded with an eight-cell Mk.41 vertical launch system (VLS) for thirty-two quad-pack Evolved Sea Sparrow Missiles (ESSM) – giving it good anti-air capability. The PN would likely be interested in the air defence upgrades as well as the Perry's existing anti-submarine warfare (ASW) capability in the form of two-triple Mk.32 launchers for the Mk.42 torpedo system.

Admiral Muhammad Afzal Tahir also mentioned that the Navy would also procure another four new built frigates – the type has not yet been chosen. The new type is expected to be larger and more capable than the Zulfiqar (F-22P) Class. No specifications or potential suppliers have been disclosed, but it is possible that it will be equipped with along the same lines as other modern frigates under development and construction around the world. The general trend for new frigates show them to have a displacement of at least 3000 tons and based off a stealthy or low RCS design. They are often equipped with eight surface-to-surface missiles; a VLS for thirty two SAM; ASW capability in the form of torpedoes or anti-submarine missiles/rockets; a helicopter deck for a 5t to 10t type; and capability to launch Unmanned Aerial and Underwater Vehicles (UAV & UUV). Frigates that fall into this category would include the Chinese Type-054A; German MEKO A-200; French Formidable and FREMM Class. Options listed by the Pakistan Navy could include any of the above, but will definitely include a heavily scaled-up F-22P variant. According to Janes, Pakistan is aiming to manufacture at least two of the four new frigates.

The Navy has a requirement for at least four corvettes. At IDEAS 2006 DCN of France proposed its Gowind 120 design – a stealth corvette based off the larger FREMM frigate. However according to the Turkish Press, it appears that the Pakistan Navy chose the Turkish MILGEM National Corvette project for the tender. The Turkish Press reported that the Pakistan Navy is interested in procuring at least 4 MILGEM, of which one would be built in Turkey and the rest in Pakistan. Compared to the French Gowind 120 design, the MILGEM has a displacement of 2000 tons compared to the Gowind's 1250. The MILGEM also has a stealthy design and unlike the Gowind 120, it has ASW capability in the form of two triple Mk.32 torpedo launchers. According to Turkish media, negotiations between Pakistan and Turkey should be underway and Pakistan would decide on the weapon systems of its corvettes. It is likely that the Pakistani MILGEM will be equipped with eight Harpoon Block II anti-ship/surface-to-surface missiles. It is unclear however whether PN MILGEM will have the twenty-one cell Rolling Airframe Missile (RAM) anti-air and Mk.32 ASW systems. Potential additions to the design include VLS SAM – such as the South Africa Naval Umkhonto for added air defence or other weapon systems in place of American counterparts.

Modernization of the Navy's fast attack craft (FAC), missile boat, mine-counter measure and auxiliary fleets will also take place. For instance the PN issued plans to procure a total of eight MRTP-33 FAC from Turkey. It also ordered four locally produced Quwaat Class missile boats. The former Chief of Naval Staff Admiral Karimullah said that plans are underway to procure two or more new mine countermeasure ships and one new auxiliary tanker.

SUBMARINE FLEET

Historically the Pakistani submarine fleet has been well equipped and qualitatively on par – if not superior – to that of the Indian Navy. Currently the PN has three Agosta-90B and two

Agosta-70 conventional diesel powered submarines. The third Agosta-90B – PNS Hamza – is equipped with MESMA Air Independent Propulsion (AIP) System. The first two Agosta-90Bs, PNS Khalid and PNS Saad will be retrofitted with the same system (AIP). According to Janes, the PN's Agosta-90Bs are armed with French BlackShark torpedoes. They are also equipped with SM-39 Exocet anti-ship missiles – and are poised to eventually carry the Harpoon Block II. German DM2A4 torpedoes have also been ordered for the Agosta-90Bs.

The Pakistan Navy will also procure another three AIP-equipped submarines of a new generation. A Request For Proposal (RFP) may have been sent sometime in 2005 or 2006 – and the top two competing firms were clearly DCN of France and HDW of Germany. At IDEAS 2006 in Karachi models of the DCN Marlin and HDW Type-214 were displayed.

The DCN Marlin was based off the successful Scorpene SSK design (six of which the Indian Navy recently ordered), but had design elements of the Barracuda Nuclear Attack submarine.

The HDW Type-214 was based off the very successful Type-209, but used the next generation fuel-cell AIP system and was compatible with the DM2A4 torpedo as well as future IDAS submarine launched missile. Major requirements in the tender were local manufacturing for all submarines as well as compatibility with the Harpoon Block II.

Although both DCN and HDW were willing to allow Pakistan produce the submarines – DCN charged extra funds for Harpoon integration. Another setback for the Marlin was that it was still under development and would be difficult to evaluate.

On April 21st 2007 the Berlin based Neues Deutschland reported that the Pakistan Navy entered negotiations with Germany for three Type-214 manufacturing kits for approximately 1.2bn Euro. If true, then this deal would mark the first German-Pakistan defence exchange valued over $1bn U.S. According to the source, the PN Type-214s would be equipped with Harpoon Block II anti-ship missiles. If the deal is finalized, then these submarines will likely be equipped with DM2A4 torpedoes as well. It is unclear whether Pakistan will procure the IDAS submarine launched missile – which could give the Type-214 anti-air capability. However an early article about the IDAS listed Pakistan as a potential customer.

The Navy also operates three Midget or X-Class submarines for Special Forces operations, torpedo attacks and mine lying. It is not yet known whether the Navy intends to replace them. However at IDEAS 2006, DCN displayed its SMX-23 light SSK design and pushed it for export. Although the PN has not shown any official interest in the SMX-23, it is worth noting that the light SSK is capable of AShW, ASW, deploy Special Forces and due to its small size, suitable for laying mines. Roughly half the size and cost of the Scorpene SSK, the SMX-23 has the potential to become a solid coastal and littoral defence asset.

AVIATION FLEET

Currently the Pakistan Navy has eight P-3C Orion Maritime Patrol Aircraft on order from the United States. The deal was valued at nearly $1bn U.S. and also includes the refurbishment and upgrade of the Navy's present two P-3 Orion. These aircraft are capable of anti-submarine and anti-surface warfare, as well as maritime reconnaissance. In late 2006 the Navy also requested three P-3 Orion aircraft equipped with the Hawkeye 2000 Airborne Early Warning (AEW) systems valued a total of approximately $855mn U.S. The new Orion and Orion-Hawkeye aircraft will give the Pakistan Navy a formidable aviation force. While the Orion is a renown and famous maritime warfare aircraft, the Hawkeye is equally as established as a good naval AEW and Control aircraft. It is possible that the Pakistan Navy will procure Link 16 (or 11) data-link sets and system to enhance coordination and communication between its aircraft, surface and sub-surface combatants.

Alongside the F-22P frigate order, the PN ordered six Z-9EC helicopters from China, the helicopter deal was valued at $150mn U.S. These helicopters can be used for anti-surface and anti-submarine warfare, as well as search and rescue and patrol operations. The Pakistan Navy has not yet disclosed plans about procuring additional helicopters of any type beyond the Z-9EC.

CHINA AND PAKISTAN'S ALL-WEATHER FRIENDSHIP

Much to the befuddlement of the rest of the world – and as ironic as it is – Communist China and Islamic Pakistan are fast friends. It's all hail to China in Pakistan and as other partnerships wither and die, these two countries continue to devote energy to strengthening their relationship. China has historically come to Pakistan's rescue with economic, political, military and nuclear assistance and perhaps what was once a relationship founded on a mutual disillusionment with India has moved toward one with more aspirational intentions on both sides.

It would appear that Pakistan has been the greater beneficiary of this friendship – from military to economic assistance, China has stood by Pakistan, but is the friendship really that sustainable? Andrew Small from the German Marshall Fund certainly seems to think so. An Asia expert, Small recently published a book examining what he calls the unusual nature of the secretive relationship between China and Pakistan and argues that it is much more promising than Pakistan's erratic ties with the U.S. And indeed, history supports this. On a visit to Pakistan earlier this year, China's Foreign Minister Wang Yi assured Islamabad that China and Pakistan were in sync on all matters and have an "iron-clad" understanding between them, one that has taken years to hone and fortify.

Wang also announced at a meeting with his Pakistani counterpart that Chinese President Xi Jinping would be visiting Pakistan soon to discuss economic cooperation and support. Indeed, Beijing's ambitious Silk Road initiative – in which the China Pakistan Economic Corridor (CPEC) is a part – running from China across South and Central Asia, makes a strong case for Chinese involvement and interest in Pakistan. The CPEC involves a major overhaul of infrastructure, with rail, roads, pipelines and ports in a bid to ease the energy crisis and increase investment in Pakistan. This is in addition to the China-Pakistan agreement on fiber optic cable that would connect Pakistan's capital with Chinese borders, along with a $6.5 billion commitment to build a new nuclear power plant in Karachi. In fact, economic opportunities for Pakistan look endless, but given the increasingly serious state of terrorism in Pakistan, some find Beijing's confidence in its "all-weather" friend a tad perplexing.

In fact, China and Pakistan function in a partnership carefully conditioned on their usefulness for each other. Beijing is mindful that Pakistan can play a significant role in China's quest to establish itself as a strategic global power. An economic corridor in Pakistan would not only allow it to connect with South and East Asia, it would also serve as an alternative transportation network for Chinese energy into the Western world. Pakistan is not the only one to benefit.

A little known but important example is the Pakistan China Free Trade Agreement signed in 2006. Trade between Pakistan and China rose quickly, and China had become Pakistan's top source of imports by 2009. China's relative importance in Pakistan's global trade has only increased, with total bilateral trade growing eight-fold in the past decade, whereas Pakistan's total trade with the world only tripled in this time period. However, trade patterns paint a troubling picture for Pakistan: While China utilized 57 percent of the tariff concessions offered by Pakistan, Pakistan's use of Chinese reductions was just 5 percent. This trickled down to local industries complaining that cheaper Chinese products were hurting high-cost local products. A second-phase China-Pakistan FTA is being negotiated, with Pakistan hoping for larger coverage and more immediate concessions. What Pakistan does not realize, however, and perhaps what Chinese negotiators use to their advantage, is that it is not such much the number of concessions, but their target.

A trade agreement with an economic giant such as China could have resuscitated Pakistan's dwindling share in the global trade market but it did not even make a dent, in part because of Pakistan's inability to ask for the right concessions. In fact, India and China's bilateral trade grew more in comparison – rising by a factor of almost 11 in the past decade – without a trade deal with the across-the-board tariff concessions that Pakistan enjoys.

While the burden of responsibility of a failed FTA cannot be placed on China's shoulders, it is important for Pakistan to recognize the essence of Chinese cooperation, which is conditional and transactional in nature. Andrew Small in an interview says: "Chinese investments are not purely for reasons of commerce or strategic economic geography – China knows that its friend is facing an uncertain future and is prepared to make these commitments in part in order to help shore the country up." What Small perhaps refrained from mentioning is that the latter is true because China's power-seeking interests are tied very closely with Pakistan's stability and China's contributions are expected to be paid for by Pakistan in kind.

Recently, not only has China wedged itself into the Afghan peace process, offering to mediate with the Taliban on behalf of Afghanistan when talks stalled, it is also using its diplomatic influence with Pakistan for more aggressive action against terrorist factions, actively assuming was once the role of Western powers. Pakistan should know that China will not be a bystander as terrorism persists on the borders of Afghanistan and Pakistan, given the threat of it spilling into China. Any assistance from China that does not serve Beijing's larger goals would be contingent on how Pakistan handles the escalating problem of terrorism in the region.

While India's growing importance to the U.S. is not a threat to Pakistan, it remains a major indicator that China is the single most important alliance that Pakistan could want. It would be extremely unfortunate for Pakistan if it failed to fully appreciate both the "worth" of China's all-weather friendship and the cost – not just economic – of losing it.

PAKISTAN'S RESURGENT SECTARIAN WAR

Sectarian violence between Sunni Deobandi and Shia Muslims in Pakistan has escalated in recent years, resulting in approximately 2,300 deaths in Pakistan's four main provinces between 2007 and 2013 and at least 1,500 deaths in the Federally Administered Tribal Areas (FATA) agency of Kurram since 2007. Local networks perpetrate most of this violence, but the sectarian phenomenon also has important ties to regional security dynamics and transnational terrorist networks. Sunni Deobandi militants that first began organizing with the support of Pakistani security services in the 1970s and 1980s have directed their violence against Pakistan's Shia minority, the Pakistani state, and the general populace.

THE BIRTH OF SUNNI AND SHIA SECTARIAN ENTREPRENEURS

Initially founded as an inclusive Muslim-majority state, Pakistan's sectarian tensions have deepened over the course of its history. Today's militant sectarian actors in Pakistan trace their origins to internal and external political trends that began in the 1970s and early 1980s. During that time, General Muhammad Zia-ul-Haq's campaign of Islamization alienated many Shias, who saw it as a majoritarian attempt to make the country more Sunni. At the same time, Iran was actively exporting its 1979 revolution to Shia communities outside Iran. By the mid-1980s, Iran-backed groups and clerics dominated religious Shia activism in Pakistan. The most notable of these groups was the Tehreek-e-Nifaz-e-Fiqh-e-Jafaria (TNFJ) led by Allama Arif ul Hussain Al-Hussaini, who demanded greater Shia autonomy within the country's legal system and endorsed the leadership of Ayatollah Ruhollah Khomeini.

Fearful of Iranian encroachment, General Zia found an ally in the Sipah-e Sahaba Pakistan (SSP), a Sunni Deobandi group founded in 1985 by Maulana Haq Nawaz Jhangvi, who was then a member of the Jamiat Ulema-e Islam party. Based in the Jhang district of Punjab, whose rural area is dominated by Shia landlords, Maulana Jhangvi positioned himself as a player in the sectarian wars regionally and nationally, engaging in both anti-Shia and anti-Iran rhetoric.

From the Fringe to the Mainstream

Allama al-Hussaini and Maulana Jhangvi were assassinated in separate attacks in 1988 and 1990, planting the seeds for targeted killings of other leaders and the emergence of structured Sunni Deobandi–Shia sectarian violence. The SSP, which now operates under the name Ahl-e Sunnat Wal Jamaat (ASWJ), grew throughout the 1990s, leaving an indelible mark on the politics and political economy of Punjab and the broader nation. Lashkar-e Jhangvi (LeJ) and Sipah-e Muhammad Pakistan (SMP), offshoots of the SSP and TNFJ, respectively, unleashed a brutal wave of violence in Punjab and Karachi in the 1990s, ultimately precipitating a crackdown by the Pakistan Muslim League government in Punjab from 1998–99.

The crackdown's long-term effects were limited; the ASWJ continues to operate openly despite a nominal ban and LeJ and Shia militant groups remain active. In Pakistan's four provinces, Shia militants have targeted SSP/ASWJ members and sympathizers, as well as Sunni Deobandi clerics and religious students. The LeJ's violence is far more prolific and indiscriminate than that of Shia militants. It has carried out repeated attacks with mass casualties, targeting Shia pilgrims and residential communities.

Despite sporadic crackdowns, the SSP/ASWJ partly owes its continued resilience to the Faustian bargains Pakistan's civilian and military leaders have made with it. Although in many cases the alli-ances appear to be initiated at the local level, outside of the control of party leaders, the ruling Pakistan Muslim League-Nawaz (PML-N) party has at times entered into unofficial partnerships with the SSP/ASWJ, motivated by both electoral considerations and a desire to keep Punjab free of militant violence. Former PML-N Punjab law minister Rana Sanaullah admitted in 2010 that he met the SSP/ASWJ chief "twice to secure votes for the upcoming by-elections." The PML-N is not unique is this regard. A number of politicians from the Pakistan Peoples Party (PPP) have also sought an ASWJ endorsement in recent elections, in part to deny the PML-N an opportunity to partner with the SSP. In 1993, the SSP joined the Punjab provincial government, led by the PPP; Sheikh Hakim Ali, a senior SSP leader, served in the PPP's Punjab provincial cabinet "despite having eight murder cases registered against him."

LeJ Fuses with Al-Qaeda and the Pakistani Taliban

Even as Pakistan's Deobandi Sunni sectarian groups have worked to enter the political mainstream—the ASWJ now positions itself as a political party and fielded at least forty candidates in the 2013 general elections—they have also developed ties to antistate terrorist organizations. The SSP/ASWJ forged initial training linkages with al-Qaeda in the 1980s. The bonds grew deeper during the 1990s, when the LeJ operated from a safe haven in Afghanistan from which it planned attacks in Pakistan. Since the September 11 attacks, LeJ has strengthened its partnerships with al-Qaeda and the TTP, supplying both groups with high-level, dual-hatted operatives, such as Qari Mohammad Zafar and Qari Hussain Mehsud. Many LeJ operatives, including Zafar—who was killed in a 2010 drone attack—fled to the FATA as al-Qaeda and similar groups faced a stiff crackdown in urban areas.

In FATA, LeJ operatives have evolved far beyond sectarian motives and opportunistic alliances. Zafar's successor, Abu Zar Azzam, has become an outspoken jihadist preacher, calling for all-out war with the Pakistani state in audio and video releases. Like Qari Hussain Mehsud, Azzam was educated at Karachi's Jamia Farooqia madrasah. LeJ fighters took part in major complex attacks in Punjab between 2007 and 2011, including a 2009 attack on the Sri Lankan cricket team.

THE RESURGENCE OF SECTARIAN VIOLENCE AMID A REGIONAL WAR

Rising conflict in the greater Middle East over the past five years has strengthened the sectarian political narrative in Pakistan and emboldened militant networks. Prime Minister Nawaz Sharif has close political ties to Saudi Arabia. In March, Riyadh provided Islamabad with $1.5 billion in aid. Pakistani officials initially sought to obscure the source of the donation. Several Shia activists the author spoke with believe that Islamabad is sending Sunni fighters to Syria. These allegations of direct governmental support for fighters have not been substantiated, but other analyses based on press reporting on foreign fighter presence suggest the number of Pakistani Shia fighters in Syria fighting on behalf of the al-Assad regime may be roughly comparable to the number of Pakistani Sunnis fighting against it.

While the Pakistani state is tilting toward the Gulf Arab Sunni camp, Pakistan-based militants are increasingly setting their eyes on Iran. In January, a TTP commander called on anti-Shia sectarian activists to join his group and kill the Shia "before they are able to flee to Iran." In February, a TTP splinter group launched the network's first attack on an Iranian installation inside Pakistan, targeting Tehran's consulate in Peshawar. In the same month, Jaish al-Adl, an Iranian Sunni Baloch insurgent group based in Pakistan, kidnapped Iranian border guards, prompting threats of reprisal strikes by Tehran.

Iran is currently believed to play a limited though significant role in Pakistan's sectarian war. It was allegedly involved in the killing of a Saudi intelligence officer in Karachi in May 2011. Karachi police officials also claim that Shia militants in the city receive training and refuge in Iran. And Tehran may be backing a new Shia political party, the Majlis Wahdat-e Muslimeen (MWM). The MWM appears less inclined to follow the Hezbollah model and more inclined to follow the peaceful approach of Bahrain's Al-Wefaq. But there are indications the party is involved in some violence: Police officials interviewed in both Karachi and Quetta linked the party to some killings of Sunni Deobandis.

Conclusions

Sunni Deobandi-Shia sectarian violence is an enduring problem in Pakistan as it is intimately linked to the broader, pervasive phenomenon of Deobandi militancy. According to a former senior Pakistani federal law enforcement official, when Deobandi militant groups seek to keep their rank and file "active," their "natural fallback position is sectarian." Foreign actors and regional conflicts have and will continue to exacerbate sectarian tensions in Pakistan. But sectarianism in Pakistan is not dependent on external influences. It has become an established industry with entrepreneurs abetted or patron-ized by a broad segment of power brokers inside Pakistan. Until it is dealt with structurally, Sunni Deobandi–Shia sectarian violence will continue. Pakistan is unlikely to see Iraq-style sectarian violence that existentially threatens the country. But the continuation of sectarian bloodshed, along with the mainstreaming of purveyors of sectarian hatred, will further radicalize elements in both Sunni Deobandi and Shia communities and consolidate Pakistan's transition toward an ugly majoritarian state.

PAKISTAN: THE RESURGENCE OF BALUCH NATIONALISM

Frédéric Grare presented his paper, "Pakistan: The Resurgence of Baluch Nationalism," which analyzes the conflict in a vast yet sparsely populated Baluchistan, a Pakistani province straddling Pakistan, Iran, and Afghanistan.

Addressing the developments since the printing of his paper, Grare emphasized that the possibility of a military intervention in Baluchistan has now materialized. Grare introduced his paper by outlining Baluchistan's significance:

- Unchecked, Baluchistan can add to the volatility of the region.
- Baluchis live all across Afghanistan, Iran and Pakistan.
- There are two military bases in Baluchistan, used by the U.S. to fight the war on terrorism.
- Baluchistan's subsoil holds vast mineral resources, 36 percent of Pakistan's total gas production, large quantities of coal, gold, copper, silver, platinum, aluminum and most importantly uranium.
- Baluchistan is the location of Pakistan's nuclear tests.
- A commercial and military port in Gwadar is under construction mainly with Chinese capital and labor. Chinese presence is perceived especially in India as a threat, and by others as a way for China to have an eye on the Middle East.

Grare explained the conflict in Baluchistan by answering three questions: what is the conflict about; who are the actors; what does it tell us about Pakistan today? Grare argued that the conflict in Baluchistan is essentially about three issues.

First, the Baluchis have been denied a fair share of their natural resources' revenues. Second, the Baluchis are demographically marginalized as manifested in the construction of the Gwadar port, the absence of technical schools and colleges in the region, and acquisition of land around the Gwadar port by Pakistan Navy and Coast Guard at a minimal, below the market price. Third, the feeling of dispossession and colonization of Baluchistan by Punjab through a predominantly Punjabi army has been reinforced through the building of cantonments in the three most sensitive areas of Baluchistan: Sui, with its gas-producing installations; Gwadar, with its port; and Kohlu, the "capital" of the Marri tribe.

Grare identified that the actors in the Baluch nationalist movement are not strictly tribal leaders. Additionally, the movement is not confined to tribal areas. The Baluchistan Student's Organization (BSO), which represents educated, but underemployed Baluchis and the young educated middle class Baluchis in the Gwadar region have been changing the sociology of the region and also the meaning of the movement. Out of some 28 Sardars (tribal chiefs), three are opposing the government—Khair Bux Marri, Ataullah Mengal, and Akbar Bugti. Marri and Bugti are fighting militarily. The three tribal chiefs now know that any division in the movement would be suicidal. Grare added that the Baluch "diaspora" in Pakistan could play a role in the Baluch nationalist movement.

Grare emphasized that ever since the start of the crisis, Islamabad has been spreading rumors about a "foreign hand" in Baluchistan. India has been suspected of wanting to forge an alliance with Afghanistan against Pakistan, the Baluch as well as the Pakistanis think that Washington would like to use Baluchistan as a rear base for an attack on Iran, and Iran is suspected of supporting Baluch activists in order to counter such a Pakistan-U.S. plot.

Some Pakistanis perceive the U.S. using its Greater Middle East initiative to dismantle the major Muslim states and redefine borders in the region. Some Baluch nationalists charge the U.S. with conspiring with the Pakistan government to put an end to Baluch claims. So far nobody has been able to prove any of these accusations.

Grare pointed that the charges by Pakistan that the Baluch rebels are financed from abroad could serve to mobilize international support for Pakistan, particularly from the U.S., and neutralize opposition to a Pakistani military intervention. Hence these charges must be understood as part of a larger effort to discredit Baluch nationalism. Grare contended that given Baluchistan is an important center for the trafficking of arms and drugs that generates income capable of financing the supply of arms and ammunition to local armed groups, it is not certain that Baluchistan really needs outside financial support.

Analyzing the outcome of the secession of Baluchistan, Grare said that an independent Baluchistan will be unstable. For Pakistan it will be a loss of natural resources, strategic depth and testing facilities. Iran and Afghanistan, both with strong Baluch minorities in their territories, will be highly concerned by an independent Baluchistan because it could revive Baluch support for a Greater Baluchistan. A change of regional boundaries will not be favorable for India since it could stimulate irredentism in Kashmir and in the territories of the Northeast.

Grare concluded that the Baluch crisis epitomizes the army's mode of governance and its relation with Pakistan's citizens and world public opinion. Pakistan is a military dictatorship that still favors military solutions over political ones and the Pakistani government is using Islam and terrorism to forge the cause of Baluchistan crisis. Grare reasoned that the Baluch cannot expect to prevail over a determined and superior government. However, he perceived the risks of prolonged guerilla as quite real. For meaningful negotiations Grare recommended the building of trust between the Baluchis and Pakistani government. Not building the cantonments and increasing the unit price of gas accorded to Baluchistan would be useful places to start.

During the question and answer section, Grare was asked how the Pakistani government should negotiate with the Baluch middle class, which is more political and ideological than the Sardars who are more concerned with the preservation of their tribal influence. Grare responded that the middle class is still emerging and has not fully materialized.

The government must negotiate with part of the representation which is in the provincial assembly and hope that these people will convey the message down to what is the real leadership of the movement. When asked if the military confrontation of BLA can be diffused by tactical concessions on issues such as the cantonments, Grare said that the Baluch are asking for no more than the respect of the 1973 constitution and tactical concessions on cantonments and the low unit price of gas accorded to Baluchistan are important initiatives for creating trust and having meaningful negotiations.

On the recommendations of the Parliamentary Sub commission, Grare said they were not implemented because of a lack of political will. The recommendations were neither revolutionary, nor sufficient to fully remedy the Baluch sense of dispossession, but if implemented they would be a step in the right direction. Grare was asked if he found in his research that as in Sindh, there is a growing acceptance in Baluchistan of the 1940 resolution (the backbone for the demand of Pakistan) as a reasonable compromise between the break up of Pakistan and a centralized dictatorial Pakistan. Grare emphasized that this is exactly what the Baluchis are asking for: the autonomy of Baluchistan within the federation.

With respect to the possible use of chemical weapons, Grare did not think this would significantly change the international involvement in the matter, for that would happen out of a larger concern for Western security and the stability of Pakistan, and the region. When asked about the need to construct cantonments and a port in the region, Grare said that these projects are enhancing the feeling of marginalization and dispossession in Baluchis and they must integrate the local population.

6

History of Afghanistan

Afghanistan, officially the Islamic Republic of Afghanistan, is a landlocked country located in the centre of Asia, forming part of South Asia, Central Asia, and Greater Middle East, it is also considered to be part of a broader West Asia. With a population of about 29 million, it has an area of 647,500 km^2 (250,001 sq mi), making it the 42nd most populous and 41st largest nation in the world. It is bordered by Pakistan in the south and the east, Iran in the west, Turkmenistan, Uzbekistan and Tajikistan in the north, and China in the far northeast.

Afghanistan has been an ancient focal point of the Silk Road and human migration. Archaeologists have found evidence of human habitation from as far back as 50,000 BC. Urban civilization may have begun in the area as early as 3,000 to 2,000 BC. Sitting at an important geostrategic location that connects the Middle East with Central Asia and the Indian subcontinent, the land has been home to various peoples through the ages and witnessed many military campaigns, notably by Alexander the Great, Genghis Khan, and in modern era Western forces. The land also served as a source from which the Greco-Bactrians, Kushans, Saffarids, Ghaznavids, Ghorids, Timurids,Mughals and many others have risen to form major empires.

The political history of the modern state of Afghanistan begins in 1709 with the rise of the Pashtuns, when the Hotaki dynasty was established in Kandahar followed by Ahmad Shah Durrani's rise to power in 1747. In the late 19th century, Afghanistan became a buffer state in the "Great Game" between the British and Russian empires. Following the Third Anglo-Afghan War of 1919 and the signing of the Treaty of Rawalpindi, King Amanullah started modernization of the country. During the Cold War, after thewithdrawal of the British from neighbouring India in 1947, the United States and the Soviet Union began spreading their influence in Afghanistan. Between 1979 and 1989, the country experienced a major war between the US-backed mujahideen forces and the Soviet-backed Afghan government in which over a million Afghans lost their lives mainly due to land-mines. This was followed by the 1990s Afghan civil war, the rise and fall of the extremist Taliban government and the 2001-present war. In December 2001, theUnited Nations Security Council authorized the creation of the International Security Assistance Force (ISAF) to help maintain security in Afghanistan and assist the Karzai administration.

The decades of war made Afghanistan the world's most dangerous country, including the largest producer of refugees and asylum seekers. While the international community is rebuilding war-torn Afghanistan, terrorist groups such as the Haqqani Network and Hezbi Islami are actively involved in a nationwide Taliban-led insurgency, which includes hundreds of assassinations and suicide attacks. According to the United Nations, the insurgents were responsible for 75% of civilian casualties in 2010 and 80% in 2011.

Etymology

The name *Afghânistân* means *"Land of the Afghans"*, which originates from the ethnonym *"Afghan"*. Historically, the name *"Afghan"* designated the Pashtun people, the largest ethnic group of Afghanistan. This name is mentioned in the form of *Abgan* in the 3rd century CE by the Sassanians and as *Avagana* (*Afghana*) in the 6th century CE by Indian astronomer Varahamihira. A people called the *Afghans* are mentioned several times in a 10th century geography book, Hudud al-'alam, particularly where a reference is made to a village: "Saul, a pleasant village on a mountain. In it live *Afghans*."

Al-Biruni referred to them in the 11th century as various tribes living on the western frontier mountains of the Indus River, which would be the Sulaiman Mountains. Ibn Battuta, a famous Moroccan scholar visiting the region in 1333, writes: "We travelled on to Kabul, formerly a vast town, the site of which is now occupied by a village inhabited by a tribe of Persians called *Afghans*. They hold mountains and defiles and possess considerable strength, and are mostly highwaymen. Their principle mountain is called Kuh Sulayman."

One prominent 16th century Persian scholar explains extensively about the Afghans. For example, he writes:

The men of Kábul and Khilj also went home; and whenever they were questioned about the Musulmáns of the Kohistán (the mountains), and how matters stood there, they said, "Don't call it Kohistán, but Afghánistán; for there is nothing there but Afgháns and dis-turbances." Thus it is clear that for this reason the people of the country call their home in their own language Afghánistán, and themselves Afgháns. — Firishta, *1560-1620 AD*

It is widely accepted that the terms *"Pashtun"* and *Afghan* are synonyms. In the writings of the 17th-century Pashto poet Khushal Khan Khattak it is mentioned:

Pull out your sword and slay any one, that says Pashtun and Afghan are not one! Arabs know this and so do Romans: Afghans are Pashtuns, Pashtuns are Afghans!

The last part of the name, *-stân* is a Persian suffix for "place", prominent in many languages of the region. The name *"Afghanistan"* is described by the 16th century Mughal Emperor Babur in hismemoirs as well as by the later Persian scholar Firishta and Babur's descendants, referring to the traditional ethnic Afghan (Pashtun) territories between the Hindu Kush mountains and the Indus River.

In the early 19th century, Afghan politicians decided to adopt the name *Afghanistan* for the entire Afghan Empire after its English translation had already appeared in various treaties with Qajarid Persia and British India. In 1857, in his review of J.W. Kaye's *The Afghan War*, Friedrich Engels describes "Afghanistan" as:

an extensive country of Asia between Persia and the Indies, and in the other direction between the Hindu Kush and the Indian Ocean. It formerly included the Persian provinces of Khorassan and Kohistan, together with Herat, Beluchistan, Cashmere, and Sinde, and a considerable part of the Punjab Its principal cities are Kabul, the capital, Ghuznee, Peshawer, and Kandahar.

The Afghan kingdom was sometimes referred to as the *Kingdom of Kabul,* as mentioned by the British statesman and historian Mountstuart Elphinstone. Afghanistan was officially recognized as a sovereign state by the international community after the signing of the 1919 Treaty of Rawalpindi.

Geography

A landlocked mountainous country with plains in the north and southwest, Afghanistan is described as being located within South Asia or Central Asia. It is part of the Greater Middle East Muslim world, which lies between latitudes 29° N and 39° N, and longitudes 60° E and 75° E. The country's highest point is Noshaq, at 7,492 metres (24,580 feet) above sea level. It has a continental climate with very harsh winters in thecentral highlands, the glaciated northeast (around Nuristan) and the Wakhan Corridor, where the average temperature in January is below "15 °C (5 °F), and hot summers in the low-lying areas of the Sistan Basin of the southwest, the Jalalabad basin in the east, and theTurkestan plains along the Amu River in the north, where temperatures average over 35 °C(95 °F) in July.

Despite having numerous rivers and reservoirs, large parts of the country are dry. The endorheic Sistan Basin is one of the driest regions in the world. Aside from the usual rain falls, Afghanistan receives snow during winter in the Hindu Kush and Pamir Mountains, and the melting snow in the spring season enters the rivers, lakes, and streams. However, two-thirds of the country's water flows into neighbouring countries of Iran, Pakistan, and Turkmenistan. The state needs more than US$2 billion to rehabilitate its irrigation systems so that the water is properly managed.

The northeastern Hindu Kush mountain range, in and around the Badakhshan Province of Afghanistan, is in a geologically active area where earthquakes may occur almost every year. They can be deadly and destructive sometimes, causing landslides in some parts oravalanche during winter. The last strong earthquakes were in 1998, which killed about 6,000 people in Badakhshan near Tajikistan. This was followed by the 2002 Hindu Kush earthquakes in which over 150 people of various regional countries were killed and over 1,000 injured. The 2010 earthquake left 11 Afghans dead, over 70 injured and more than 2,000 houses destroyed.

The country's natural resources include: coal, copper, iron ore, lithium, uranium, rare earth elements, chromite, gold, zinc, talc, barites, sulfur, lead, marble, precious and semi-precious stones, natural gas, and petroleum among other things. In 2010, US and Afghan government officials estimated that untapped mineral deposits located in 2007 by the US Geological Survey are worth between $900 bn and $3 trillion.

At 652,230 square kilometres (251,830 sq mi), Afghanistan is the world's 41st largest country, slightly bigger than France and smaller than Burma, about the size of Texas in the United States. It borders Pakistan in the south and east, Iran in the west, Turkmenistan, Uzbekistan and Tajikistan in the north, and China in the far east.

History

Excavations of prehistoric sites by Louis Dupree and others suggest that humans were living in what is now Afghanistan at least 50,000 years ago, and that farming communities in the area were among the earliest in the world. An important site of early historical activities, many say that Afghanistan compares to Egypt in terms of the historical value of its archaeological sites.

Afghanistan is at a unique nexus point where numerous civilizations have interacted and often fought. It has been home to various peoples through the ages, among them theancient Iranian peoples who established the dominant role of Indo-Iranian languages in the region. At multiple points, the land has been incorporated within large regional empires, among them the Achaemenid Empire, the Macedonian Empire, the Indian Maurya Empire, the Islamic Empire and the Sassanid Empire.

Many kingdoms have also risen to power in what is now Afghanistan, such as the Greco-Bactrians, Kushans, Hephthalites, Kabul Shahis, Saffarids, Samanids, Ghaznavids,Ghurids, Kartids, Timurids, Mughals, and finally the Hotaki and Durrani dynasties that marked the political origins of the modern state of Afghanistan.

Pre-Islamic period

Archaeological exploration done in the 20th century suggests that the geographical area of Afghanistan has been closely connected by the culture of and trade with neighbouring regions to the east, west, and north. Artifacts typical of the Paleolithic, Mesolithic, Neolithic, Bronze, and Iron ages have been found in Afghanistan. Urban civilization may have begun as early as 3000 BCE, and the early city of Mundigak (near Kandahar in the south of the country) may have been a colony of the nearby Indus Valley Civilization.

After 2000 BCE, successive waves of semi-nomadic people from Central Asia moved south into the boundaries of modern Afghanistan, among them were many Indo-European-speakingIndo-Iranians. These tribes later migrated further south to India, west to what is now Iran, and towards Europe via the area north of the Caspian. The region was calledAriana.

The ancient Zoroastrianism religion is believed by some to have originated in what is now Afghanistan between 1800 and 800 BCE, as its founder Zoroaster is thought to have lived and died in Balkh. Ancient Eastern Iranian languages may have been spoken in the region around the time of the rise of Zoroastrianism. By the middle of the 6th century BCE, the Achaemenid Persians overthrew the Medians and incorporated Afghanistan (Arachosia,Aria and Bactria) within its boundaries. An inscription on the tombstone of King Darius I of Persia mentions the Kabul Valley in a list of the 29 countries he had conquered.

Alexander the Great and his Macedonian army arrived in the area of Afghanistan in 330 BCE after defeating Darius III of Persia a year earlier in the Battle of Gaugamela. Following Alexander's brief occupation, the successor state of the Seleucid Empire controlled the area until 305 BCE when they gave much of it to the Indian Maurya Empire as part of an alliance treaty.

Alexander took these away from the Aryans and established settlements of his own, but Seleucus Nicator gave them to Sandrocottus (Chandragupta), upon terms of intermarriage and of receiving in exchange 500 elephants. —Strabo, *64 BC – 24 AD*

The Mauryans brought Buddhism from India and controlled the area south of the Hindu Kush until about 185 BCE when they were overthrown. Their decline began 60 years after Ashoka's rule ended, leading to the Hellenistic reconquest of the region by the Greco-Bactrians. Much of it soon broke away from the Greco-Bactrians and became part of the Indo-Greek Kingdom. The Indo-Greeks were defeated and expelled by the Indo-Scythians in the late 2nd century BCE.

During the 1st century BCE, the Parthian Empire subjugated the region, but lost it to their Indo-Parthian vassals. In the mid to late 1st century CE the vast Kushan Empire, centered in modern Afghanistan, became great patrons of Buddhist culture. The Kushans were defeated by the Sassanidsin the 3rd century CE. Although various rulers calling themselves Kushanshas (generally known as the Indo-Sassanids) continued to rule at least parts of the region, they were probably more or less subject to the Sassanids.

The late Kushans were followed by the Kidarite Huns who, in turn, were replaced by the short-lived but powerful Hephthalites, as rulers in the first half of the 5th century. The Hephthalites were defeated by Khosrau I in CE 557, who re-established Sassanid power in Persia. However, in the 6th century CE, the successors to the Kushans and Hepthalites established a small dynasty in Kabulistan called Kabul Shahi.

Islamization and Mongol invasion

Between the fourth and nineteenth centuries, much of modern Afghanistan was known by the regional name as Khorasan. Two of the four main capitals of Khorasan (i.e. Balkh, Merv, Nishapur and Herat) are now located in modern Afghanistan, while Kandahar, Zabulistan, Ghazni and Kabulistan formed the frontier between Khorasan and Hindustan. The land inhabited by the Afghan tribes (i.e. ancestors of modern Pashtuns) was called Afghanistan, which loosely covered the area between the Hindu Kush and the Indus River, with the Sulaiman Mountains being the center. Arab Muslims brought the message of Islam to the western area of what is now Afghanistan during the 7th century and began spreading eastward, some of the native inhabitants they encountered accepted it while others revolted. Afghanistan at that time was Zoroastrian, Buddhist and Hindu, with smaller populations of Jews, Christians and others.

The Shahi rulers lost their Kabul capital in around 870 AD after it was conquered by the Saffarid Muslims of Zaranj. Later, the Samanids extended their Islamic influence into the Hindu Kush area from Bukhara in the north. It is reported that Muslims and non-Muslims lived side by side.

"Kábul has a castle celebrated for its strength, accessible only by one road. In it there areMusulmáns, and it has a town, in which are infidels from Hind." —Istahkrí, *921 AD*

Afghanistan became one of the main centers in the Muslim world during the Islamic Golden Age. By the 11th century the Ghaznavids had finally Islamized all of the remaining non-Muslim areas, with the exception of the Kafiristan region. They were replaced by the Ghurids who expanded and advanced the already powerful empire.

In 1219 AD, Genghis Khan and his Mongol barbariansoverran the region. His troops are said to have annihilated the Khorasanian cities of Herat and Balkh. The destruction caused by the Mongols depopulated major cities and forced many of the locals to revert to an agrarian rural society.

Mongol rule continued with the Ilkhanate in the northwest while the Khilji dynasty controlled the Afghan tribal areas south of the Hindu Kush, until the invasion of Timur who established the Timurid dynasty in 1370. During the Ghaznavid, Ghurid, and Timurid eras, Afghanistan produced many fine Islamic architectural monuments as well as numerous scientific and literary works.

Babur, a descendant of both Timur and Genghis Khan, arrived from Central Asia and captured Kabul from the Arghun dynasty, and from there he began to seize control of the central and eastern territories of Afghanistan.

He remained in Kabulistan until 1526 when he and his army invaded Delhi in India to replace the Afghan Lodi dynasty with the Mughal Empire. From the 16th century to the early 18th century, Afghanistan was part of three regional kingdoms: the Khanate of Bukhara in north, the Shi'a Safavids in the west and the remaining larger area was ruled by the Mughal Empire.

ISLAMIC EMIRATE OF AFGHANISTAN

The Islamic Emirate of Afghanistan, was founded in 1996 when the Taliban began their rule of Afghanistan and ended with their fall from power in 2001. Even at the peak of their influence, the Taliban never controlled the entire area of Afghanistan, as about 10% of the country in the northeast was held by the United Islamic Front for the Salvation of Afghanistan.

History

The Taliban and its rule arose from the chaos of post-Soviet Afghanistan. It began as an Islamic fundamentalist politico-religious movement composed of students in the Helmand and Kandaharregion of Afghanistan. Overwhelmingly local ethnic Pashtuns, the Taliban blended Pashtunwalitribal code with elements of Deobandi Islamic teaching to form an anti-Western, anti-modern, and highly restrictive Islamic fundamentalist ideology with which it ruled. Spreading from Kandahar, the Taliban eventually seized Kabul in 1996. By the end of 2000, the Taliban were able to capture 90% of the country, aside from the opposition (Afghan Northern Alliance) strongholds primarily found in the northeast corner of Badakhshan Province. The Taliban sought to impose a strict interpretation of Islamic *Sharia law* and were later implicated as supporters of mujahideen, most notably by harbouring Osama bin Laden's Al-Qaeda network.

During the five-year history of the Islamic Emirate, much of the population experienced restrictions on their freedom and violations of their human rights. Women were banned from jobs, girls forbidden to attend schools or universities. Those who resisted were punished instantly. Communists were systematically eradicated and thieves were punished by amputating one of their hands or feet. Meanwhile, the Taliban managed to nearly eradicate the majority of the opium production by 2001.

Following the Taliban's harsh treatment of Afghanistan's Shia minority, Iran stepped up assistance to the Northern Alliance. Relations with the Taliban deteriorated further in 1998 after Taliban forces seized the Iranian consulate in Mazari Sharif and executed Iranian diplomats. Following this incident, Iran almost went to war with the Taliban regions of Afghanistan but intervention by the United Nations Security Council and the United States prevented an imminent Iranian invasion.

International relations

Only Pakistan, Saudi Arabia, and the United Arab Emirates recognized the Taliban government. The state was not recognised in the UN. Turkmenistan, however, was known to have held official meetings and agreements with Taliban government ministers.

One reason for lack of international recognition was the Taliban's disregard for international law as demonstrated by their actions on taking power. For example, one of the first acts of the Islamic Emirate was the murder of the former President of Afghanistan, Mohammad Najibullah. Before the Taliban had even taken control of Afghanistan's capital they sent out a squad to arrest, torture, mutilate and murder Najibullah, leaving his body hanging from a street lamp outside the presidential palace for two days. As Najibullah was staying in the United Nations compound in Kabul, this was a violation of international law. As a further example, the Taliban regime was also heavily criticised for the murder of Iranian diplomats in Afghanistan in 1998. The Taliban supported the Islamic militants operating in Chechnya, Kashmir and Xinjiang, thus antagonizing Russia, India and the People's Republic of China simultaneously.

Sanctions

In 1999, the UN Security Council established a sanctions regime to cover individuals and entities associated with Al-Qaida, Osama bin Laden and/or the Taliban. Since the US Invasion of Afghanistan in 2001, the sanctions were applied to individuals and organizations in all parts of the world, also targeting former members of the Taliban government.

On January 27, 2010, a United Nations sanctions committee removed five former senior Taliban officials from this list, in a move favoured by Afghan President Karzai. The decision means the five will no longer be subject to an international travel ban, assets freeze and arms embargo. The five men, all high-ranking members of the Taliban government:

- Wakil Ahmad Muttawakil, former foreign minister.
- Fazal Mohammad, former deputy minister of commerce.
- Shams-us-Safa Aminzai, former Taliban foreign affairs press officer.
- Mohammad Musa Hottak, former deputy minister of planning.
- Abdul Hakim, former deputy minister of frontier affairs.

All had been added to the list in January or February 2001. Mohammed Omar continues to speak in the name of this Emirate.

COOPERATION ON AFGHANISTAN WITH SAUDI ARABIA

Pakistan and Saudi Arabia have created a deep strategic partnership on a variety of issues one of the more important being Afghanistan. After Musharraf's coup in October 1999, the Saudi capital Riyadh was the first foreign capital Pervez Musharraf visited, to signify the importance he gave to PAK-Saudi relations.

President Musharraf honored King Abdullah by conferring upon him Pakistan's highest civil award, Nishan-e-Pakistan, in a colorful investiture ceremony at the presidential palace. On 21 Jan 2007, the Custodian of the Two Holy Mosques King Abdullah conferred the King Abdul Aziz Medallion, the Kingdom's top honor, on Pakistani President Gen. Pervez Musharraf during a ceremony at his palace in Riyadh.The first Pakistani leader ever to receive this highest Saudi honor.

Al-Qaeda

Ayman al-Zawahiri was the second and last "emir" of Egyptian Islamic Jihad. In 1998 al-Zawahiri formally merged Egyptian Islamic Jihad into bin Laden's organization. He is often described as a "lieutenant" to Osama bin Laden, though bin Laden's chosen biographer has referred to him as the "real brains" of al-Qaeda. Ayman al-Zawahiri is believed to be hiding in Pakistan's Federally Administered Tribal Areas by some analysts while other observers believe he might be hiding in major urban areas in Pakistan or elsewhere. From 1996 to 2001 Osama Bin Laden and Ayman al-Zawahiri became a virtual state within the Taliban state. Bin Laden sent Arab fighters to join the fight against the United Front, especially his so-called 055 Brigade. Arab militants under Bin Laden were responsible for some of the worst massacres in the war, killing hundreds of civilians in areas controlled by the United Front. A report by the United Nations quotes eyewitnesses in many villages describing Arab fighters carrying long knives used for slitting throats and skinning people. Meanwhile fighters of Bin Laden's Brigade 055 were known for committing collective suicide before running risk of being taken prisoners by enemy forces themselves.

Strategic Cooperation with the Islamic Movement of Uzbekistan (IMU)

The Islamic Movement of Uzbekistan (IMU) is a militant group formed in 1991 with strong ties to Al Qaeda. It is estimated that the IMU in the late 1990s was approximately 2000 men strong, and that they contributed around 600 fighters to the Taliban's offensive against Massoud, participating in the siege of Taloqan, where they fought alongside Bin Laden's 055 Brigade. They were operating out of bases in Taliban-controlled areas of northern Afghanistan. In 2001 the IMU was largely destroyed while fighting alongside the Taliban against the United States-led coalition forces in Afghanistan.

An unknown number of their fighters escaped with remnants of the Taliban to Waziristan in Pakistan where they created a follow-up organization. The IMU's longterm leader Tahir Yuldashev was killed as a result of an August 27, 2009, U.S. predator airstrike in South Waziristan. Abu Usman succeeded him as the new leader of the IMU. Today there are an estimated 2,500 to 4,000 IMU fighters based in Pakistan's tribal regions and in Afghanistan.

BACKGROUND AND HISTORY

Taliban rise to power

After the fall of the communist Najibullah-regime in 1992, the Afghan political parties agreed on a peace and power-sharing agreement (the Peshawar Accords). The Peshawar Accords created the Islamic State of Afghanistan. From the first day of its founding until late 1994, the newly-created Islamic State of Afghanistan (ISA) came under attack by Gulbuddin Hekmatyar's Hezb-i Islami militia armed, financed and instructed by neighbouring Pakistan. Afghanistan expert Amin Saikal concludes in *Modern Afghanistan: A History of Struggle and Survival*:

Pakistan was keen to gear up for a breakthrough in Central Asia. Islamabad could not possibly expect the new Islamic government leaders to subordinate their own nationalist objectives in order to help Pakistan realize its regional ambitions. Had it not been for the ISI's logistic support and supply of a large number of rockets, Hekmatyar's forces would not have been able to target and destroy half of Kabul.

Abdul Rashid Dostum and his Junbish-i Milli militia joined an alliance with Hekmatyar in early 1994. In addition, Saudi Arabia and Iran – as competitors for regional hegemony – supported Afghan militias hostile towards each other. According to Human Rights Watch, Iran was assisting the Shia Hazara Hezb-i Wahdat forces of Abdul Ali Mazari, as Iran was attempting to maximize Wahdat's military power and influence. Saudi Arabia supported the Wahhabite Abdul Rasul Sayyaf and his Ittihad-i Islami faction. Conflict between the two militias soon escalated into a full-scale war. The capital city Kabul saw extremely violent fighting during that period. Power was highly decentralized.

Meanwhile, southern Afghanistan was neither under the control of foreign-backed militias nor the government in Kabul, but was ruled by local leaders such as Gul Agha Sherzai and their militias. In 1994, the Taliban (a movement originating from Jamiat Ulema-e-Islam-run religious schools for Afghan refugees in Pakistan) also developed in Afghanistan as a politico-religious force, reportedly in opposition to the tyranny of the local governor. In 1994, the Taliban took power in several provinces in southern and central Afghanistan.

In late 1994, most of the militia factions (Hezb-i Islami, Junbish-i Milli and Hezb-i Wahdat) which had been fighting in the battle for control of Kabul were defeated militarily in Kabul by forces of the Islamic State's Secretary of Defence Ahmad Shah Massoud. Bombardment of the capital came to a halt. Massoud tried to initiate a nationwide political process with the goal of national consolidation and democratic elections, also inviting theTaliban to join the process. The Taliban declined. They started shelling Kabul in early 1995 but were defeated by forces of the Islamic State government under Secretary of Defence Ahmad Shah Massoud. Taliban offensive, wrote in a 1995 report:

This is the first time in several months that Kabul civilians have become the targets of rocket attacks and shelling aimed at residential areas in the city.

The Taliban's early victories in 1994 were followed by a series of defeats that resulted in heavy losses.

On September 26, 1996, as the Taliban with military support by Pakistan and financial support by Saudi Arabia prepared for another major offensive, Massoud ordered a full retreat from Kabul. The Taliban seized Kabul on September 27, 1996, and established the Islamic Emirate of Afghanistan. The Islamic State government remained the internationally recognized government of Afghanistan. The Taliban's Islamic Emirate received recognition only from Saudi Arabia, Pakistan and the United Arab Emirates.

Creation of the United Front

Ahmad Shah Massoud and Abdul Rashid Dostum, two former archenemies, created the United Front (Northern Alliance) against the Taliban that were preparing offensives against the remaining areas under the control of Massoud and those under the control of Dostum. The United Front included beside the dominantly Tajik forces of Massoud and the Uzbek forces of Dostum, Hazara factions and Pashtun forces under the leadership of commanders such as Abdul Haq, Haji Abdul Qadir, Qari Baba or diplomat Abdul Rahim Ghafoorzai. From the Taliban conquest in 1996 until November 2001 the United Front controlled roughly 30% of Afghanistan's population in provinces such as Badakhshan, Kapisa, Takharand parts of Parwan, Kunar, Nuristan, Laghman, Samangan, Kunduz, Ghôr and Bamyan. This union did not consist of a "Northern Alliance" thus only the "northern states" of Afghanistan, but included resistance forces from all parts and all major ethnicities of the country.

Massoud did not intend for the United Front to become the ruling government of Afghanistan. His vision was for the United Front to help establish a new government, where the various ethnic groups would share power and live in peace through a democratic form of government.

Taliban massacres

According to a 55-page report by the United Nations, the Taliban, while trying to consolidate control over northern and western Afghanistan, committed systematic massacres against civilians. UN officials stated that there had been "15 massacres" between 1996 and 2001. They also said, that, these have been highly systematic and they all lead back to the [Taliban] Ministry of Defence or to Mullah Omar himself. "The Taliban especially targeted Shias or Hazaras. Many civilians fled to the area of Massoud. The National Geographic concluded: "The only thing standing in the way of future Taliban massacres is Ahmad Shah Massoud."

CHANGE IN U.S. POLICY TOWARDS AFGHANISTAN

During the Clinton administration the U.S. had no clear policy towards Afghanistan until 1998-1999 and tended to favor Pakistani policies. In 1997, U.S. State Department's Robin Raphel told anti-Taliban leader Ahmad Shah Massoud to surrender to the Taliban. Massoud answered that as long as he controlled an area the size of his hat he would continue to defend it from the Taliban. Robin Raphel eventually became a lobbyist and adviser at Cassidy & Associates.

The firm had a $1.2 million contract with the Musharraf military regime of Pakistan. At Cassidy & Associates she lobbied and advised Congress and the State Department for Pakistan on issues such as Afghan policy, Pakistan's relations with India, judicial independence and U.S. perceptions and congressional views of the Pakistan government. In late 2009 Raphel was (again) appointed to the Af-Pak region as deputy to Richard Holbrooke, the late US. Special Representative to Afghanistan and Pakistan, by the Obama administration. Raphel will be the main person overlooking the $1.5 billion U.S. aid package "for non-military purpose" to Pakistan.

At one point in the war, in 1997, the Taliban were vulnerable and the road to the capital, Kabul, was wide open. Two top foreign policy officials in the Clinton administration flew to northern Afghanistan to convince – without success – the United Front not to take advantage of an opportunity to make crucial gains against the Taliban. Before the United Front could strike, Assistant Secretary of State Rick Indefurth and American U.N. Ambassador Bill Richardson flew to northern Afghanistan and tried to convince the leadership of the United Front that this was not the time for an offensive. Instead, they insisted this was the time for a cease-fire and an arms embargo. At the same time Pakistanis began a "Berlin-like airlift to resupply and re-equip the Taliban", financed with Saudi money.

United States policy towards Afghanistan changed after the 1998 United States embassy bombings. Subsequently, Osama Bin Laden was indicted for his involvement in the embassy bombings and in 1999 both the United States and the United Nations enacted sanctions against the Taliban via United Nations Security Council Resolution 1267 which demanded the Taliban surrender Osama Bin Laden for trial in the United States and close all Al Qaeda bases in Afghanistan. In the meantime, the only collaboration between Massoud and another U.S. intelligence service, the Central Intelligence Agency (CIA), consisted of an effort to trace Osama bin Laden following the 1998 embassy bombings. The U.S. and the European Union provided no support to Massoud for the fight against the Taliban.

A change of policy regarding support to Massoud, lobbied for by CIA officers who had visited Massoud, was underway during 2001. According to Steve Coll's book *Ghost Wars* (which won the 2005 Pulitzer Prize for General Non-Fiction):

The CIA officers admired Massoud greatly. They saw him as a Che Guevara figure, a great actor on history's stage. Massoud was a poet, a military genius, a religious man, and a leader of enormous courage who defied death and accepted its inevitability, they thought.... In his house there were thousands of books: Persian poetry, histories of the Afghan war in multiple languages, biographies of other military and guerrilla leaders. In their meetings

Massoud wove sophisticated, measured references to Afghan history and global politics into his arguments. He was quiet, forceful, reserved, and full of dignity, but also light in spirit. The CIA team had gone into the Panshjir as unabashed admirers of Massoud. Now their convictions deepened. —Steve Coll in *Ghost Wars, 2004*

CIA lawyers, working with officers in the Near East Division and Counter-terrorist Center, began to draft a formal, legal presidential finding for Bush's signature authorizing a new covert action program in Afghanistan, the first in a decade that sought to influence the course of the Afghan war in favor of Massoud. Richard A. Clarke, chair of the Counter-Terrorism Security Group under the Clinton administration, and later an official in the Bush administration, allegedly presented a plan to incoming Bush administration official Condoleezza Rice in January 2001.

A change in policy was finalized in August 2001. In late August 2001, the Bush administration, to pressure the Taliban to hand over leading al-Qaeda operatives, agreed on a plan to start giving support to the anti-Taliban forces of Ahmad Shah Massoud who sought to create a democratic form of government in Afghanistan. Massoud until then had not received any meaningful support from Western countries. In a meeting by the Bush administration's top national security officials it was agreed that the Taliban in negotiations would be presented with a final ultimatum to hand over Osama bin Laden and other leading al-Qaeda operatives. If the Taliban refused, covert military aid would be channeled by the U.S. to anti-Taliban groups. If both those options failed, "the deputies agreed that the United States would seek to overthrow the Taliban regime through more direct action."

9 September 2001

On his visit to Europe in March 2001 Ahmad Shah Massoud had warned that his intelligence had gathered information about a large-scale attack on U.S. soil being imminent.

Massoud's intelligence staff is aware that the attack against the U.S. will be on a scale larger than the 1998 embassy bombings, which killed over two hundred people and injured thousands.

On 9 September 2001, Massoud, then aged 48, was the target of a suicide attack by two Arabs posing as journalists detonating a bomb hidden in their video camera during an interview in Khoja Bahauddin, in the Takhar Province of Afghanistan. Massoud died in a helicopter taking him to a hospital. The funeral, though in a rather rural area, was attended by hundreds of thousands of mourning Afghans.

Massoud had survived countless assassination attempts over a period of 26 years. The assassination of Massoud is considered to have a strong connection to the 11 September 2001, attacks, which killed nearly 3,000 people, and which appeared to be the terrorist attack that Massoud had warned against in his speech to the European Parliament several months earlier. International experts and members of the United Front such as Amrullah Saleh feared that without Massoud the anti-Taliban resistance would be overrun by the Taliban.

11 September 2001

On 11 September 2001, in the early morning, a series of coordinated attacks took place on United States soil. Four commercial passenger jet airliners were hijacked. The hijackers intentionally crashed two of the airliners into the Twin Towers of the World Trade Center in New York City, killing everyone on board and many others working in the buildings. Both buildings collapsed within two hours, destroying nearby buildings and damaging others. The hijackers crashed a third airliner into the Pentagon in Arlington, Virginia, just outside Washington, D.C. The fourth plane crashed into a field near Shanksville in rural Pennsylvania after some of its passengers and flight crew attempted to retake control of the plane, which the hijackers had redirected toward Washington, D.C to target the White House, or the Capitol. There were no survivors from any of the flights.

Nearly 3,000 people and the 19 hijackers died in the attacks. According to the New York State Health Department, 836 responders, including firefighters and police personnel, have died as of June 2009.

The United States identified members of the al-Qaeda movement based in Afghanistan as the perpetrators of the attacks.

Legal basis for war

The United Nations Charter, to which all the Coalition countries are signatories, provides that all UN member states must settle their international disputes peacefully and no member nation can use military force except in self-defence. The United States Constitution states that international treaties, such as the United Nations Charter, that are ratified by the U.S. are part of the law of the land in the U.S., though subject to effective repeal by any subsequent act of Congress (i.e., the "leges posteriores priores contrarias abrogant" or "last in time" canon of statutory interpretation). The United Nations Security Council (UNSC) did not authorize the U.S.-led military campaign in Afghanistan (Operation Enduring Freedom).

Defenders of the legitimacy of the U.S.-led invasion argue that U.N. Security Council authorization was not required since the invasion was an act of collective self-defence provided for under Article 51 of the UN Charter, and therefore was not a war of aggression. Critics maintain that the bombing and invasion of Afghanistan were not legitimate self-defence under Article 51 of the UN Charter because the 9/11 attacks were not "armed attacks" by another state, but rather were perpetrated by groups of individuals or non-state actors, and that these attackers had no proven connection to Afghanistan. Further, it is their opinion that even if a state had perpetrated the 9/11 attacks, no bombing campaign would constitute self-defence; the necessity for self-defence must be "instant, overwhelming, leaving no choice of means, and no moment for deliberation."

President George W. Bush was authorized by Congress on 14 September 2001, by legislation titled Authorization for Use of Military Force Against Terrorists which was passed and signed on 18 September 2001, by both President Bush and congress. This legislation authorized the use of United States Armed Forces against those responsible for the attacks on 11 September 2001. The authorization granted the President the authority to use all "necessary and appropriate force" against those whom he determined "planned, authorized, committed or aided" the 11 September attacks, or who harbored said persons or groups.

The Bush administration, for its part, did not seek a declaration of war by the U.S. Senate, and labeled Taliban troops as supporters of terrorists rather than soldiers, denying them the protections of the Geneva Convention and due process of law.

This position was successfully challenged in the U.S. Supreme Court and questioned even by military lawyers responsible for prosecuting affected prisoners. On 20 December 2001, more than two months after the U.S.-led attack began, the UNSC authorized the creation of an International Security Assistance Force (ISAF) to take all measures necessary to fulfill its mandate of assisting the Afghan Interim Authority in maintaining security. Command of the ISAF passed to NATO on 11 August 2003.

2001: Initial attack

On 20 September 2001, U.S. president George W. Bush addressed the United States Congress and demanded that the Taliban deliver Osama bin Laden and destroy bases of al Qaeda. On 5 October 2001, the Taliban offered to try Bin Laden in an Afghan court, so long as the United States provided what it called "solid evidence" of his guilt, but the U.S. would not hand over its evidence to the Taliban . So on 7 October 2001, the U.S. government launched military operations in Afghanistan. Teams from the CIA's Special Activities Division (SAD) were the first U.S. forces to enter Afghanistan and begin combat operations. They were soon joined by U.S. Army Special Forces from the 5th Special Forces Group and other units from USSOCOM. On 7 October 2001, airstrikes were reported in the capital, Kabul (where electricity supplies were severed), at the airport, at Kandahar (home of the Taliban's Supreme Leader Mullah Omar), and in the city of Jalalabad. CNN released exclusive footage of Kabul being bombed to all the American broadcasters at approximately 5:08 pm October 7, 2001.

At 17:00 UTC, President Bush confirmed the strikes on national television and Prime Minister of the United Kingdom Tony Blair also addressed the UK. Bush stated that Taliban military sites and terrorist training grounds would be targeted. In addition, food, medicine, and supplies would be dropped to "the starving and suffering men, women and children of Afghanistan".

US officials rejected a new offer from the Taliban to hand over Osama bin Laden to a third country for trial if the Americans halted the bombing of Afghanistan. A prerecorded videotape of Osama bin Laden had been released before the attacks in which he condemned any attacks against Afghanistan. Al Jazeera, theArabic satellite news channel, reported that these tapes were received shortly before the attack.

British and American special forces worked jointly to liberate Herat in November 2001. These forces worked with Afghan opposition groups on the ground, in particular the Northern Alliance. The United Kingdom, Canada and Australia also deployed forces and several other countries provided basing, access and overflight permission.

The U.S. was able to track al-Qaeda's number three at the time Mohammed Atef who was one of the most wanted, when Atef was killed, along with his guard Abu Ali al-Yafi'i and six others, in a U.S. air-strike on his home near Kabul during the U.S. invasion of Afghanistan at some time between 14–16 November 2001. This was one of America's first and largest victories during the early stages of the war.

Air campaigns

"Having begun the war with the greatest imaginable reservoir of moral authority, the U.S. was on the verge of letting it slip away through high-level attacks using the most ghastly inventions its scientists could come up with." —Stephen Tanner, "Afghanistan: A Military History from Alexander the Great to the War against the Taliban"

Bombers operating at high altitudes well out of range of antiaircraft guns dropped bombs at Afghan training camps and Taliban air defenses. U.S. aircraft, including Apache helicopter gunships from the 101st Combat Aviation Brigade, operated with impunity throughout the campaign with no losses due to Taliban air defenses.

The strikes initially focused on the area in and around the cities of Kabul, Jalalabad, and Kandahar. Within a few days, most Taliban training sites were severely damaged and the Taliban's air defenses were destroyed. The campaign then focused on command, control, and communication targets which weakened the ability of the Taliban forces to communicate. However, the line facing the Afghan Northern Alliance held, and no tangible battlefield successes had yet occurred on that front. Two weeks into the campaign, the Northern Alliance demanded the air campaign focus more on the front lines.

The next stage of the campaign began with carrier based F/A-18 Hornet fighter-bombers hitting Taliban vehicles in pinpoint strikes, while other U.S. planes began cluster bombing Taliban defenses. For the first time in years, Northern Alliance commanders finally began to see the substantive results that they had long hoped for on the front lines.

At the beginning of November, the Taliban front lines were bombed with daisy cutter bombs, and by AC-130gunships. The Taliban fighters had no previous experience with American firepower, and often even stood on top of bare ridgelines where Special Forces could easily spot them and call in close air support. By 2 November, Taliban frontal positions were devastated, and a Northern Alliance march on Kabul seemed possible for the first time. However, according to author Stephen Tanner, "After a month of the U.S. bombing campaign rumblings began to reach Washington from Europe, the Mideast, and Pakistan where Musharraf had requested the bombing to cease.

Having begun the war with the greatest imaginable reservoir of moral authority, the U.S. was on the verge of letting it slip away through high-level attacks using the most ghastly inventions its scientists could come up with." Then US-President George W. Bush went to New York City on 10 November 2001, "where the wreckage of the World Trade Center still smoldered with underground fires", to address the United Nations and told the assembled nations that not only the United States are in danger of further attacks of the 9/11 terrorists, but also every other countries in the world. Tanner writes: "His words had impact. Most of the world renewed its support for the American effort, including commitments of material help from Germany, France, Italy, Japan and other countries."

Fighters from al-Qaeda took over security in the Afghan cities, demonstrating the instability of the Taliban regime. Meanwhile, the Northern Alliance and their Central Intelligence Agency/Special Forces advisers planned the next stage of their offensive. Northern Alliance troops would seize Mazari Sharif, thereby cutting off Taliban supply lines and enabling the flow of equipment from the countries to the north, followed by an attack on Kabul itself.

Areas most targeted

During the early months of the war the U.S. military had a limited presence on the ground. The plan was that Special Forces, and intelligence officers with a military background, would serve as liaisons with Afghan militias opposed to the Taliban, would advance after the cohesiveness of the Taliban forces was disrupted by American air power.

The Tora Bora Mountains lie roughly east of Afghanistan's capital Kabul, which is itself close to the border with Pakistan. American intelligence analysts believed that the Taliban and al-Qaeda had dug in behind fortified networks of well-supplied caves and underground bunkers. The area was subjected to a heavy continuous bombardment by B-52 bombers. The U.S. forces and the Northern Alliance also began to diverge in their objectives. While the U.S. was continuing the search for Osama bin Laden, the Northern Alliance was pressuring for more support in their efforts to finish off the Taliban and control the country.

Battle of Mazar-i Sharif

The battle for Mazari Sharif was considered important, not only because it is the home of the Shrine of Hazrat Ali or "Blue Mosque", a sacred Muslim site, but also because it is the location of a significant transportation hub with two main airports and a major supply route leading into Uzbekistan. It would also enable humanitarian aid to alleviate Afghanistan's looming food crisis, which had threatened more than six million people with starvation. Many of those in most urgent need lived in rural areas to the south and west of Mazar-i-Sharif. On 9 November 2001, Northern Alliance forces, under the command of generals Abdul Rashid Dostum and Ustad Atta Mohammed Noor, swept across the Pul-i-Imam Bukhri bridge, meeting some resistance, and seized the city's main military base and airport. U.S. Special Operations Forces (namely Special Forces Operational Detachment A-595, CIA paramilitary officers and Air Force Combat Control Teams) on horseback and using Close Air Support platforms, took part in the push into the city of Mazari Sharif in Balkh Province by the Northern Alliance. After a bloody 90-minute battle, Taliban forces, who had held the city since 1998, withdrew from the city, triggering jubilant celebrations among the townspeople whose ethnic and political affinities are with the Northern Alliance.

The Taliban had spent three years fighting the Northern Alliance for Mazar-i-Sharif, precisely because its capture would confirm them as masters of all Afghanistan. The fall of the city was a "body blow" to the Taliban and ultimately proved to be a "major shock", since the United States Central Command (CENTCOM) had originally believed that the city would remain in Taliban hands well into the following year, and any potential battle would be "a very slow advance".

Following rumors that Mullah Dadullah was headed to recapture the city with as many as 8,000 Taliban fighters, a thousand American 10th Mountain Soldiers were airlifted into the city, which provided the first solid foothold from which Kabul and Kandahar could be reached. While prior military flights had to be launched from Uzbekistan or Aircraft carriers in the Arabian Sea, now the Americans held their own airport in the country which allowed them to fly more frequent sorties for resupply missions and humanitarian aid. These missions allowed massive shipments of humanitarian aid to be immediately shipped to hundreds of thousands of Afghans facing starvation on the northern plain.

The American-backed forces now controlling the city began immediately broadcasting from *Radio Mazar-i-Sharif,* the former Taliban *Voice of Sharia*channel on 1584 kHz, including an address from former President Burhanuddin Rabbani.

LEGAL HISTORY OF AFGHANISTAN

The population of Afghanistan is 80–85% *sunnis* and 15–20% *shei'ite.* The majority of*sunnis* in Afghanistan are followers of the *hanafi* school and the *Shias* follow the *jafari*jurisprudence.

In the 1950's and 1960's the rulers started to modernize the justice system in line with the Western world, hence during this process of consolidation, *Hanafi* version of *Shari'a* law along with the customary laws provided the foundation for the legal system in Afghanistan. Islamic scholars acted as Judges in the state courts. During the process of modernization, a lot of these laws were also codified, since then, the state law rather than the Islamic law began to be the primary source of the law.

Thus, Afghanistan substantially altered its structure of governance through the 1964 constitution, the political atmosphere during the time was relatively peaceful and hence there was public participation at the time of making the constitution.

In the 1964 constitution, Article 69 explicitly stated that in the event of no codified law, the*Hanafi* jurisprudence of the *Shari'a* law will be considered as the law. Thus this justice system tried to reconcile between the Islamic *Shari'a* law and the modern state law, it regulated the interaction between the both. State law was recognized as the primary source of law and the Shari'a law to be the secondary source of law. The impact of this transition in reality is minimal; the corruption embedded in the legal system and the lack of faith in the state authority distanced people from formal legal structures.

Later, the reforms that were introduced during the communist regime were totally at odds with both Islam and Afghan traditions, hence the whole system of governance and its judicial reforms (decrees) were rejected by the people, and instead they took to the local traditional institutions for the purposes of dispute resolution.

After the collapse of the Marxist government, the Mujahideen government (1992–1996) declared*Shari'a* as the substructure of their "Islamic State of Afghanistan". They attempted to impose a totalitarian theocracy. The Taliban'stheocratic regime (1996–2001) imposed an even more regressive version of *Shari'a*

POST 2014 SCENARIO

The impact of the withdrawal of international troops remains to be seen and the opinions of analysts and other experts vary. Dr Gordon told us the most likely scenario was "somewhere towards status quo and partial meltdown in some areas, but with a central degree of authority and stability". The UN has forecasted "a continued escalation of violent conflict fuelled by the departure of foreign security forces in country and subsequent increased humanitarian need, coupled with nominal humanitarian access or assistance."

Mercy Corps, an NGO working across Afghanistan and funded by DFID for its work in Helmand, was concerned by the potential spread of insecurity as tranches were handed over to ANSF, and the ISAF presence reduced. It told us that without a relatively secure environment, it was unlikely that economic and development progress would be achieved or maintained and that if fighting and conflict spread at the local level, the economy would almost certainly suffer.

Security during and after transition depends on a number of variables, including the capacity of the ANSF in 2014, the support and the role of the ISAF contributing countries and the military advisers that remain on after 2014. Naysan Adlparvar, a researcher on Afghanistan, said peace hinged on: the amount, continuity and modalities of aid committed to Afghanistan; sources of growth; the emerging investment climate; the outcome and acceptability of the pending presidential elections; the role played by regional powers including Pakistan; and whether a political settlement with the Taliban, and other armed groups, is achieved and accepted by the Afghan people.

While much of Afghanistan's future economic stability depends on an improvement, or at minimum a halt, to the continued deterioration, of security, it also depends on continued financial support from the international community. The World Bank expects economic growth to slow up to 2025, and said that "sudden sharp drops in aid can be particularly destabilising by changing perceptions of the Government's strength and encouraging political actors and armed groups to challenge the state's authority."

Afghanistan has one of the highest aid dependencies in the world with 71% of its GDP funded by external assistance. Key donors have made significant, if reduced, pledges to support both the security forces as well as development and humanitarian assistance. As part of the $4.1billion pledged annually for security forces at the NATO Summit held in Chicago in May 2012, the British Government has pledged to provide £70million (approximately $110million) annually. The Afghan Government aims to assume responsibility for these costs by 2024. The Tokyo Conference resulted in donors pledging $16billion in civilian aid to Afghanistan up to 2015—a 35% decrease from current funding levels.

There is also a concern that as a result of the withdrawal of international combat forces there will be a reduction in spending by the military which currently bolsters the Afghan economy. There will no longer be the high level of demand for food and provisions from local Afghan businesses which supply the foreign military forces and there will also be the loss of wages for civilian staff, security guards and interpreters who work for ISAF. A dramatic fall in GDP at the point of transition would undermine security, fuel perceptions of the international community turning its back on the country and ultimately threaten stability.

ISAF troop-contributing countries (including the UK) should therefore quantify the likely economic impact of military withdrawal and commit to spend part of the peace dividend they gain when they bring troops home on ODA to Afghanistan, particularly in the years immediately following withdrawal. It is currently unclear where any reduction in aid after 2014 will be focused or how quickly aid will decline.

There is a risk of both security and development being underfunded, with a resultant deterioration in public services. Global Witness projected that "a reduction in foreign development assistance will correlate directly to a reduction in the Government's ability to provide services, infrastructure projects, Government salaries, and security [...] There is a significant risk to development gains made in the past ten years if the transition is not carefully planned, and alternative and sustainable sources of funding are not secured."

Dr Gordon said that one of his main concerns was if the amount of international oversight of Kabul's expenditure was reduced there would be a further reduction of money flowing from Kabul down to the district level. He predicted that if that occurred it would have a dramatic impact on governance arrangements and make it more likely that other patronage systems would become more dominant and the informal sector of governance would end up dominating the formal. It is not just a potential decrease in aid money and the drawdown of troops that is likely to affect the economy. The World Bank noted: Recent performance has been on a downward trend [...] transition presents serious threats to growth and economic stability, but these do not directly stem from declining aid itself. Key economic vulnerabilities are risks of drought (which would adversely affect volatile agricultural production) and of falling business confidence as a result of worsening insecurity, corruption, governance and uncertainty over Afghanistan's political future.

Impact at the local level is likely to vary, with provinces heavily dependent on aid tied to security objectives and on funding from the PRTs likely to be most severely affected. Mercy Corps highlighted that a large percentage of construction and related industries in Helmand were significantly bolstered by contracts awarded by the PRT. These range from the building of police checkpoints, road repair and school construction to repairs and maintenance of generators and electrical apparatus. It believed that without an international presence providing funding and overseeing these contracts the number and value would sharply decrease. Those which remained were likely to be awarded to a small number of companies, often based outside of Helmand and even Afghanistan, that have political support or links to Government officials. This meant that the construction boom that Helmand had experienced was likely to stall and previously working men of fighting age would be faced with fresh economic challenges.

A concern we heard whilst in Afghanistan was that the young and educated Afghans were already preparing to leave due to fear of what was going to happen post 2014. Ahmed Rashid believed that the exodus had already started and that this would have a detrimental effect on the civil service in which they were often working as well as the economy as it was losing its skilled labour.

As this chapter demonstrates, the situation in Afghanistan is very complex. There are great uncertainties about the political, security and economic future of Afghanistan, notably: the outcome of the 2014 elections; whether there will be a political settlement; economic growth; and the role of Afghanistan's neighbouring countries. In the light of these uncertainties DFID will need to be able to adapt. DFID will also need to continue to lead donors in pledging and disbursing aid so that there will not be any sudden drops in funding which could exacerbate an extremely fragile situation. Based on the assessment of the likely economic impact of military withdrawal, the UK Government should be prepared to do whatever it can to address this potential shortfall in spending including urging other governments to increase their aid commitments to Afghanistan to fill the economic gap.

THE *MUJAHEDIN* GOVERNMENT AND RISE OF THE TALIBAN

The fall of Najibullah exposed the differences among the *mujahedin* parties. The leader of one of the smaller parties (Afghan National Liberation Front), Islamic scholar Sibghatullah Mojadeddi, was president during April-May 1992. Under an agreement among the major parties, Rabbani became president in June 1992 with agreement that he would serve until December 1994. He refused to step down at that time, saying that political authority would disintegrate without a clear successor. That decision was strongly opposed by other mujahedin leaders, including Gulbuddin Hikmatyar, a Pashtun, and leader of the Islamist conservative Hizb-e-Islam Gulbuddin *mujahedin*party. Hikmatyar and several allied factions began fighting to dislodge Rabbani. Rabbani reached an agreement for Hikmatyar to serve as Prime Minister, if Hikmatyar would cease the shelling Kabul that had destroyed much of the western part of the city. However, because of Hikmatyar's distrust of Rabbani, he never assumed a working prime ministerial role in Kabul.

In 1993-1994, Afghan Islamic clerics and students, mostly of rural, Pashtun origin, formed the Taliban movement. Many were former *mujahedin* who had become disillusioned with conflict among *mujahedin* parties and had moved into Pakistan to study in

Islamic seminaries ("madrassas") mainly of the "Deobandi" school of Islam. Some say this interpretation of Islam is similar to the "Wahhabism" that is practiced in Saudi Arabia. Taliban practices were also consonant with conservative Pashtun tribal traditions. The Taliban's leader, Mullah Muhammad Umar, had been a fighter in Khalis's Hezb-i-Islam party during the anti-Soviet war—Khalis' party was generally considered moderate Islamist during the anti-Soviet war, but Khalis and his faction turned against the United States in the mid-1990s. Many of his fighters, such as Mullah Umar, followed Khalis' lead. Umar, a low-ranking Islamic cleric, lost an eye in the anti-Soviet war.

The Taliban viewed the Rabbani government as weak, corrupt, and anti-Pashtun, and the four years of civil war between the *mujahedin* groups (1992-1996) created popular support for the Taliban as able to deliver stability. With the help of defections, the Taliban peacefully took control of the southern city of Qandahar in November 1994. Upon that capture, Mullah Umar ordered the opening of the Qandahar shrine containing the purported cloak used by the Prophet Mohammad; he reportedly donned the purported cloak briefly in front of hundreds of followers.

By February 1995, it was approaching Kabul, after which an 18-month stalemate ensued. In September 1995, the Taliban captured Herat province, bordering Iran, and imprisoned its governor, Ismail Khan, ally of Rabbani and Masoud, who later escaped and took refuge in Iran. In September 1996, new Taliban victories near Kabul led to the withdrawal of Rabbani and Masoud to the Panjshir Valley north of Kabul with most of their heavy weapons; the Taliban took control of Kabul on September 27, 1996. Taliban gunmen subsequently entered a U.N. facility in Kabul to seize Najibullah, his brother, and aides, and then hanged them.

TALIBAN RULE (SEPTEMBER 1996-NOVEMBER 2001)

The Taliban regime was led by Mullah Muhammad Umar, who held the title of Head of State and "Commander of the Faithful." He remained in the Taliban power base in Qandahar and almost never appeared in public, although he did occasionally receive high-level foreign officials. Al Qaeda leaders Osama bin Laden relocated from Sudan to Afghanistan, where he had been a recruiter of Arab fighters during the anti-Soviet war, in May 1996. He at first was located in territory in Nangarhar province controlled by Hezb-i-Islam of Yunus Khalis (Mullah Umar's party leader) but then had free reign in Afghanistan as the Taliban captured nearly all the territory in Afghanistan. Umar reportedly forged a political and personal bond with Bin Laden and refused U.S. demands to extradite him. Like Umar, most of the senior figures in the Taliban regime were Ghilzai Pashtuns, which predominate in eastern Afghanistan. They are rivals of the Durrani Pashtuns, who are predominant in the south.

The Taliban lost international and domestic support as it imposed strict adherence to Islamic customs in areas it controlled and employed harsh punishments, including executions. The Taliban authorized its "Ministry for the Promotion of Virtue and the Suppression of Vice" to use physical punishments to enforce strict Islamic practices, including bans on television, Western music, and dancing. It prohibited women from attending school or working outside the home, except in health care, and it publicly executed some women for adultery. In what many consider its most extreme action, and which some say was urged by Bin Laden, in March 2001 the Taliban blew up two large Buddha statues carved into hills above Bamiyan city, considering them idols.

U.S. Policy Toward the Taliban During Its Rule/Bin Laden Presence

The Clinton Administration opened talks with the Taliban after it captured Qandahar in 1994, and engaged the movement after it took power. However, the Administration was unable to moderate the Taliban's policies and relations worsened. The United States withheld recognition of Taliban as the legitimate government of Afghanistan, formally recognizing no faction as the government. The United Nations continued to seat representatives of the Rabbani government, not the Taliban. The State Department ordered the Afghan embassy in Washington, DC, closed in August 1997. U.N. Security Council Resolution 1193 (August 28, 1998) and 1214 (December 8, 1998) urged the Taliban to end discrimination against women. Women's rights groups urged the Clinton Administration not to recognize the Taliban government. In May 1999, the Senate-passed S.Res. 68 called on the President not to recognize an Afghan government that oppresses women.

The Taliban's hosting of Al Qaeda's leadership gradually became the Clinton Administration's overriding agenda item with Afghanistan. In April 1998, then-U.S. Ambassador to the United Nations Bill Richardson (along with Assistant Secretary of State Karl Inderfurth and NSC senior official Bruce Riedel) visited Afghanistan, but the Taliban refused to hand over Bin Laden. They did not meet Mullah Umar.

After the August 7, 1998, Al Qaeda bombings of U.S. embassies in Kenya and Tanzania, the Clinton Administration began to strongly pressure the Taliban to extradite him, imposing U.S. sanctions on Taliban-controlled Afghanistan and achieving adoption of some U.N. sanctions as well. On August 20, 1998, as a response to the Africa embassy bombings, the United States fired cruise missiles at alleged Al Qaeda training camps in eastern Afghanistan, but Bin Laden was not hit. Some observers assert that the Administration missed several other opportunities to strike him, including a purported sighting of him by an unarmed Predator drone at a location called Tarnak Farm in Afghanistan in the fall of 2000. Clinton Administration officials said that domestic and international support for ousting the Taliban militarily was lacking.

The "Northern Alliance" Congeals

The Taliban's policies caused different Afghan factions to ally with the Tajik core of the anti-Taliban opposition—the ousted President Rabbani, Ahmad Shah Masoud, and their ally in the Herat area, Ismail Khan. Joining the Tajik factions in the broader "Northern Alliance" were Uzbek, Hazara Shiite, and even some Pashtun Islamist factions. Virtually all the figures mentioned remain key players in politics in Afghanistan, sometimes allied with and at other times adversaries of President Hamid Karzai. The Soviet occupation-era parties remain relatively intact informally, although they do not remain organized under those prior names. (Detail on these figures is in CRS Report RS21922, *Afghanistan: Politics, Elections, and Government Performance*, by Kenneth Katzman.)

Uzbeks/General Dostam. One major faction was the Uzbek militia (the Junbush-Melli, or National Islamic Movement of Afghanistan) of General Abdul Rashid Dostam. Frequently referred to by some Afghans as one of the "warlords" who gained power during the anti-Soviet war, Dostam first joined those seeking to oust Rabbani during his 1992-1996 presidency, but later joined him and the other Northern Alliance factions opposed to the Taliban.

Hazara Shiites. Members of Hazara tribes, mostly Shiite Muslims, are prominent in Bamiyan, Dai Kundi, and Ghazni provinces of central Afghanistan and have been the object of repression and disparagement by Afghan Pashtuns. The Hazaras have tended to serve in working class and domestic household jobs, although more recently they have been prominent in technology jobs in Kabul, raising their economic status. During the various Afghan wars, the main Hazara Shiite militia was Hizb-e-Wahdat (Unity Party, composed of eight groups). In 1995, the Taliban captured and killed Hizb-e-Wahdat's leader Abdul Ali Mazari. One of Karzai's vice president's Karim Khalili, is a Hazara. Another prominent Hazara faction leader, Mohammad Mohaqeq, is a Karzai critic.

Pashtun Islamists/Sayyaf. Some Pashtuns joined the Northern Alliance. Abd-i-Rab Rasul Sayyaf headed a Pashtun-dominated hardline Islamist *mujahedin* faction (Islamic Union for the Liberation of Afghanistan, *Ittihad Islami*) during the anti-Soviet war. Even though he is an Islamist conservative, Sayyaf viewed the Taliban as selling out Afghanistan to Al Qaeda. Sayyaf is politically close to Saudi Arabia, whose leaders perceived a domestic threat from bin Laden.

LEGAL PLURALISM IN AFGHANISTHAN

Jirga and *Shura* fall outside the purview of state institutions, the chthonic law that is adjudicated upon in such institutions is diverse due to different ethnicities and varies with regions, it isn't a uniform system of law, however it plays a significant role in dispute resolution.

Prolonged conflict in the society, multiple constitutions and a lack of centralized authority propelled people, particularly people living in the rural areas to take up to non-state chthonic law, rural population constitutes eighty percent of the Afghan population and hence one cannot dismiss the pervasive and binding effect of chthonic law in Afghanistan.

Even today, Hamid Karzai's government is largely composed of the old war lords of Northern alliance, and hence due to the lack of separation of powers people are still dependent on the local non state entities for the purposes of security and justice.

The reasons as to why people prefer chthonic law over the state law boils down to the following:

a) Chthonic law focuses on substantive justice instead of procedural justice;
b) It focuses on compensation and reconciliation instead of punishment;
c) The parties have a sense of faith in the institution and hence are bound by it.

Pashtuns are the dominant ethnic tribe in Afghanistan, their chthonic law is the pasthunwali, it is an amalgamation of *Shari'a* law, customs and ethical values of the tribe. The decision making process in a *jirga* is driven by consensus rather than voting; parties to the dispute and the communities meet for the resolution of a dispute. It has an appeal procedure as well, the first level of appeal is taken to another *jirga* with more elder members, the second level of appeal is taken to a tribal assembly which has representatives of pashtuns from other lineages.

In a Shura, the *Shari'a* plays a significant role when compared to a *jirga*, it is composed of imams and the "local religious figures" for the resolution of dispute, the local practices of the geography play a major role in dispute resolution. Now, with the emergence of a constitution, there surfaces a problem of deeply embedded legal pluralism, the question then remains, how do we reconcile the state and non state entities? Specifically in a culture which lacks constitutional morality. The normative laws guiding a constitutionally validated judiciary would inevitably come into conflict with the diverse normative framework of a non state entity.

United States Institute of Peace proposes the interaction of both, in cases where chthonic law isn't in congruence with the state law, the state should ensure that the chthonic law doesn't violate "the basic human rights" or "principles within the law", thus the government should act as a bridge between the both, the model posits that the government should prescribe the areas where non state institutions can be beneficial and work positively, the state shall have supremacy on important realms such as criminal law and property law, the rationale for such supremacy is the conception that the state's objective is to further justice and hence it must have finality over issues of such issues of significance, the *jirgas* have their own conceptions of justice, but however the model ascribes finality and supremacy to the state conception's of justice.

Wardak on the other hand proposes for an active human rights unit along with *jirga/shura* and the formal legal institutions. The role of the human rights unit is to interact with the educational institutions at the local level for the production of material pertaining to issues that are culturally sensitive in nature and sensitise people on human rights abuses such as domestic violence and so on, thus it works at the ground level. The formal mechanism of the state on the other hand is to deal with civil issues that are usually not dealt by the informal mechanisms and other major criminal offences. It is to aid the informal institutions and the human rights unit in their functioning.

In some way, both the models hierarchize the institutions at hand, despite giving due recognition to chthonic institutions, major powers are given to the state instilled formal legal institutions; however the ground reality remains that, even in the matters pertaining to major criminal offences, the mechanisms adopted by the informal institutions secure more authority.

Hence, the judge then, while assessing the decisions must weigh it in terms of two different normative frameworks: legal and chthonic. He must analyse the extent to which it is consistent or comes into contradiction with such frameworks. While doing so, he must also incorporate into his decisions, the universal principles of international human rights and the *shari'a* law. A standard set of priori rules will not be able to resolve the conflicts that arise due to legal pluralism; hence an assessment has to be done on a case-by-case basis depending upon the facts and circumstances of each case.

The constitution of Afghanistan also provides for fundamental rights such as the freedom of expression, presumption of innocence, right to liberty, right to form social organization, and the right to legal defence if accused of an offence under the law ; the philosophy of fundamental rights is to encapsulate human rights, the aim of the state is to protect the fundamental rights, thus the discourse of fundamental rights can also serve as a framework to evaluate the decisions of *jirga/shura*. A concern can be raised if there is a deviation of fundamental right.

The state may as well identify major avenues i.e. Issues related to women, major criminal offences etc. that could potentially give space for conflict and then oversee the rulings of*jirga/ shura* pertaining to such matters.

Judicial review needn't always be one sided, decisions can also be made from the vantage point of chthonic law.

For an instance, in the south African case of Bangindawo and Other v Head of Nyanada Regional Authority & Another, the court while deciding on the role of a traditional ruler- who was a judge and the legislator, opined that such duality could hamper judicial independence, however, it was careful enough to not impose the western notion of separation of powers and held that, such duality can be allowed as the adherents of such customary law trust the impartiality of the ruler when he is a judge. Mechanisms have to be developed to provide for the working multiple legal systems, trying to annihilate entities outside the purview of state can turn counter productive.

Now, we are going to examine the legal history of Islamic law in Afghanistan and track the making of the current constitution.

7

Afghan Armed Forces

The Afghan Armed Forces are the military forces of the Islamic Republic of Afghanistan. They consist of the Afghan National Army and the Afghan Air Force. Being a landlocked country, Afghanistan has no navy. The President of Afghanistan is the Commander-in-Chief of the military, acting through the Ministry of Defense. The National Military Command Center in Kabul serves as the headquarters of the Afghan armed forces. The military of Afghanistan currently has around 200,000 active soldiers, which are expected to reach 260,000 in the coming years.

The current Afghan military originates in 1709 when the Hotaki dynasty was established in Kandahar followed by the Durrani Empire. The Afghan armed forces fought many wars with the Safavid dynasty and Maratha Empire from the 18th to the 19th century. It was re-organized by the British in 1880, when the country was ruled by Amir Abdur Rahman Khan. It was modernized during King Amanullah Khan's rule in the early 20th century, and upgraded during King Zahir Shah's forty-year rule. From 1978 to 1992, the Soviet-backed Afghan army fought with multi-national mujahideen groups who were being funded by the United States and Saudi Arabia while trained by the Pakistani Armed Forces. After President Najibullah's resignation in 1992 and the end of Soviet support, the military dissolved into portions controlled by different warlord factions and the mujahideen took control over the government. This era was followed by the rise of the Pakistan-backed Taliban regime, who established a military force on the basis of Islamic sharia law.

After the removal of the Taliban and the formation of the Karzai administration in late 2001, the military of Afghanistan was gradually rebuilt by NATO military alliance, mainly by the United States Armed Forces. Despite early problems with recruitment and training, it is becoming effective in fighting against the Taliban insurgency. As of 2014, it is becoming able to operate independently from US-led NATO forces. As a major non-NATO ally, Afghanistan continues to receive billions of dollars in military assistance from NATO, mainly from the United States.

HISTORY

Afghans have served in the militaries of the Ghaznavids (963–1187), Ghurids (1148–1215), Delhi Sultanate (1206–1527), Mughals (1526–1858) and the Persian army. The current Afghan military traces its origin to the early 18th century when the Hotaki dynasty rose to power in Kandahar and defeated the Persian Safavid Empire at the Battle of Gulnabad in 1722.

"The sun had just appeared on the horizon when the armies began to observe each other with that curiosity so natural on these dreadful occasions. The Persian army just come out of the capital, being composed of whatever was most brilliant at court, seemed as if it had been formed rather to make a show than to fight. The riches and variety of their arms and vestments, the beauty of their horses, the gold and precious stones with which some of their harnesses were covered, and the richness of their tents contributed to render the Persian camp very pompous and magnificent.

On the other side there was a much smaller body of soldiers, disfigured with fatigue and the scorching heat of the sun. Their clothes were so ragged and torn in so long a march that they were scarce sufficient to cover them from the weather, and, their horses being adorned with only leather and brass, there was nothing glittering about them but their spears and sabres..." —Jonas Hanway, *1712–1786*

When Ahmad Shah Durrani formed the Durrani Empire in 1747, his Afghan army fought a number of wars in the Punjab region of Hindustan during the 18th to the 19th century. One of the famous battles was the 1761 Battle of Panipat in which the Afghans invaded and decisively defeated the Hindu Maratha

Empire. The Afghans then engaged in wars with the Punjabi Sikh Empire of Ranjit Singh, which included the Battle of Jamrud in which Hari Singh Nalwa was killed by Prince Akbar Khan. During the First Anglo-Afghan War, British India invaded Afghanistan in 1838 but withdraw in 1842. During the three years a number of battles took place in different parts of Afghanistan.

The first organized army of Afghanistan (in the modern sense) was established after the Second Anglo-Afghan War in 1880 when the nation was ruled by Emir Abdur Rahman Khan. Traditionally, Afghan governments relied on three military institutions: the regular army, tribal levies, and community militias. The regular army was sustained by the state and commanded by government leaders. The tribal or regional levies - irregular forces - had part-time soldiers provided by tribal or regional chieftains. The chiefs received tax breaks, land ownership, cash payments, or other privileges in return. The community militia included all available able-bodied members of the community, mobilized to fight, probably only in exceptional circumstances, for common causes under community leaders. Combining these three institutions created a formidable force whose components supplemented each other's strengths and minimized their weaknesses.

After the Third Anglo-Afghan War ended, the reforming King Amanullah did not see the need for a large army, instead deciding to rely on Afghanistan's historical martial qualities. This resulted in neglect, cutbacks, recruitment problems, and finally an army unable to quell the 1929 up-rising that cost him his throne. However, under his reign, the small Afghan Air Force was formed in 1924. The Afghan armed forces were expanded during King Zahir Shah's reign, reaching a strength of 70,000 in 1933.

Following World War II, Afghanistan briefly received continued military support from the British government under the Lancaster Plan from 1947–1947, until the partition of India realigned British priorities in the region. Afghanistan refused to join the 1955 United States-sponsored Baghdad Pact; this rebuff did not stop the United States from continuing its low-level aid program, but it was reluctant to provide Afghanistan with military assistance, so Daoud turned to the Soviet Union and its allies for military aid, and in

1955 he received approximately US$25 million of military matériel. In addition, the Soviet bloc also began construction of military airfields in Bagram, Mazar-e-Sharif, and Shindand. By the 1960s, Soviet assistance started to improve the structure, armament, training, and command and control arrangements for the military. The military reached a strength of 98,000 (90,000 army and 8,000 air force) by this period.

After the exile of King Zahir Shah in 1973, President Daud Khan forged stronger ties with the Soviets by signing two highly controversial military aid packages for his nation in 1973 and 1975. For three years, Afghan armed forces and police officers received advanced Soviet weapons, as well as training by the KGB and Soviet commandos. Due to problems with local political parties in his country, President Daud Khan decided to distance himself from the Soviets in 1976. He made Afghanistan's ties closer to the Greater Middle East and the United States instead.

From 1977 to 1978, the Afghan armed forces conducted joint military training with the Military of Egypt. In April 1978 there was a coup, known as the Saur Revolution, orchestrated by members of the government loyal to the People's Democratic Party of Afghanistan (PDPA). This led to a full-scale Soviet invasion in December 1979, led by the 40th Army and the Airborne Forces. In 1981 the total strength of the army was around 85,000 troops according to The New York Times. The army had around 35-40,000 soldiers, who was mostly conscripts, the air force had around 7,000 soldiers and if put together all military personnel in 1984, the total strength of the Afghan military was around 87,000 in 1984.

Throughout the 1980s, the Afghan military was heavily involved in fighting against the multi-national Mujahiddin rebel groups who were largely funded by the United States and trained by the Pakistani Armed Forces. The rebel groups were fighting to force the Soviet Union to withdraw from Afghanistan as well as to remove the Soviet-backed government of President Mohammad Najibullah. Due to large number of defectors, the Afghan armed forces in 1985 was reduced to around 47,000. The air force had over 150 combat aircraft with about 7,000 officers who were watched over by an estimated 5,000 Cuban and Czechoslovak advisers.

Weapons supplies were made available to the Mujahideen through numerous countries; the United States purchased all of Israel's captured Soviet weapons clandestinely, and then funnelled the weapons to the Mujahideen, while Egypt upgraded their own army's weapons, and sent the older weapons to the militants, Turkey sold their World War II stockpiles to the warlords, and the British and Swiss provided Blowpipe missiles and Oerlikon anti-aircraft guns respectively, after they were found to be poor models for their own forces. China provided the most relevant weapons, likely due to their own experience with guerrilla warfare, and kept meticulous record of all the shipments.

Following the Soviet withdrawal in 1989 the Democratic Republic of Afghanistan continued to deal with attacks from the Mujahiddin. For several years the Afghan army had actually increased their effectiveness past levels ever achieved during the Soviet military presence. But the government was dealt a major blow when Abdul Rashid Dostum, a leading general, switched allegiances to the Mujahideen in 1992 and together they captured the city of Kabul. By 1992 the national army fragmented into regional militias under local warlords because of the fall of the Soviet Union which stopped supplying the army and later in 1992 when the Afghan government lost power and the country went into a state of anarchy.

"The fall of the Moscow-backed regime in 1992 disintegrated the state as well as the army. Bits and pieces of the fragmented military either disappeared or joined the warring factions that were locked in a drawn-out power struggle. The warring factions were composed of odd assortments of armed groups with varying levels of loyalties, political commitment, professional skills, and organizational integrity." —Ali A. Jalali, 2002

After the fall of Najibullah's regime in 1992, private militias were formed and the nation began to witness a civil war between the various warlords, including Ahmad Shah Massoud, Gulbuddin Hekmatyar, Abdul Rashid Dostum, Abdul Ali Mazari, Ismail Khan, and many others. They received logistics support from foreign powers including Russia, Pakistan, India, Iran, China, France, Canada and the United States. When the Taliban took power in 1996, all the warlords fled Kabul to the north or neighboring countries. With the backing and support of the Pakistani Armed Force, the Taliban began creating a new military force purely based on Islam's Sharia law.

The Taliban maintained a military during their period of control. The Taliban Army possessed over 400 T-54/55 and T-62 tanks and more than 200 Armoured personal carriers. The Afghan Air Force under the Taliban maintained five supersonic MIG-21MFs and 10 Sukhoi-22 fighter-bombers. In 1995, during the 1995 Airstan incident, a Taliban fighter plane captured a Russian transport. They also held six Mil Mi-8 helicopters, five Mi-35s, five L-39Cs, six An-12s, 25 An-26s, a dozen An-24/32s, an IL-18, and a Yakovlev.

CURRENT ORGANIZATION

After the formation of the Karzai administration in late 2001, a unified Afghan Army was gradually reestablished by the United States and its allies. Initially, a new Afghan National Army (ANA) was created, along with an Army Air Corps. This air corps later became the Afghan Air Force (AAF). Commandos and special forces, including the ANA Commando Brigade, were also formed. Training was managed initially by the U.S. Office of Military Cooperation, followed by other U.S. organisations and then Combined Security Transition Command-Afghanistan, and is now being run by the NATO Training Mission-Afghanistan.

The AAF was very significant before and during the 1980s but by late 2001, the number of aircraft available was minimal. The United States and its allies quickly eliminated any remaining strength or ability of the Taliban to operate aircraft.

With the occupation of airbases by American forces it became clear how destitute the air force had been since the withdrawal of the Soviet Union. Most aircraft were only remnants rusting away for a decade or more. Many others were relocated to neighboring countries for storage purposes or sold cheaply. The AAF was reduced to a very small force while the country was torn by civil war. It is currently being rebuilt and modernized by the US-led multinational Combined Air Power Transition Force of the US-led international Combined Security Transition Command - Afghanistan (CSTC-A).

There has been significant progress toward revitalization of the national military in the last decade, with two official branches established. The ANA and AAF became under the Afghan Ministry of Defense, which forms the basic military force. By 2006, more than 60,000 former militiamen from around the country have been disarmed. Most heavy weapons from Panjshir, Balkh, Nangarhar and other areas were seized by the Afghan government. In 2007, it was reported that the DDR programmes had dismantled 274 paramilitary organizations, reintegrated over 62,000 militia members into civilian life, and recovered more than 84,000 weapons, including heavy weapons. But the New York Times reported in October 2007 this information in the context of a reported rise in the number of hoarded weapons in the face of what has been seen as a growing Taliban threat, even in the north of the country.

The ANA Commando Battalion was established in 2007. The Afghan National Development Strategy of 2008 explained that the aim of DIAG (Disbandment of Illegal Armed Groups) was to ban all illegal armed groups in all provinces of the country. Approximately 2,000 such groups have been identified and most of them have surrendered to the Afghan government or joined the nation's military.

The NATO-trained ANA is organized into 31 Kandaks, or Battalions, 28 of which are considered combat ready. Seven regional corps headquarters exist. The National Military Academy of Afghanistan was built to provide future officers, it is modeled after the United States Military Academy at West Point, New York. The Afghan Defense University (ADU) is located in Kabul province and consists of a headquarters building, classrooms, dining facility, library, and medical clinic. In addition to this, an $80 million central command center was built next to the Hamid Karzai International Airport. In 2012, Afghanistan became a Major non-NATO ally.

Sizable numbers of ANA officers are sent to be trained in India either at the Indian Military Academy in Dehradun, the National Defence Academy near Pune or the Officers Training Academy in Chennai. The Indian Military Academy which has been in existence since 1932, provides a 4 year degree to army officers, while the National Defence Academy is a tri-service college provides a 3 year degree after which officers undergo a 1 year specialization in their respective service colleges. The Officers Training Academy on the other hand provides a 49 week course to Graduate officer candidates. In 2014 the number of Afghan officers in training in India was nearly 1,100. A Total of 1,200 Afghan officers have been trained up to 2013.

The total manpower of Afghanistan's military was around 164,000 in May 2011. By September 2014 it has reached 195,000. Its air force has about 100 refurbished aircraft, which includes Lockheed C-130 Hercules and Pilatus PC-12s military transport aircraft as well as Mil Mi-17 and Mi-24 helicopters. It also includes trainers such as Aero L-39 Albatros and Cessna 182 turbos. The manpower of the Afghan Air Force is around 3600, including 450 pilots, mainly trained during the Communist era. It also has small number of female pilots.

SENIOR OFFICERS

- Defense Minister, General Bismillah Khan Mohammadi
- Defense Ministry Spokesman, Major General Mohammad Zahir Azimi
- Chief of Staff of the General Staff (CoGS), Lieutenant General Sher Mohammad Karimi
- Vice Chief of the General Staff (VCoGS),
- Deputy Chief of the General Staff (DoGS), Lieutenant General Mohammad Ikram
- Command Sergent Major of the ANA, Sergeant Major Roshan Safi
- General Staff Chief of Personnel (GSG1), Major General Abdul Abdullah
- General Staff Chief of Intelligence (GSG2), Major General Abdul Khaliq Faryad

- General Staff Chief of Operations (GSG3), Major General Afzal Aman
- General Staff Chief of Logistics (GSG4), Lieutenant General Azizuddin Farahee
- General Staff Chief of Plans (GSG5), Major General Jan Kahn
- General Staff Chief of Communications (GSG6), Major General Mehrab Ali
- General Staff Chief of Doctrine & Training (GSG7), Major General Kushiwal
- General Staff Chief of Engineering (GSEng), Major General Muslim Amid
- General Staff Inspector General, Major General Jalandar Shah
- Surgeon General, Lieutenant General Dr. Abdul Qayum Tutakhail
- Afghan Air Force Commander, Major General Mohammad Dawran
- Ground Forces Commander, Lieutenant General Murad Ali Murad
- 201st Selab ("Flood") Corps Commander, Major General Mohammad Rahim Wardak
- 203rd Tandar ("Thunder") Corps Commander, Major General Abdul Khaleq
- 205th Atal ("Hero") Corps Commander, Major General Sher Mohammad Zazai
- 207th Zafar ("Victory") Corps Commander, Major General Jalandar Shah Behnam
- 209th Shaheen ("Falcon") Corps Commander, Major General Murad Ali
- 215th Maiwand Corps Commander, Major Gen. Sayed Malouk
- Afghan National Army Training Command, Major General Aminullah Karim
- ANA Special Operations Command, unknown officer

- ANA Recruiting Command, Lieutenant General Mohammad Eshaq Noori
- Headquarters Security and Support Brigade, Brigadier General Sadiq
- Command and General Staff College, Major General Rizak
- National Military Academy of Afghanistan, Major General Mohammad Sharef
- Kabul Military Training Centre, Brigadier General Mohammad Amin Wardak

BASES AND EQUIPMENT

Large number of military bases are found all cross the country, including major ones in Kabul, Kandahar, Herat, Balkh, Nangarhar, Khost, Paktia, Paktika, Maidan Wardak, Ghazni, Farah, and many other provinces. Some of these were built by the United States Army Corps of Engineers (USACE) while others by ISAF and Afghans. It was reported in 2010 that there were at least 700 military bases inside Afghanistan but more were expected to be built in the coming years. About 400 of these were used by Americans and ISAF forces with the remaining 300 or so by Afghan National Security Forces.

During the 1950s and 1960s, Afghanistan purchased moderate quantities of Soviet weapons to keep the military up to date. It was mainly Sukhoi Su-7, MiG-21 fighter jets, T-34 and Iosif Stalin tanks, SU-76 self-propelled guns, GAZ-69 4x4 light trucks of jeep class (in many versions), ZIL-157 military trucks, Katyusha multiple rocket launchers, and BTR-40 and BTR-152 armored personnel carriers. Also included were PPSh-41 and RPK machine guns. After King Zahir Shah's exile in 1973, President Daoud Khan made attempts to create a strong Afghan military in the Greater Middle East-South Asia region. Between 1973 to 1978, Afghanistan obtained more sophisticated Soviet weapons such as Mi-4 and Mi-8 helicopters, Su-22 and Il-28 jets. In addition to that the nation possessed great many T-55, T-62, and PT-76 tanks along with huge amounts of AKM assault rifles ordered. Armored vehicles delivered in the 1970s also included: ZIL-135s, BMP-1s, BRDM-1s, BTR-60s, UAZ-469, and GAZ-66 as well as large quantities of small arms and artillery.

Under the Democratic Republic of Afghanistan (1978–1992), weapon deliveries by the Soviets were increased and included Mi-24 helicopters, MiG-23 fighter aircraft, ZSU-23-4 "Shilka" and ZSU-57-2 anti-aircraft self-propelled mounts, MT-LB armored personnel carriers, BM-27 "Uragan" and BM-21 "Grad" multiple-launch rocket systems and FROG-7 and Scud launchers. Some of the weapons that were not damaged during the decades of wars are still being used today, while the remainder have probably been sold on the black market.

Camp Leatherneck in Helmand province under construction in 2011. It was officially transferred to Afghan Armed Forces in October 2014..

The United States has provided billions of dollars in military aid. One package included 2,500 Humvees, tens of thousands of M-16 assault rifles and body armoured-jackets. It also included the building of a national military command center as well as training compounds in several provinces of the country. Canadian Forces supplied some ANA soldiers surplus C7 assault rifles but the Afghans returned the Canadian-made C7 in favor of the American-made M16 rifle, reason being that parts between the two rifles, despite being similar, are not fully interchangeable.

Besides NATO, Afghanistan has been increasingly turning to India and Russia for assistance. Both countries have supported the Northern Alliance, with funding, training, supplies and medical treatment of wounded fighters, against the Taliban prior to 2002. India has been helping with several billion dollars invested in infrastructure development projects in Afghanistan besides the training of Afghan officers in India, but has been reluctant to provide military aid due to fears of antagonizing its regional rival Pakistan. In 2013, After years of subtle reminders, the Afghan government sent a wish list of heavy weapons to India. The list includes as many as 150 battle tanks T-72, 120 (105 mm) field guns, a large number of 82 mm mortars, one medium lift transport aircraft AN-32, two squadrons of medium lift Mi-17 and attack helicopters Mi-35, and a large number of trucks. In 2014, India signed a deal with Russia and Afghanistan where it would pay Russia for all the Heavy equipment requested by Afghanistan instead of directly supplying them. The deal also includes the refurbishment of heavy weapons left behind since the Soviet war.

In March 2008, the *New York Times* reported that in the past 12 months, the main supplier of munitions to Afghanistan's army and police forces was an AEY, Inc., a company headed by a 22-year old Efraim E. Diveroli, an Israeli-American from Florida whose vice president was a licensed masseur. The *Times* reported that much of the ammunition was defective, and appeared to involve illegal arms dealing. The company obtained more than 100 million cartridges from stocks in Eastern European countries including Albania, Bulgaria, Montenegro, and Romania.

The United States has also been largely responsible for the growth of the Afghan Air Force, as part of the Combined Air Power Transition Force, from four aircraft at the end of 2001 to about 100 as of 2011. Types include Lockheed C-130 Hercules and Pilatus PC-12 transport aircraft as well as Mi-17 troop-carrying helicopters and Mi-35 attack helicopters. The aircrew are being trained by an American team. The American intention is to spend around $5 billion by 2016 to increase the force to around 120 aircraft.

As the number of Afghan Armed Force is growing rapidly so is the need for more aircraft and vehicles. It was announced in 2011 that the military of Afghanistan would be provided with 145 multi-type aircraft, 21 helicopters and 23,000 various type vehicles. As a Major non-NATO ally, Afghanistan is able to purchase and receive weapons from the United States without restrictions. In the meantime, the Afghan military began seeking latest fighter aircraft and other advanced weapons. Defense Minister Wardak explained that "what we are asking to acquire is just the ability to defend ourselves, and also to be relevant in the future so that our friends and allies can count on us to participate in peacekeeping and other operations of mutual interest."

THE U.S. ARMY IN AFGHANISTAN OPERATION ENDURING FREEDOM

The terrorist attacks on America on 11 September 2001 awakened the country from its habitual peacetime slumber. Slow to anger, Americans traditionally spend most of their time pursuing personal goals, each with his or her own version of the American dream. But for many, the events of 11 September quickly burned into their consciousness, changing their lives in ways that only slowly began to register. As the nation mourned, it did so with the realization that sadness would give way to anger, and anger to justice. Almost immediately, in fact, the U.S. armed forces led the way in beginning a new type of war: a war on terrorism. Gradually, all elements of national power were focused on this struggle-intelligence, diplomacy, public health, security, and even financial and economic institutions. The first goal of the new war was discovering who these terrorists were, where they trained, who trained them, and where they lived so that America could destroy them and their infrastructure. The leaders of the United States determined that it was necessary to "drain the swamps" in which the terrorists lived. A partial answer to these questions was quickly apparent: the worst of the swamps that harbored the al Qaeda terrorists was in Afghanistan.

Strategic Setting

Afghanistan by the early twenty-first century was in shambles. Even in the best of times the tribal structure of the country prevented the functioning of a strong central government. The decentralized political structure precluded the creation of a thriving state. Economically, Afghanistan was poor, but until the 1970s it was surprisingly self-sufficient. However, the Soviet invasion and contested occupation from 1979 to 1989 destroyed what political and economic structures were in place. This struggle left an estimated 1.3 million Afghans dead or missing and created approximately 5.5 million refugees. The United States and much of the world community condemned the Soviet Union's war but did little directly to confront them. However, U.S. intelligence agencies covertly supplied arms and money to the Afghan *mujahadeen*, or holy warriors, and even provided training in some highly sophisticated arms, such as the very effective Stinger shoulder-fired antiaircraft missile.

With the departure of the Soviets in 1989 and the collapse of the puppet president they left behind, the United States' interest in Afghanistan waned and the country lapsed into near anarchy. The increase in open factional fighting in 1992 continued Afghanistan's time of troubles, leading to the rise of the *Taliban* group beginning in 1996.

The Taliban consisted of Muslim fundamentalists who sought to return the country to strict Islamic rule using whatever brutality was necessary in the process. Most of the country was under Taliban control by 2001 except for some small areas held by Northern Alliance forces in the Panjshir Valley northeast of Kabul and a few scattered pockets of resistance in the northwest of the country. Much of the opposition to the Taliban was divided along ethnic and geographic lines. The Northern Alliance was composed mainly of ethnic minorities such as the *Tajiks* and *Uzbeks* from the northern and western parts of the country. In contrast, the Taliban drew its strength from the majority *Pashtun* tribes in the southern and eastern portions of the country. Along with the attempt to institute a strict Islamic rule, the Taliban provided an open haven to some of the worst terrorist groups of the world, including Osama bin Laden's al Qaeda organization.

After the attacks on Americans in September 2001, the United States quickly uncovered clues as to the identity and organizational affiliation of the suicide terrorists who crashed planes into the World Trade Center towers and the Pentagon. However, knowing that al Qaeda was responsible for the attacks, and that al Qaeda was based primarily in Afghanistan, was one thing. How to attack it was another. Afghanistan is an immense, land-locked country approximately the size of Texas with a population of around 24 million. It is a land of massive mountain ranges and remote valleys in the north and east and near desert-like conditions on the plains to the south and west. Road and rail communications nets were minimal and in disrepair. The rough terrain had been one of the major obstacles the Soviet troops faced during their war, and it would provide challenges to any U.S. military effort.

The United States had attempted to attack the terrorists in Afghanistan before. In 1998 the Clinton administration had launched cruise missiles against known or suspected terrorist training camps after terrorists attacked several U.S. embassies.

This handful of cruise missiles, however, did little more than stir up the hornet's nest. Only troops on the ground would be able to locate and kill the terrorists. However, without sea or air lines of communications, the movement of large numbers of conventional troops to the area with the missions of seizing terrain or locating and killing terrorists seemed a nearly impossible task. Reflecting that assessment, both Taliban and al Qaeda leaders seemed smugly safe in their faraway mountain strongholds. Nevertheless, within a month of the September 11th attacks the U.S. Army had deployed forces to Central Asia to confront the terrorists on their own ground. One of the first of these units was the 5th Special Forces Group (Airborne) from Fort Campbell, Kentucky. The unique talents and skills of this Special Operations unit would be tapped to penetrate this terrorist redoubt and assist the Northern Alliance in overthrowing the Taliban and rooting out the al Qaeda.

Operations

During initial combat operations in northern Afghanistan as part of Operation ENDURING FREEDOM, Army Special Forces (SF) was tested to a degree not seen since the Vietnam War. With little time to prepare for this mission, SF teams were to land by helicopter deep in hostile territory, contact members of the Northern Alliance, coordinate their activities in a series of offensives, bring the entire might of U.S. air power to bear on Taliban and al Qaeda forces, and change the government of Afghanistan so that the country was no longer a safe haven for terrorists. They accomplished all this, and more, in the space of a few months. While the details of many of their operations remain classified, the general outline is clear.

Army operations in Afghanistan focused first on obtaining a suitable operational base outside the country but close enough to infiltrate Special Forces teams into their targeted areas of operations. Because of earlier contacts with the government of Uzbekistan, this occurred rather rapidly and U.S. forces began arriving at an old Soviet airbase near Karshi Kandabad in south-central Uzbekistan in the fall of 2001. The 5th Special Forces Group (Airborne), stationed in Fort Campbell, Kentucky, formed the core of Joint Special Operations Task Force NORTH, called Task Force (TF) DAGGER, under the command of Col. John Mulholland. In addition to the 5th Special Forces Group personnel, the task force included aviators from the 160th Special Operations Aviation Regiment (SOAR), also stationed at Fort Campbell, and Special Tactics personnel from the Air Force Special Operations Command headquartered at Hurlburt Field, Florida. To assist in base security, and to provide a quick reaction force of heavily armed infantrymen, the 1st battalion of the 87th Infantry, 10th Mountain Division (Light), also deployed to Karshi Kandabad.

Once in place, TF DAGGER was directed to conduct special operations in support of a number of Northern Alliance (NA) commanders in Afghanistan and to work with them to gain their active assistance in overthrowing the Taliban regime. Representatives of other U.S. government agencies who had long-standing ties with many of these organizations served as advance elements for the Special Forces. However, much of the military burden would fall on Army Special Forces and Special Operations aviators. They planned to quickly establish contact with three of the most powerful of the NA faction leaders, Generals Abdur Rashid Dostum, Mullah Daoud, and Fahim Khan. Assisted by U.S. air support, each would be encouraged to expand his footholds in northern Afghanistan and to provide a base for follow-on U.S. operations before the onset of winter. Winter in Afghanistan made mountain passes virtually impassible, and even air support was often adversely affected by the winds and storms of the harsh Afghan climate. For political purposes, the Special Forces teams were divided among the various faction warlords as equally as possible, since the United States did not want to give the impression of favoring one of these long-term rivals, now temporary allies, over the other. This policy impacted on the timetable of inserting teams, with some being held up, at times for days, awaiting the successful insertion of another team into a rival's territory. Afghanistan's inherent tribalism and factional splits could never be ignored despite the common enemy.

The concept of the operation in Afghanistan was to land teams first into the Mazar-e Sharif and Bagram-Kabul areas, followed almost simultaneously by insertions into the Kondoz-Taloqan region. Once these areas were secured, the plan was to move teams to liberate Kandahar, the center of the Taliban movement. Then the focus would shift to a likely area of enemy concentration in the Tora Bora Mountains. DAGGER leaders realized, however, that any success could ultimately lead to the scattering of the enemy forces into even more remote areas.

TF DAGGER launched its first teams into Afghanistan in mid-October. The first twelve-man SF team infiltrated into northern Afghanistan to the south of the key city of Mazar-e Sharif via helicopter on 19 October 2001.

This insertion, and the ones that followed, were stories in their own right. The flights were in modified CH-47s, all conducted at night, into mountains up to 16,000 feet high with clouds, rain, and even sandstorms dramatically limiting visibility. The insertions were highly dangerous even for the best aviators in the Army, the pilots of the 160th SOAR. Despite these risks, all insertions were accomplished without major incident, although there were a number of close calls from the high mountains and enemy ground fire.

After a two-and-a-half-hour hazardous journey through high mountains and extremely poor weather, the first SF team reached its landing zone south of the city of Mazar-e Sharif, where they linked up with the local warlord, General Dostum. Dostum was an old regional power broker who alternately allied himself with and then betrayed Afghans, Soviets, and the Taliban. He was considered a ruthless warlord with a strong power base centered around Mazar-e Sharif. After conferring with him, the team split into two elements to better assist Dostum's scattered forces against the Taliban.

From 19 to 24 October the Special Forces team operated in a split team manner. One element, Team Alpha, rode on horseback north into the mountains near Keshendeh Bala along with General Dostum to help him plan the attack on Mazar-e Sharif. The other half of the team, the Bravo element, moved south into the nearby Alma Tak Mountains to attack the Taliban in the southern Darya Suf Valley.

Team Alpha quickly began helping Dostum directly by calling in close air support (CAS) from U.S. B-1 and B-52 bombers and F-14, 15, 16, and 18 fighter-bombers. At first, however, the team was not permitted to move forward close enough to the Taliban positions to be most effective; Dostum was afraid they would be killed or captured. According to one Special Forces observer, on several occasions he told the team leader "500 of my men can be killed, but not one American can even be injured or you will leave." As a result, the team had to call CAS from a distance of eight to ten kilometers away from the targets, looking across the Darya Suf gorge with weather conditions often hampering visibility. It was extremely hazy most of the time, making it difficult to visually acquire targets even with binoculars and spotting scopes. Eventually, the trust barrier was broken when it became obvious the team could take care of itself. Choosing observation posts (OPs) at their own discretion, often regardless of the element of danger, the men of Team Alpha quickly became more effective.

The massive close air support brought down by Special Forces had a huge and immediate psychological effect on the Taliban, causing panic and fear, and a correspondingly positive effect on General Dostum's men. Starting on 22 October, Team Alpha, traveling on horseback in support of Dostum's cavalry, decisively demonstrated to the Afghans the U.S. commitment to their cause. From an OP near the villages of Cobaki and Oimatan, team members began systematically calling in CAS missions. In one eighteen-hour period they destroyed over twenty armored and twenty support vehicles using close air support. At first the Taliban responded by reinforcing its troops, sending reserves into the area from Sholgara, Mazar-e Sharif, and Kholm. All that did was provide more targets for the CAS aircraft circling overhead and called into action by the SF team on the ground. Numerous key command posts, armored vehicles, troop concentrations, and antiaircraft artillery pieces were destroyed.

Meanwhile, the Bravo element of the team, also mounted on horseback, moved south into the Alma Tak Mountain range to link up with one of Dostum's subordinate commanders in the southern Darya Suf Valley and prevent the enemy from assisting its forces in the north. They would continue to interdict and destroy Taliban forces in these mountains until 7 November, destroying over sixty-five enemy vehicles, twelve command bunker positions, and a large enemy ammunition storage bunker.

The work of Teams Alpha and Bravo quickly eroded the initial Taliban defensive positions. Many Taliban vehicles were destroyed, and hundreds of troops were killed. The survivors fled for their lives north to Mazar-e Sharif. In pursuit, Dostum's forces began to conduct old-fashioned cavalry charges into the northern Darya Suf and Balkh Valleys. During these attacks SF team members were in the forefront of the action, often on horseback, even though only one member of the team had ever ridden extensively before.

Soon the Northern Alliance troops approached a critical pass just south of Mazar-e Sharif. It was a natural choke point, and the enemy was there in force. Dostum's force could not go farther without massive fire support. Moving over treacherous terrain by horse and foot, SF elements moved into a forward mountain OP, and on 9 November they engaged Taliban defenses on the north side of the pass with close air support. Their efforts resulted in the destruction of several vehicles, a number of antiaircraft guns, and numerous troop concentrations. Coming under direct effective enemy BM-2 1 multiple rocket launcher fire on two separate occasions, they continued to engage Taliban forces with B-52 strikes. It was the heavy bombers that finally broke the back of the Taliban defenders, who now began streaming in retreat to Mazar-e Sharif and beyond.

With the way to victory opened up to him by Special Forces, General Dostum secured the city of Mazar-e Sharif on 10 November. Riding with Dostum into the heart of the city, the SF team watched as local Afghan citizens lined the streets, cheering and bringing gifts to Dostum. This triumphal progress into the city ended at the medieval fortress of Quali Jangi, where Dostum established his headquarters in the eastern entryway. The remaining sections became temporary prisoner holding areas. The fortress had been General Dosturn's headquarters when he was in command of the city prior to Taliban rule. More important, the capture of Mazar-e Sharif was the first major victory for the U.S.-led coalition in the war in Afghanistan, giving it a strategic foothold and an airport in northern Afghanistan.

Raid on Kandahar

While the campaign was under way in the north, U.S. forces also struck in the southern part of the country in the heart of the Taliban movement near Kandahar. On the night of 19-20 October Rangers and other Special Operations Forces (SOF) soldiers conducted airborne and air assault operations against several sites in Kandahar. Four MC-130 aircraft dropped 199 Rangers of the 3d Battalion, 75th Ranger Regiment (-), onto a desert landing strip southwest of Kandahar, code-named Objective RHINO. Assisted by circling AC-130 Spectre gunships, the Rangers quickly secured their objective. Then the soldiers and attached psychological operations (PSYOP) loudspeaker teams moved toward a nearby enemy compound and cleared it without resistance. Having secured the landing zone, they assisted follow-on helicopter forces of SOF soldiers that had additional raids to conduct in the area. In all, the Rangers and SOF soldiers spent almost five-and-a-half hours on the ground with only a few minor injuries. Although the tactical results of the raid were mixed, the Taliban was shown that U.S. forces could strike anywhere and anytime and that no location in Afghanistan was a safe haven any longer. Later, when U.S. marines landed in that same area on 25 November, they would establish a new base on the Ranger landing zone, called Camp RHINO.

The Capture of Kabul

Simultaneously with the Special Forces team's insertion into the Mazar-e Sharif region, another team infiltrated into northeastern Afghanistan to contact the Northern Alliance forces dug in on the Shamali Plains just south of the entrance to the strategic Panjshir Valley. The situation in this region, only fifty miles north of the capital city, Kabul, had been static for close to five years. Northern Alliance forces controlled an old Soviet air base at Bagram on the Shamali Plains. The opposing Taliban forces could not penetrate the defensive minefields near the base nor attack into the rich Panjshir Valley to the northeast. The valley had been the stronghold of Ahmed Shah Masood, the revered leader of the Northern Alliance assassinated by al-Qaeda agents on 9 September 2001, an act that had almost destroyed the Northern Alliance. The Special Forces teams now sought out local successors, Generals Fahim Khan and Bismullah Khan.

Having infiltrated into Afghanistan during the night of 19-20 October, the team linked up with the two Northern Alliance cornmanders on 21 October at Bagram air base and began looking for vantage points on the plains to call in close air support. They soon found an ideal position and established an observation post in the old air traffic control tower for the airfield. From that location, they could clearly see the Taliban positions in the Shamali Plains spread out before them and immediately began calling in air strikes on the entrenched enemy. From 21 October through 14 November 2001, the Special Forces directed almost continuous CAS missions against the dug-in enemy. The constant air attacks degraded the Taliban/al Qaeda command and control, killed hundreds of entrenched front-line troops, and disrupted their support elements. General Fahim Khan was encouraged to begin thinking about an immediate move against Kabul while the enemy was in disarray.

The Northern Alliance leaders originally planned a multiday, five-phased operation to take the Afghan capital. However, it soon became apparent to them that their foes were so weakened by U.S. air strikes that operations could be accelerated. When the attack was launched on 13 November, the enemy defenses quickly crumbled. By noon on the first day of the offensive, the operation had achieved all of its phase three objectives. Twenty-four hours later, to the surprise of the world press and the delight of the Northern Alliance, General Khan's ground forces liberated Kabul without incident. The Taliban and al Qaeda had fled in disarray toward Kandahar in the south and into the supposed sanctuary of the nearby Tora Bora Mountains to the east near Jalalabad. By early December U.S. troops were assisting in a ceremony reopening the U.S. embassy in Afghanistan's capital.

As the enemy abandoned its positions in the northeast and northwest sections of the country, the U.S. focus shifted to the central northern area around Taloqan-Kondoz, to the east of Mazar-e Sharif. SF teams had infiltrated into the area on 8 November and moved quickly to link up with General Daoud, a prominent Northern Alliance warlord who had gained fame fighting the Soviet invaders.

By 11 November the SF soldiers had established observation posts overlooking the defensive positions around Taloqan and were prepared to call in close air support for Daoud. However, before any air strikes could be arranged, Daoud launched his offensive and his front lines quickly moved out of the OP's line of sight. By the end of the night of 11 November, Taloqan had fallen with little resistance. A major victory had occurred almost without a fight, based solely, it seemed, on Daoud's new confidence in U.S. support and air power.

After the fall of Taloqan, the Special Forces continued its primary mission of assisting Daoud's combat operations with CAS as he began moving west, toward the city of Kondoz. To ensure nearly continuous air support, the twelve-man SF team split into three elements. On any given day one element would be on or forward of the front lines directing air strikes. A second element would be recovering from its operations the previous day, while a third element would be preparing for its operations the next day. Thus the team established a rotation cycle that enabled them to maintain a round-the-clock air strike capability on enemy positions blocking the advance to Kondoz.

Up to this point General Daoud had met very little opposition from the Taliban. On 13 November he met his first heavy resistance when one of his commanders attacked enemy positions to the west of Taloqan without orders, triggering a Taliban counterattack. After receiving both direct heavy-weapons fire and indirect tank fire, the SF element for that day repositioned to a different OP, called in air strikes on the Taliban, and helped Daoud repel the attack. However, this marked increase in Taliban resistance altered Daoud's plan of attack. Instead of trying to blitz through the Taliban all the way to Kondoz, he entrenched his forces and decided to use heavy U.S. air attacks to weaken the Taliban, either establishing the conditions for a successful attack or forcing them to surrender.

For the next ten days the Special Forces called in air support to pound Taliban entrenched positions in and around Khanabad and Kondoz. Over the course of these operations, SF-directed air strikes destroyed 12 tanks, 51 cargo trucks, 44 bunker complexes, and numerous other vehicles and supply dumps while inflicting losses on the Taliban/al Qaeda of around 2,000 killed or wounded.

By the end of eleven days of intense bombing, the enemy began crumbling and General Daoud captured the nearby city of Khanabad. He next prepared to move directly on Kondoz but decided to try a little diplomacy first, initiating talks with the Taliban leaders in that city. Seeing that their position was hopeless, they agreed to surrender on 23 November. Kondoz, the last Taliban stronghold in northern Afghanistan, was under Northern Alliance control.

At this point the wholesale surrender of the Taliban forces began to cause problems. Over 3,500 Taliban troops surrendered in the Kondoz area, and these prisoners were added to the hundreds more already under Northern Alliance control after the fall of Mazar-e Sharif. The thousands of prisoners from Kondoz were moved quickly, without even being thoroughly searched, to join the prisoners of General Dostum in the Quali Jangi fortress in Mazar-e Sharif. The large number of enemy prisoners and their inexpert handling led to difficulties almost immediately. Most of the prisoners were concentrated in a portion of the Quali Jangi fortress when U.S. intelligence officers started to interrogate them. During this process some 600 of the "detainees" disarmed the guards and took over the prison compound.

The rebellion sparked an immediate crisis. Two U.S. intelligence officers were trapped, one eventually escaping and the other murdered by his captors. In response, nearby SF soldiers organized a team of U.S. and British Special Forces to infiltrate the facility and bring back any friendly personnel held by enemy forces. As they neared the prison, they began taking heavy fire, including RPG (rocket-propelled grenade) rounds exploding in the team's immediate vicinity. The SF team requested close air support even though it would be in the "danger close" range and there was a possibility that bomb fragments would hit them even if their call for fire was accurate. Before the operation was complete, five U.S. and one British soldier would be wounded by an errant 2,000-pound bomb that landed too close.

Throughout the next three days the SF team exchanged fire with the rebels and used laser designator devices to illuminate their positions for air strikes and nighttime howitzer and 40-mm. cannon attacks from circling AC-130 Spectre gunships. It was during this period that they received notification that Johnny "Mike" Spann, one of the captured intelligence agents, had been killed. The crisis also prompted the first introduction of conventional troops into Afghanistan with the insertion of a small Quick Reaction Force (QRF) of infantry from Charlie Company, 1st Battalion, 87th Infantry, of the 10th Mountain Division operating out of Uzbekistan. The 1st Platoon helped secure the perimeter around the fortress to prevent enemy escapes and was available to provide any additional firepower that might be needed. Concurrently, the company headquarters and the 3d Platoon from C Company secured a landing zone at the Mazar-e Sharif airfield and assisted in the triage and evacuation of casualties. Once the mission had ended, the 1st Platoon remained in Afghanistan to provide security and a QRF in support of the Special Forces forward operating base soon established in that key northern city.

After five days of constantly engaging the prisoners with fire and maneuver, the coalition forces brought the battle to an end only when the last holdout bunkers in the fortress were flooded with water. The remaining prisoners-cold, wet, and hungry-surrendered. Out of the more than 600 prisoners at the facility, about 500 had been killed, reflecting the bitterness of the struggle. Those surrendering included the "American Taliban," John Walker Lindh, who had joined the movement sometime before 11 September.

During the Mazar-e Sharif and Taloqan-Kondoz campaigns with the Northern Alliance forces, Army SF soldiers effectively liberated six provinces of Afghanistan, including the key cities of Mazar-e Sharif, Meymanah, Sar-e Pol, Sheberghan, Heyratan, Auybak, Kondoz, Khanabad, Taloqan, and over fifty other towns. To accomplish this feat, they had traveled by horse, all-terrain vehicle, pickup truck, and on foot along hazardous mountain trails, often at night and in all extremes of weather, through hundreds of miles of mountains, gorges, hills, and valleys. They did all of this in about a month with only a few U.S. casualties, while inflicting thousands of casualties on the enemy and completing the destruction of Taliban and al Qaeda defensive positions in the north, including the liberation of Kabul.

With the liberation of most of the northern portion of Afghanistan and the recapture of Kabul, it was critical that the United States begin to take steps to assist the people of this war-torn country. Already the Americans had attempted to blend humanitarian concerns with military operations. While the fighting was under way, for example, C-17 cargo aircraft loaded with humanitarian daily rations (special meals without meat products and thus suitable for strict Muslims) dropped hundreds of thousands of food packets from the skies to cut-off refugee camps to mitigate what was feared could become a humanitarian disaster. In addition, PSYOP leaflets dropped in numerous locations offered rewards for fugitive Taliban and al Qaeda leaders, informed the Afghan people about their forthcoming liberation, and warned them of the dangers of unexploded ordnance and mines. Civil Affairs teams with Task Force DAGGER began assessing humanitarian needs even as the fighting was winding down in northern Afghanistan. And, with the capture of Kabul, the Central Command established a Combined Joint Civil Military Operations Task Force (CJCMOTF) to coordinate the efforts of relief organizations in Kabul and to work to establish Coalition Humanitarian Liaison Cells (CHLCs) in many population centers. The work of restoration had begun even while the campaign to retake the remainder of Afghanistan continued.

While Special Operations forces fought alongside the Northern Alliance, the U.S. Central Command (CENTCOM) established the theater architecture to command and control a sustained land campaign. In October 2001 General Tommy R. Franks, combatant commander of U.S. Central Command, designated the U.S. Third Army, or U.S. Army Forces Central Command (ARCENT), to provide command and control for ongoing operations as the

Combined Forces Land Component Command (CFLCC). Commanded by Lt. Gen. Paul T. Mikolashek, Third Army headquarters had deployed to Egypt just days prior to the 9/11 terrorist attacks to provide oversight of the biannual BRIGHT STAR exercise. Upon completion of BRIGHT STAR on 13 November, the headquarters deployed from Egypt to Camp Doha, Kuwait, where it officially assumed responsibilities as the CFLCC on 20 November. CENTCOM authorized General Mikolashek to immediately "direct and synchronize land operations to destroy al Qaeda and prevent the reemergence of international terrorist activities in Combined Joint Area-Afghanistan," as well as to conduct humanitarian operations and create conditions for a peaceful, stable Afghanistan.

In order for the CFLCC to accomplish this ambitious mission, additional Army support forces were deployed to the Gulf region and Central Asia to support Operation ENDURING FREEDOM. These forces included the 513th Military Intelligence Brigade, the 11th Signal Brigade, the 92d Engineer Battalion (Heavy), the 561st Logistical Task Force, the 507th Combat Support Group (-), and the 59th Military Police Company. Many of these elements had to provide support from outside of Afghanistan since the Central Command was under pressure to limit the "footprint" of American troops on the ground in that country, in part to avoid looking like an occupying power and repeating the mistakes of the Soviet Union in Afghanistan two decades earlier.

To coordinate support activities at Bagram Airfield in Afghanistan, in November the CFLCC formed an ad hoc group called Task Force BAGRAM. This task force was organized around the 3d Mobile Liaison Team under the provisional command of Col. Robert Kissel. Kissel's mission was to establish his headquarters at Bagram, coordinate the repair of the 8,000-foot runway built by the Soviets, and establish a key support base close to Kabul for follow-on missions. BAGRAM joined another task force at Bagram: Task Force BOWIE, commanded by Brig. Gen. Gary L. Harrell. BOWIE was a joint and interagency task force with an intelligence fusion cell reporting directly to the commanding general of Central Command.

The buildup of forces in Central Asia led CFLCC to request further augmentation to position a command and control node closer to the actual fighting.

CFLCC asked for the equivalent of a division tactical command post to serve as the CFLCC (Forward) headquarters, which would operate initially from the forward operating base at Karshi Kandabad in Uzbekistan.

On 25 November the 10th Mountain Division (Light), stationed at Fort Drum, New York, and commanded by Maj. Gen. Franklin L. "Buster" Hagenbeck, received orders to deploy to Central Asia for the mission. Initially constrained by the number of forces already deployed in Bosnia, Kosovo, and the Persian Gulf and by the force cap in place for the Afghanistan region, the division organized a small, 159-man command post for the mission. On 12 December the 10th Mountain Division headquarters officially assumed duties as the CFLCC (Forward) at Karshi Kandabad.

The mission of CFLCC (Forward) was to command and control Army forces, less Special Operations forces, in the Combined and Joint Area of Operations, Afghanistan (CJOA). General Hagenbeck's first priorities were to ensure support for ongoing Special Forces operations, to oversee repair of the damaged airstrip at Mazar-e Sharif, and to open a ground line of communications into that key city. Using the few resources available, primarily from the units organized under the 507th Combat Support Group's logistical task force, CFLCC (Forward) pushed needed supplies into Afghanistan and oversaw the demining and reconstruction of the Mazar-e Sharif airfield by Army and Air Force engineers.

The headquarters also worked with Uzbek officials and Afghan General Dostum to open both sides of the Freedom Bridge near Terrnez, Uzbekistan. The Soviet-built bridge had been closed since the Afghan civil war in the 1980s and 1990s. This land route provided a critical pathway for the smooth flow of supplies and humanitarian aid from Central Asia into northern Afghanistan. The road was opened by late December. These command and control and logistical steps greatly facilitated the posturing of coalition forces for future operations and for the stabilization of the northern portion of Afghanistan.

Two Approaches to Kandahar

Following the tactical successes in northern Afghanistan, Kandahar, far to the south, was to be the next U.S. objective. Military planners suspected that it would be the hardest city to take. The populous city was a long way from the Northern Alliance strongholds in the north, was of a different ethnic makeup-Pashtuns, not Tajiks-and was the spiritual and political center of the Taliban movement. With few opposition leaders or forces in the area to work with, its capture might take months, or even be delayed until spring. Still, two separate SF elements infiltrated into the region and approached the city from the north and the south, with their supported host nation commanders picking up support all along the way.

The first Special Forces team was inserted north of Kandahar, near the village of Tarin Kowt, on 14 November. There, they linked up with Hamid Karzai and a small number of his followers. Karzai, a charismatic Pashtun tribal leader born near Kandahar, was both pro-western and anti-Taliban, a rare combination. As such, he was vital to U.S. plans for establishing an anti-Taliban front in the region. However, he almost did not survive his first brush with the foe.

On 16 November, in an engagement two days after their arrival, the SF team had to act quickly to save Karzai's resistance group. Fearing Karzai's potential power, Taliban leaders had moved about 500 soldiers north from Kandahar to crush him. In response, Karzai deployed his handful of men near the village of Tarin Kowt but relied heavily on his new U.S. allies to provide close air support. As U.S. planes pounded the approaching Taliban convoy guided by SF teams on the ground, the Afghan opposition fighters rallied and repulsed the Taliban attack. The Taliban, apparently stunned by the air assault, retreated in disarray.

Having gained a breathing space, the SF team began working closer with Karzai's small force to equip, train, and prepare it for the move south. Feeling that time was crucial, Karzai agreed to move toward Kandahar as soon as possible. Accordingly, his tiny Afghan force, initially little more than thirty-five "well meaning" supporters-a force that would eventually grow to an "armed mob" of almost 800 men-began moving southeast around 30 November from Tarin Kowt, through narrow passes along what was virtually a goat path, toward the village of Petaw.

Karzai's men spent a few days resting at Petaw while the SF brought in weapons, food, and clothing for the growing army. Then, on 2 December, the army moved south toward the village of Sayd Alim Kalay, the site of a critical bridge over a dry riverbed. By that time Mr. Karzai had been notified of his selection as head of the interim government of Afghanistan, making it critical to move quickly to Kandahar and increasing the pressure on the attached Special Forces to ensure that the movement was successful.

Karzai's forces quickly routed the small force of Taliban soldiers holding the village near the eastern end of the bridge, but they could not take the well-defended bridge itself. For the next two days, despite the steady drone of close air support missions, the Taliban successfully defended the crossing. The tenacious defense was even marked by occasional enemy counterattacks through the dry riverbed in an attempt to gain a foothold on the other side. Each time the enemy attempted a counterattack, the alert SF team would bring in more air missions and, in conjunction with Karzai's soldiers, drive it back.

On the morning of 4 December Karzai's force began its preparations for an all-out attack to take the bridge. After final coordination with the Afghans, the combined army of Special Forces soldiers and Afghan irregulars loaded onto pickup trucks and drove to battle. Each pickup was packed with a band of Afghan warriors with an assortment of weapons (machine guns, AK-47s, and RPGs) hanging out of the back. Some crew-served weapons were mounted on the vehicles, making the convoy look like, in the words of one SF observer, a combination traveling circus and Somali war party.

The Special Forces team directed air strikes on the enemy-held ridge opposite them, but the enemy responded with heavy and accurate fire on the attacking force and again attempted a flanking counterattack over the dry gulch. Under SF guidance, the Afghans put direct fire on the attackers and drove them back. Three times the determined Taliban soldiers tried to cross, but each time the fire of Karzai's forces turned them back. Meanwhile, the SF team on the ridge continued to call down punishing air attacks onto the enemy positions. One SF soldier was wounded; but having failed to dislodge the combined SFI/Afghan force, the Taliban finally withdrew. That night the Taliban pulled back a few kilometers; the next morning Karzai's forces captured the bridge and established a foothold on the other side.

That next day, 5 December, the U.S. effort suffered a serious setback. While the Special Forces were observing operations from the ridgeline near the bridge and calling in close air support, a stray 2,000-pound Joint Direct Attack Munition (JDAM) bomb landed in the middle of the SF position. The soldiers were literally blown off their feet. Three Americans were killed and dozens wounded, along with many of their Afghan allies. They called for a MEDEVAC and patched up the survivors as they waited. The same helicopters that came in to evacuate the wounded brought in another SF team to fill in for the broken team. The mission went on despite the tragedy, but it resulted in the worst U.S. casualty figure in the war up to that time and the most damaging friendly fire incident.

As the SF teams were recovering from the bomb accident, Karzai's negotiators finalized an agreement for the surrender of the Taliban forces across the river and for the surrender of the entire city of Kandahar. On 6 December the force began moving again toward the now open city.

While Karzai and his SF element were making their way toward Kandahar from Tarin Kowt, another Special Forces team was advancing on the city from the south with a different opposition group. That team had infiltrated into the Shin Narai Valley southeast of Kandahar near the Pakistan border on the night of 18 November, quickly joining the local anti-Taliban leader, Gul Sharzai. Sharzai, the former governor of Kandahar, had led one of the groups against the Soviets and had been equally unhappy with the Taliban regime. Although he, like Karzai, welcomed the team as tangible proof of U.S. support for his operations, his force was heavily outnumbered by the local Taliban and in a vulnerable position. The SF team moved quickly to provide weapons and food to support his army of close to 800 tribesmen.

Once reinforced, Sharzai also proved amenable to advancing on Kandahar. During the night of 21 November Sharzai sent a delegation led by his brother to meet with the local Taliban representative to negotiate their surrender and ensure safe passage out of the valley for his forces. Unfortunately, the mission proved abortive, with the "truce party" taken under fire by the Taliban. There were no casualties, but Sharzai was forced to change his movement plans to avoid an early, and disruptive, battle.

Instead, his force bypassed the Taliban strongpoint, moving north from the Shin Narai Valley and then west through the Arghastan wadi district to Takht-e Pol located on Highway 4 south of the Kandahar Airport. Believing that intermediate firefights might only disrupt his movement and sap his strength, Sharzai remained fixed on Kandahar and the hope that his governorship might be restored.

On the morning of 22 November the group departed the valley, moving slowly. The convoy consisted of over 100 vehicles of many different types, including pickups, large transport ("jinga") trucks, and even farm tractors pulling trailers. The movement to Takht-e Pol took a little over two days and was virtually unopposed until the second night. By that time the group had moved into a small, bowl-shaped valley just east of Highway 4, approximately six kilometers from Takht-e Pol. When Sharzai sent a delegation into the town to negotiate for the surrender of the local Taliban, the Special Forces moved two CAS elements forward with the Afghan commander, covering the town from a ridge overlooking the negotiations. The Taliban, refusing to surrender, suddenly ambushed Sharzai's small security force. Immediately the SF requested air support and used it to break up the ambush, allowing the forward friendly elements to withdraw safely. However, shortly thereafter the Taliban began moving vehicles from Highway 4 to firing positions behind several ridgelines near Sharzai's force and began to attack with machine-gun and RPG fire. With the SF directing new air strikes against those forces, the Taliban quickly retreated and shortly thereafter, abandoned the entire Takht-e Pol area. It took only a few bombing missions to knock the fight out of them.

The next morning, 24 November, Sharzai's forces entered Takht-e Pol with little resistance, severing the main highway between Kandahar and Chaman, Pakistan. Immediately Sharzai established checkpoints to the north and south along the highway. The northern checkpoint was almost in sight of the major airport at Kandahar. The next day that checkpoint received indirect fire from the airport, leading the SF to establish a forward OP on a nearby ridgeline secured by a 100-man friendly Afghan force. During the next week the team was able to overlook the airport and direct air strikes onto the enemy forces operating between the ridgeline and the airfield.

Feeling that the Taliban was too strong and his own forces too weak, Sharzai waited for the air strikes to weaken the enemy. The Taliban countered by firing artillery and rockets onto the ridgeline and the village of Takht-e Pol. The airport appeared heavily defended by ground forces, as well as antiaircraft artillery and missiles. Nevertheless, relentless air strikes slowly eroded the defenders. During this same week Taliban forces began to move north from Spin Boldak, a small town to the south, along Highway 4 to defensive positions in a large wadi approximately five kilometers from the southern element of Sharzai's army; they never posed much of a threat. They were also probably deterred by the sudden presence of a U.S. Marine Corps force that established a defensive position, nicknamed Camp RHINO, some thirty-five miles southwest of Kandahar on 25 November.

By early December Sharzai had positioned his troops for an all-out attack on the airport. The Taliban probed his forces with a number of small counterattacks from the west, using a series of dry canals to mask their movement. Sharzai's men, supported by U.S. air power, repelled the attackers and even seized a number of enemy positions around the canals. Finally, on 7 December, Sharzai began his assault on the airfield. His forces moved carefully to the entrance of the airfield but unexpectedly found no resistance. Then, suddenly, he received a call on his satellite phone informing him that the Taliban had completely evacuated Kandahar as a result of Karzai's negotiations. He immediately gathered his personal security force and, along with a small SF element, sped into the city toward the governor's mansion, his former home. The remainder of the SF elements followed the next day and moved into the governor's mansion with Sharzai. The city had fallen without a shot, and Karzai subsequently confirmed Sharzai as the governor of the city.

While some SF soldiers were operating around Kandahar, others were pursuing enemy forces elsewhere. After the fall of Kabul, al Qaeda and Taliban forces had retreated into major strongholds in the Tora Bora Mountains south of Jalalabad near the Pakistani border, some of the most rugged terrain in the world. The terrorists had controlled the area for years, digging hundreds of caves and refuges and establishing their training camps. In addition to being intimately familiar with the area, they had emplaced extensive fortifications and stockpiled weapons and ammunition to fight a protracted defense. With large numbers of well-supplied, fanatical al Qaeda troops dug into extensive fortified positions, Tora Bora appeared to be an extremely tough target.

To make matters worse, the local anti-Taliban forces were even more disorganized than those in other areas. Not only were they divided into mutually hostile factions, but also each faction was deeply distrustful of American aims. However, given the few U.S. troops available in the country, Central Command had no readily available alternative to using Afghan forces for any timely attack on the region. At the time, the U.S. Marines had established only a small forward base at RHINO, south of Kandahar, and only a reinforced company of the 10th Mountain Division was at Bagram and Mazar-e Sharif. No other forces were readily available for use. Central Command and the headquarters of the Third U.S. Army generated numerous plans for the introduction of some U.S. conventional troops into the Tora Bora fight as blocking elements, but none were executed.

The mission fell to Special Forces working with an indigenous Afghan force. The Task Force DAGGER commander directed several SF teams to enter into the Tora Bora region in early December, meet with the local Afghan anti-Taliban commander, Hazrat Ali, and coordinate his attacks on the caves with U.S. airpower.

The forces of Hazrat Ali were a heterogeneous mixture of Northern Alliance soldiers loyal to Ali but whose fighting qualities were somewhat mixed. Yet lack of time and a U.S. policy that dictated the use of indigenous forces in ground operations as much as possible made the use of Ali's forces important. The SF teams were only to provide them advice and assistance with air support, not to lead them into battle. The plan was to send the Afghan forces up into the Tora Bora Mountains to assault al Qaeda positions located in a well-protected canyon. The latest intelligence placed senior al Qaeda leaders, possibly even Osama bin Laden, in that area.

The SF teams moved south out of Jalalabad, planning to set up an observation post along the high ground near the canyon. They were accompanied by a small Afghan security element to protect them while they were calling down air strikes. The movement up into the Tora Bora Mountains proved slow and hazardous. After a short trip in the ubiquitous pickup trucks, the teams were forced to unload and move forward on foot with burros carrying their packs. Moving into mountains where the altitude varied from 10,000 to 12,000 feet, they progressed slowly over rocky and narrow paths.

Initially, the team set up an OP on the canyon's western ridgeline and immediately began calling down air strikes, forcing the al Qaeda to move away, out of direct sight, into an even smaller canyon. Another SF team then moved to set up a smaller OP on the eastern side of the ridgeline, giving them direct observation of the new enemy concentration. The two teams then coordinated their air strikes from both sites, leaving the al Qaeda nowhere to turn.

For seventeen straight hours the SF teams rained fire onto enemy positions as the Afghan forces of Hazrat Ali began moving into the canyon. After this preparatory fire they began hitting targets of opportunity over the course of the next several days. The fight continued into the night. Each night, as the enemy forces would light their campfires to try and keep warm, the teams used their thermal imagers and brought in more bombs and fire missions, including a number of attacks by AC-130 Spectre gunships.

The enemy fought stubbornly. Each day Ali's forces would take advantage of U.S. air power and advance into the canyon, and each evening they would fall back. Much of the same ground would have to be taken again the next day. This went on for eight days and nights, as the enemy pocket grew smaller and smaller. Ali's force soon tired of the constant action and relaxed the pressure on the enemy, with U.S. forces and air support attempting to take up the slack. By the time the Tora Bora fighting slowly ground to a halt in mid-December, the SF soldiers had called in hundreds of air strikes, dropping thousands of tons of munitions and killing hundreds of enemy troops. A few al Qaeda were captured, but most of them fought to the death or slipped away into the relative safety of nearby Pakistan. The whereabouts of Osama bin Laden, or even whether he had been in the Tora Bora region in the first place, remained a mystery.

With the capture of Kabul and Kandahar and the destruction of organized resistance in Tora Bora, Afghanistan was now in effect liberated. It had taken fewer than sixty days of concentrated military operations and only a few hundred soldiers to seize the country from the Taliban and its terrorist allies. U.S. Army forces, now augmented with small teams of Civil Affairs personnel and the newly arrived 3d Brigade, 101st Airborne Division, still faced the challenge of finding an elusive and potentially deadly residual guerrilla force. Army elements increasingly turned to assessing the humanitarian situation in their local areas, coordinating allied humanitarian initiatives such as the establishment of a Jordanian hospital at Mazar-e Sharif, gathering intelligence on al Qaeda and Taliban remnants, and ensuring that liaison was established with the newly emerging Afghan government.

Detainee operations surfaced as another task for CFLCC (Forward) to plan and manage. After the recapture of the Quali Jangi fortress, the prisoners who survived that uprising were transported and jailed with other detainees inside a run-down prison in the town of Sheberghan, west of Mazar-e Sharif. The prisoners were of various nationalities, and CENTCOM wanted them carefully screened to determine whether any key Taliban or al Qaeda leaders had been captured. General Hagenbeck assigned the task to Col. Kevin V. Wilkerson, commander of the 10th Mountain Division's 2d Brigade. Wilkerson and a portion of his staff had only recently joined the headquarters and now set to work planning the mission. Wilkerson quickly formed Task Force COMMANDO, a force that included his headquarters as a command and control element; Capt. Nelson Kraft's Charlie Company, 1st Battalion, 87th Infantry, for security; and interrogation, medical, and military police elements to screen, handle, and treat the prisoners. The task force flew into the Mazar-e Sharif airfield from 24 to 26 December, procured host nation vehicles for transportation, and convoyed to Sheberghan on 28 December.

Task Force COMMANDO established liaison with General Dostum, set up a hasty base camp near the warlord's headquarters outside the town, and began the screening process. Wanting to avoid any potential for a prisoner uprising similar to that at Quali Jangi, Wilkerson developed strict prisoner procedures to ensure the security of the screening process. For over two weeks Task Force COMMANDO screened the prisoners. Those deemed to have valuable intelligence were evacuated to the temporary holding facility set up at Kandahar, prior to shipment to Guantanamo Bay, Cuba, for further interrogation. Wilkerson's men accomplished the mission without incident.

Another example of unfinished business from combat operations was the siege of Kandahar hospital. With the fall of the city in December, a number of wounded and captured al Qaeda soldiers had been moved into the hospital for treatment. Having been inadequately screened for weapons by their Afghan guards, once at the hospital a number had pulled out grenades and weapons, taken hostages, and vowed never to be taken alive. Anxious to avoid casualties, the newly established local government decided to wait them out. The doctors continued to treat the patients, even while the al Qaeda fanatics clutched live grenades to their chests and threatened them. Attempts to starve them out were undermined by Taliban sympathizers who smuggled food into the hospital. After a month the government turned to the local Special Forces team to train a small Afghan volunteer militia group in how to retake the building. Commander Lali, a brave Afghan soldier respected by his men, led the indigenous force. Working closely with Lali's men, the SF helped develop a plan and ran them through a series of rehearsals.

Finally, on 27 January the hospital was closed off and the Afghans moved in with the SF team hovering nearby in support. The initial breach of the hospital wing around 0830 was met with a hail of gunfire, and several of the militia were wounded. Falling back, the operation settled into a stalemate that lasted for nearly twelve hours. The militia, despite five of them being wounded, reorganized and rearmed and, assisted by SF snipers, stormed down a corridor as several of the al Qaeda, true to their threat, used their last grenades to blow themselves up. Those that continued to fight were shot and killed. Six al Qaeda died during the operation, but no Afghan or American soldier was killed. It was a bloody end to the standoff, as all attempts to induce them to surrender had failed. An SF officer remarked at the time: "Up to the last minute, we told every man to surrender. But none of them listened. These Arabs fought to the death." It was, in his words, a "very hard gunfight."

While these loose ends were being dealt with, attention in other parts of the country now turned to locating and destroying concealed al Qaeda and Taliban forces, which was easier said than done. Afghanistan is the size of Texas and has hundreds of square miles of virtually impenetrable mountains and valleys connected by unmapped paths and trails. U.S. forces faced the further problem of what to do with the enemy once they found him. Afghanistan had no army, and it would take time to build one, while U.S. forces numbered fewer than 2,000. The 3d Brigade of the 101st Airborne Division was at the Kandahar airport, replacing the marines; elements of the 1st Battalion, 87th Infantry, 10th Mountain Division, were at Bagram, serving both as a base security force and as a quick reaction force. Any major combat operations would stretch these forces to their limit. Yet, a disciplined and reliable ground blocking force was a vital component of any future attempt to destroy guerrilla concentrations. For example, while the attack on the Tora Bora caves complex in December 2001 had successfully destroyed an enemy strongpoint and cleared hundreds of caves, many al Qaeda soldiers had slipped away into Pakistan despite an attempt by Pakistani forces to prevent their movement across that border.

Following the Tora Bora battles, U.S. intelligence began searching for other concentrations of enemy forces. SF elements, including the newly arrived Task Force K-BAR consisting of Navy SEALS (Sea, Air, Land commandos), foreign Special Forces, and elements of the 3d Special Forces Group (Airborne) from Fort Bragg, North Carolina, conducted a series of raids. Soldiers from TF K-BAR and TF DAGGER hit a number of potential enemy locations in the Zawar Kili cave complex, in Deh Rawod, Ali Kheyl, and other locations, mostly in the area south and west of the Tora Bora Mountains. Simultaneously the focus of U.S. intelligence slowly shifted toward this area, in particular the Paktia province and the Gardiz-Khowst-Orgun-e triangle. The people in this area were Taliban sympathizers, reported as tolerating the continued presence of al Qaeda fighters. Indications were growing that there was a major concentration of enemy forces in the Shahi Kowt Valley of this province. The attempt to deal with this enemy force was code-named Operation ANACONDA.

Operation ANACONDA

ANACONDA grew rapidly to include participants from almost every type of American, coalition, and indigenous unit in Afghanistan at the time. The operation was directed at a major concentration of what was thought to number between 200 and 500 terrorists in the Shahi Kowt Valley and was fought from 2 to 19 March 2002.

The Shahi Kowt Valley, south of the city of Gardiz, runs north to south just to the west of a major mountain range about one hundred miles south of Kabul near the Pakistani border. The local terrain determined the conduct of the operation. There were two main approaches to the valley, one from the northwest and the other from the southwest around a major ridgeline just to the west of the valley known as Tergul Ghar, which U.S. troops nicknamed the Whale. Just outside and to the northwest of the valley is a smaller ridgeline called little Tergul Ghar, nicknamed the Little

Whale. These two major terrain features dominated the two approaches to the valley. The valley, approximately five kilometers wide and ten kilometers long, shelters three villages named Shir Khan Kheyl, Babulkhel, and Marzak. These villages constituted Objective REMINGTON during ANACONDA.

Much of the valley is approximately 8,000 feet in elevation, with the surrounding peaks exceeding 11,000 feet. The valley's higher eastern mountain range is pierced by only a few main routes and dozens of smaller goat paths. Near the southern end is a mountain peak called Takur Ghar with excellent observation over both the valley and a number of the exit routes. (*Figure*) All in all, the valley was surrounded by formidable terrain, making the area difficult-nearly impossible-to isolate.

The first real confirmation of enemy forces in strength in the Shahi Kowt Valley had come not from air reconnaissance or other sophisticated collection means, but rather through the efforts of a Special Forces team on the ground with the radio call sign "Texas 14." Working closely with local Afghan forces, Texas 14 attempted to conduct a ground reconnaissance of the valley in late January, only to turn back after their Afghan security forces warned them of a major enemy concentration.

After digesting Texas 14's report, U.S. forces began focusing other intelligence assets on that area. Initial results suggested as many as 150-200 foreign fighters in the Shahi Kowt Valley area. Subsequent intelligence estimates would vary widely, with some reports placing the number as high as 800-1,000 enemy combatants in the valley and along the nearby mountain ridges. U.S. surveillance assets also uncovered a number of caves in the valley thought to contain terrorist weapons caches. The various sources of information, however, often proved misleading and contradictory, and no one was really sure of enemy strength in the valley.

Initially, TF DAGGER considered the option of attacking into the valley using only SF teams leading a few hundred Afghan military forces they had trained. However, as the number of enemy projected to occupy the valley began to climb, the Special Forces asked for planners from the conventional units. Quickly the plan grew to include additional troops from the 10th Mountain Division (Light Infantry) and 101st Airborne Division (Air Assault). By mid-February a total of 6 Special Forces "A" Teams of 12 men each, 3 SF command and control elements, 3 other Special Operations task forces, and a U.S. infantry brigade of 3 battalions were involved, along with nearly a thousand Afghan Military Forces (AMF) trained by the Special Forces. The planning effort, and command and control of the forces involved in the operation, was assumed by Combined Joint Task Force MOUNTAIN under the command of the 10th Mountain Division commander, General Hagenbeck, on 15 February.

The Plan for ANACONDA

Operation ANACONDA'S scheme of maneuver called for isolation and encirclement of the valley area, followed by converging attacks to destroy al Qaeda forces. A mixture of Afghan militia, U.S. and coalition Special Operations, and conventional forces would establish three sets of concentric rings astride enemy escape routes before the main strike into terrorist defenses in the valley. Around D minus 3, coalition Special Operations forces, including elements of Task Force 64 (Australian Special Air Service) and Task Force K-BAR, would begin infiltrating into surveillance positions located five to seven kilometers from the objective area, where they could observe enemy movement and call for close air support against spotted enemy targets. At D minus 1, about 600 SF-led Afghan forces, TF ANVIL, would move into position along major enemy routes of retreat. Then, on D-day, the CJTF MOUNTAIN would air-assault elements of the 101st Airborne and 10th Mountain Divisions (TF RAKASSAN) into an inner ring of blocking positions along the eastern side of the valley. Simultaneously TF HAMMER, about 260 Special Forces and AMF, would attack around the southern end of the Whale and into the valley as the main effort, while a secondary effort set up a blocking position near the Little Whale at the northern entrance to the valley with about forty AMF and Special Forces soldiers. The goal was to hit the enemy hard enough to kill or capture as many of the al Qaeda as possible and to squeeze the survivors out of the valley into the blocking positions where they would then be eliminated. Those that somehow escaped the trap would be tracked using air and ground reconnaissance assets as they moved along the various "ratlines" through safe houses and refuges in an attempt to reach Pakistan.

Task Force ANVIL, the outer blocking force, would move from the cities of Khowst and Orgun-e at D minus 1. From Khowst, the forces of Kamil Khan, approximately 300 strong, would travel west along Axis IRON about thirty-five kilometers. From Orgun-e, Zakim Khan's forces, with another 200 or so fighters, would move about fifty kilometers along Axis METAL. They would establish blocking positions code-named CHEVY, FORD, HONDA, JEEP, DODGE, and OLDSMOBILE that covered the main exfiltration routes out of the valley.

As the main effort force, Task Force HAMMER would depart Gardiz just before H-hour on D-day and drive thirty-five kilometers southwest along Axis STEEL. The force would then divide into two elements and approach the valley, moving southeast about ten kilometers toward the valley entrances along Axes BRASS and COPPER.

The smaller, northern element of TF HAMMER would proceed along Axis BRASS and stop at Phase Line EMERALD to await the preliminary air strikes on the objective before moving to establish a blocking position just north of the valley. The second HAMMER element was to move along Axis COPPER and similarly wait on Phase Line EMERALD for the supporting air strikes before assaulting and clearing the three villages on Objective REMINGTON: Shir Khan Kheyl, Babulkhel, and Marzak. Simultaneously, Task Force RAKASSAN, consisting of the 3d Brigade of the 101st Airborne Division and the 1st Battalion, 87th Infantry, 10th Mountain Division, would air-assault two battalions (-) into Blocking Positions (BP) AMY, BETTY, CINDY, DIANE, EVE, GINGER, and HEATHER to the east of the valley, To assist in watching smaller possible escape routes from the valley, three other U.S. and combined Special Operations task forces would conduct special reconnaissance missions along likely escape trails.

As the time for the commencement of offensive operations grew closer, CJTF MOUNTAIN orchestrated the arrival of the necessary forces and supplies. Beginning on 20 February, a combination of fixed and rotary-wing aircraft moved Task Force RAKASSAN and Task Force 64 soldiers from Kandahar to the forward operating base at Bagram. CJTF MOUNTAIN established its command post at Bagram on the following day and assumed command of all forces for the operation. Concurrently, U.S. logisticians began to build up the necessary supplies, especially fuel for the helicopters, to support the operation. Fuel was particularly difficult to stockpile, since there was a lack of usable ground routes to bring it to Bagram and all of it had to come in by air. Supply personnel resorted to "wet wing" operations (siphoning fuel directly from aircraft fuel tanks into ground storage facilities) from U.S. Air Force C-17 aircraft to fill fuel bladders at Bagram air base. The CJTF MOUNTAIN staff monitored all movements of forces, coordinated the necessary rehearsals, and watched the fluctuating weather conditions. General Hagenbeck initially set D-day for 28 February but was forced to postpone the start for two days due to inclement weather.

Special Operations forces, meanwhile, had several vital tasks to perform prior to the start of the operation. As early as D minus 11, some Special Operations reconnaissance assets infiltrated into the valley, where they began clandestinely to scout enemy positions. On 27 February the Australians of Task Force 64 moved to the Gardiz area from Bagram and began to infiltrate into reconnaissance positions to the south of the valley. Special Forces soldiers with Commander Zia worked on training their Afghan allies in basic tactics and weaponry. Their training efforts were hampered by constantly changing numbers of recruits, the need to identify and train squad and platoon leaders, and problems in obtaining a timely supply of the necessary equipment, especially weapons, for their troops.

The Operation

On D minus 1, 1 March, the TF ANVIL elements moved out from Orgun-e and Khowst and established the external Afghan blocking positions without incident. However, increased enemy activity in the valley seemed to indicate that the enemy forces were aware that something was afoot.

On D-day, 2 March, TF HAMMER departed Gardiz at midnight local time and hit the first checkpoint along Axis STEEL on schedule. However, as the trucks moved off the main road and onto the muddy track that was the main approach route to the valley, things began to go wrong. One of the large jinga trucks tipped over, halting the convoy. After cross-loading the troops and equipment, the convoy began to move out again, only to have other vehicles become stuck, break down, or tip over. Hours were consumed extricating the vehicles or moving loads from broken-down or stuck trucks onto different, by now even more overloaded, trucks. Some trucks were abandoned and others were only driven out of the mud by soldiers throwing hundreds of combat rations (MREs) under the wheels for traction. Many of the Afghan soldiers finally set out for Phase Line EMERALD on foot.

As the troops approached EMERALD along the northern and southern routes, they were suddenly taken under fire. On the northern approach route, what at first appeared to be enemy mortar fire struck the lead SF vehicle, killing one American and wounding three others. A subsequent investigation discovered that the vehicle was accidentally hit by friendly fire from a circling AC-130. Two of Zia's men were also killed in that incident, and twelve to fifteen were wounded. With the whole northern force only around forty strong to begin with, almost half that element was now out of action and the rest were under continuing enemy fire. The American and Afghan wounded were evacuated by helicopter, but that took almost two hours; it was at least another hour before additional Afghan forces could be brought out of the southern element to reinforce the northern force. This movement was complicated since the southern element, just short of Phase Line EMERALD, was also under attack by enemy mortars and artillery all during this time.

The deadly rounds and subsequent halt as the situation was reevaluated were fatal to the momentum of the attack. It became obvious that the enemy had good observation posts on the Whale that allowed him to spot all friendly movements. Also, the planned U.S. air strikes that were to assist Zia were poorly coordinated and generally ineffective. Expecting a hail of bombs, Zia's men watched as only a handful hit enemy positions on the Whale, causing no slackening in enemy mortar and artillery fire. Commander Zia and his men initially held up well, but after many hours of enemy bombardment with no way to answer back and ineffective or nonexistent close air support, their morale began to suffer. Due in part to events elsewhere on the battlefield, air support consistently failed to arrive throughout the day. TF HAMMER received only one additional CAS mission and one Apache fire support mission throughout that long day despite its designation as the main effort.

While the drama west of the valley unfolded, TF RAKASSAN began its air assault with the first of two planned lifts of seven helicopters each into its assigned blocking positions. After a pre-assault bombardment of targets along the eastern ridge of the valley, AH44 Apache helicopters swept down the valley and engaged enemy targets as CH-47 Chinook helicopters dropped off infantrymen at their designated landing zones. From the start, however, the units began taking heavy enemy fire. Nevertheless, the infantrymen of Task Force RAKASSAN immediately moved to occupy their positions and engage the al Qaeda fighters in the valley and in the heights above them. By noon American forces had occupied six of seven assigned blocking positions. However, a sudden shift in the weather blocked a number of the passes between Bagram Airfield and the valley with fog and prevented the arrival of the second lift of troops for several hours. Thus the positions were at half strength for some time and under nearly constant mortar attacks.

Enemy mortars were particularly effective against the 10th Mountain Division's 1st Battalion, 87th Infantry, soldiers trying to occupy BPS GINGER and HEATHER. The soldiers of Charlie Company began taking small-arms fire as soon as the helicopters had deposited them on their landing zones (LZs). As the 1st and 2d Platoons attempted to move off the LZs toward their designated blocking positions at HEATHER and GINGER, respectively, the enemy opened up with RPG and machine-gun fire. Both platoons were forced to take cover, but the 1st Platoon moved forward and established itself on BP HEATHER. Suddenly, the enemy dropped a succession of mortar rounds onto their position, wounding the

1st Platoon leader, his platoon sergeant, and eight others. Almost half the troops on BP HEATHER were casualties. The battalion 120-mm. mortars accompanying the 2d Platoon were set up and began returning fire but fairly soon ran out of rounds. The 2d Platoon was also being hit; and the Charlie Company commander, Captain Kraft, pulled his men back and put them in a company strongpoint in a nearby crater. This single strongpoint attempted to control both avenues of approach down the valley that were supposed to be blocked by BPS HEATHER and GINGER.

During the next eighteen hours the soldiers of Charlie Company fought back al Qaeda attempts to outflank them and overrun their position. Conserving ammunition, the 10th Mountain soldiers defeated every attempt but took additional casualties. Lt. Col. Paul LaCamera, commander of 1st Battalion, 87th Infantry, and his battalion tactical command post had accompanied C Company on the assault and set up their operations near BP HEATHER. This command post was also hit and suffered six casualties during the course of the day. By the end of the day some twenty-five soldiers of the 10th Mountain Division were wounded, four very seriously. The enemy fire slackened by nightfall, and the light fighters were able to use their night vision goggles to dominate the battlefield.

Much of the enemy fire against the attempt to establish BPS GINGER and HEATHER was coming from the nearby village of Marzak, just to the northwest of the positions. After repeated overflights of the town by unmanned aerial vehicles revealed enemy fighters but no indications of civilians, General Hagenbeck declared the village hostile and directed air strikes onto the town. A series of bombing runs virtually obliterated the village.

It was soon apparent that the original main effort under Commander Zia was not going to make any headway against the tenacious foe. As darkness approached, the SF commander with Zia's forces consulted with Zia and the Task Force DAGGER commander, Colonel Mulholland; they all agreed that it was time to fall back, regroup, and come back to fight another day. As darkness began to fall, Zia's weary men loaded up onto what trucks they had left and returned to their home base at Gardiz.

As the second helicopter lift finally brought in additional troops to reinforce each battle position early the following morning, the situation in the valley began to stabilize. Five AH-64 Apache helicopters had acquitted themselves well in the fight, attacking enemy troop concentrations, observation posts, and firing positions. However, they also took heavy ground fire themselves; by the end of the day only one undamaged Apache was flying. As Task Force RAKASSAN'S commander, Col. Frank Wiercinski, later stated, "The weapon that changed the face of the battle for us was the Apache." Nevertheless, with close air support still poorly coordinated and slow and artillery support not available, the actions of the Apaches were the one bright spot of fire support during a long day. After hours of bombardment and over twenty wounded, the 1st Battalion, 87th Infantry, soldiers trapped near BP GINGER were pulled out at nightfall, leaving a major exit from the valley open. Reconnaissance assets and air strikes attempted to cover this gap, especially the well-placed special reconnaissance teams of Task Force 64, but it was not the same as maintaining a blocking position in the GINGER valley itself. This region became the focus of several days' bombing attacks in an attempt to deny the enemy exit from or entry into the valley.

The next day General Hagenbeck issued new instructions to guide operations for continuing the attack. Consequently, TF RAKASSAN units prepared a modified plan. The new scheme of maneuver called for RAKASSAN'S 2d Battalion, 187th Infantry, to attack toward the heights of the ridge to the east of the valley and begin systematically to clear the ridge of the enemy. The reserve 1st Battalion, 187th Infantry, would air-assault into the northernmost landing zone with the mission of moving from battle position to battle position, north to south, linking up with each position and clearing the ridgeline between positions.

This operation began in the early hours of 4 March, but the going for the soldiers was slow. The rocky terrain was broken, and the altitude quickly exhausted anyone not acclimatized to it. Still, by the end of the day advance elements of TF RAKASSAN had already pushed down as far as BP DIANE and linked up with those U.S. elements still in place from the air assault of 2 March.

Nearly simultaneously, Army Special Forces helped Commander Zia launch a small AMF reconnaissance element onto the northern portion of the Little Whale to watch enemy movements in the valley as renewed air strikes hit Objective REMINGTON. In addition, sixteen Apaches from the 3d Battalion, 101st Aviation; five AH-1W Cobras from the 13th Marine Expeditionary Unit's Composite Aviation Squadron; and a number of Air Force A-10s flying from bases in Pakistan joined the fight.

The majority of the attention on the battlefield on 3-4 March, however, focused on a firefight on Takur Ghar, a mountain to the southeast of the valley. There, on the night of 3 March, Special Operations had attempted to insert a Special Reconnaissance team nearly on top of what turned out to be an enemy-held position and a Navy SEAL had fallen out of the helicopter as it was hit by enemy fire. The helicopter moved away about eight kilometers before having to set down, but the SEAL was left behind to face certain death or capture. A small SEAL reaction force was quickly inserted to locate him, but an alert enemy drove them off the hill. Then, just before dawn on the fourth, a larger quick reaction force of about twenty-five Rangers inserted into the area aboard two helicopters. One helicopter set down directly on top of the mountain and was taken under fire and disabled, killing three Rangers and an aviation crewman almost immediately. The other helicopter set down several hundred meters away at another LZ with its Ranger load. These Rangers were forced to move slowly up the steep slopes of Takur Ghar as their comrades were engaged in sharp fighting at the top. After several hours the two elements linked up and killed the remaining al Qaeda on the mountain, only to be engaged by enemy reinforcements moving toward the position. During a fierce, daylong fight the Rangers were able to hold onto their positions but suffered from intense enemy mortar and small-arms fire that wounded several more soldiers. The Ranger force located the body of the dead SEAL and established defensive positions to wait for extraction at nightfall. However, the cold during the long day sapped the strength of the casualties; and one of the wounded, an Air Force medic, died. All the Rangers and Special Operations soldiers were finally rescued after darkness fell on 4 March, but at a final cost for the United States of 7 dead: 4 Army, 2 Air Force, and 1 Navy. The fight on Takur Ghar was the most deadly firefight during Operation ANACONDA.

Over the next few days TF RAKASSAN elements continued to move slowly down the ridgeline from BP DIANE to Objective GINGER, an area to the east of the blocking position of the same name, clearing all the caves and potential enemy positions along the way. The al Qaeda fighters the American infantry encountered along the way skillfully used the terrain to mask their positions and movement and employed mortars to advantage but could never muster a coordinated attack of any great size. They tried to reinforce their forces in the valley, but to no avail. As TF RAKASSAN soldiers fought down the eastern ridge, they killed numerous al Qaeda, cleared over 129 caves and 40 buildings, and destroyed 22 heavy weapons emplacements.

Due to the enemy strength in the valley, it became apparent that more than Zia's attenuated forces, by now only around 200 strong, would be needed to clear Objective REMINGTON. The Afghan defense minister, Fahim Khan, was contacted, and he selected one of his best generals, Gul Haidar, to lead a mixture of Afghan infantry, motorized infantry, and tanks-about 700 soldiers in all-down from Kabul to join the fight. Gul Haidar was a battle-tested veteran of the war with the Soviets, and his forces were the closest equivalent of a conventional military force available to the Afghans at the time.

By 10 March all of Gul Haidar's elements were in place near the northern entrance to the valley; after a quick reconnaissance of the area, some of Haidar's men charged and seized the northern half of the Whale ridgeline. With his flank thus secured, Haidar moved his main body of troops into the northern end of the valley on the eleventh.

The next day, 12 March, tanks and armored personnel carriers attacked straight down through the valley and moved quickly to clear the villages of Shir Khan Kheyl and Babulkhel. While Haidar attacked from the north, Commander Zia sent his reconstituted Afghan force into the valley from the south and began clearing the village of Marzak. The three villages were quickly taken, as the enemy had already fled; only two wounded prisoners were captured.

Meanwhile, Task Force SUMMIT, built around the 1st Battalion, 87th Infantry, 10th Mountain Division, replaced elements of the 101st Division as the main effort and continued the drive south to Objective GINGER. Under the command of Colonel LaCamera, TF SUMMIT reached its objective by the thirteenth and was extracted after only light enemy contact. The next day Task Force COMMANDO, consisting of elements from Colonel Wilkerson's 2d Brigade, 10th Mountain Division; that division's 4th Battalion, 31st Infantry; and the 3d Battalion, Princess Patricia's Canadian Light Infantry, air-assaulted onto the Whale to conduct a series of sensitive site exploitation missions to locate any remaining enemy or supply caches. This phase of ANACONDA was code-named Operation HARPOON. After TF COMMANDO completed clearing the Whale, it continued exploitation operations into the Objective GINGER and GINGER pass areas. From 13 to 19 March Task Force COMMANDO killed a few remaining al Qaeda, found and destroyed huge caches of weapons and ammunition, and seized a great deal of valuable intelligence from cave hideouts. Meanwhile, CJTF MOUNTAIN targeted a number of intelligence platforms against suspected enemy safe houses in the nearby Naka Valley, some twenty kilometers to the southeast of the Shahi Kowt Valley. Special Operations elements subsequently scouted the valley without finding any al Qaeda. Declaring the entire operation highly successful, General Franks, the commander of Central Command, declared Operation ANACONDA officially over on 19 March.

For the first time in the war, the al Qaeda had indeed stood and fought. They had occupied well-camouflaged, dug-in fighting positions with overhead cover and large stocks of food and ammunition. They had excellent forward observation posts that provided early warning and observation for placing well-targeted mortar and artillery onto any coalition forces coming into the valley. The initial U.S.-led Afghan ground attack failed in part due to poor air support, a lack of artillery, and, most damning, a more numerous and aggressive enemy than anticipated. Despite focusing all available intelligence collection assets, including many highly sophisticated national assets, on a relatively small square of ground in Afghanistan, the United States was still unable to gain an accurate picture of enemy size, strength, and intentions.

Nevertheless, the operation was successful and many al Qaeda were killed. Although estimates of enemy dead varied from a low of 100 to a high of as many as 1,000, an unknown number of al Qaeda probably were able to flee into the surrounding hills and then into safe havens in the Pakistan tribal regions. Still, the enemy had been located, forced into a losing battle, and killed or forced to flee without his large equipment or stockpiles of supplies. In a guerrilla war, that counts for much. The al Qaeda lost many of its most experienced and most aggressive fighters in this operation. Subsequent U.S. troops, including additional Special Forces units and elements of the 82d Airborne Division and XVIII Airborne Corps, have not faced enemy concentrations of this magnitude or aggressiveness to date. Nevertheless, military operations continue in that troubled land, accompanying attempts to ensure political stability and encourage economic reconstruction.

Analysis

U.S. Army forces, operating closely with allied Afghan units, were decisive in defeating the Taliban and their al Qaeda allies and in liberating Afghanistan in a few short weeks in late 2001. The high level of training and dedication to duty of American forces overcame all obstacles and delivered a heavy blow against terrorism. In the earliest phases of the operation, Special Forces was clearly the force of choice to achieve dramatic results with only a handful of soldiers on the ground. When later backed up by the conventional power of U.S. air assets and the air assault and infantry assets of the Army, the mix proved decisive. All of these elements came together in Operation ANACONDA, a major success in locating and defeating remnant forces of al Qaeda. In Operation ENDURING FREEDOM, American military power delivered a fatal blow to the Taliban and their al Qaeda allies for a major victory in the war on terrorism.

Too much, however, should not be drawn from the easy collapse of the Taliban. The United States had heavy assistance from its Northern Alliance allies, who had their own political aims in mind. They were, in essence, a surrogate ground army that proved quite effective when provided some coordination elements and air power assistance. These circumstances are so unique that one should be leery of applying any "new model" of warfare wholesale without considering all the unique elements of any other situation. Nonetheless, the soldiers of the U.S. Army, assisted by the Air Force, Navy, and Marines, proved that the application of discrete military power, regardless of geographical obstacles, could have an impact far out of proportion to the number of forces on the ground.

The U.S. Army proved again that it could fight throughout the spectrum of conflict as it moved from unconventional warfare to conventional operations and back again as circumstances warranted. The Army, working with all the services and numerous other governmental agencies, also proved that the United States would pursue its enemies wherever they fled or tried to hide, even to the farthest reaches of one of the most remote countries in the world.

8

Military Withdrawal from Afghanistan

America has been at war in Afghanistan for more than 13 years, as long as the Civil War, Spanish-American War, World Wars I and II and Korean War combined. U.S. troop levels peaked at 140,000 in 2010. More than 2,200 Americans died in a conflict reflecting little more than purposeless inertia.

The U.S. is leaving, but not entirely and maybe not soon. Warned NATO commander Gen. Philip Breedlove in January, "We are going to continue to have casualties." The formal combat mission might be over, but combat is not.

Defense Secretary Ashton Carter said the administration hopes to strengthen its relationship with Kabul. The president, said Carter, "Is considering a number of options to reinforce our support for [Afghan] President [Ashraf] Ghani's security strategy."

Roughly half of the 10,600 American troops were supposed to leave by the end of the year, with the rest scheduled to depart in 2016. But the administration has cancelled this year's withdrawal. Carter said he wanted to "make sure this progress sticks." Alas, by that standard American forces might never leave.

Washington intervened in Afghanistan with two overriding objectives: Destroy al-Qaeda and oust its Taliban hosts. The U.S. quickly fulfilled both goals. But then the Bush administration lost interest, using terrorism as an excuse to oust Iraq's Saddam Hussein.

America's best opportunity to create a stable and peaceful Afghanistan was in 2002 and 2003, after the Taliban had been largely dispersed. But the Bush administration fixated on Iraq even though Saddam Hussein had nothing to do with 9/11. The administration quickly withdrew military resources from Afghanistan, allowing Osama bin-Laden and other al-Qaeda leaders to escape and the Taliban to regroup.

Instead of ending Washington's half-hearted misadventure at nation-building, the Obama administration twice doubled down in a desperate attempt to recoup lost ground. Some progress was made, but when I visited I found only limited confidence in private.

Washington and its allies built a large government bureaucracy and security force in Kabul, but on a potential foundation of sand. The Afghan government is noted for venality, incompetence and corruption. The military's performance has improved but remains uneven at best; police behavior is much worse.

Despite high international expectations the Kabul government was unable to hold a fair and free election last year. The Obama administration negotiated an extra-constitutional power-sharing agreement between President Ashraf Ghani and "Chief Executive" Abdullah Abdullah.

Unsurprisingly, it proved difficult to implement and public dissatisfaction has grown. The government still could outshine its predecessor, admittedly a low standard, but even that will require extraordinary statesmanship — a virtue never in high supply in Kabul.

Nor does the Ghani government rule the country. Wrote John Sifton of Human Rights Watch: "In many parts of Afghanistan, governors or members of parliament run their own militias under the banner of [Afghan Local Police], using the pretext of fighting insurgents to terrorize the local population." The role of warlords, especially old Mujahideen leaders, bedevils Afghanistan. Indeed, First Vice President Abdul Rashid Dostum is loathed by Pashtuns for allegedly massacring 2,000 Taliban fighters in 2001.

Nevertheless, the administration celebrated Ghani's election since he signed the (U.S.) Bilateral Security Agreement and (NATO) Status of Forces Agreement which Hamid Karzai had rejected. Ghani's approval allowed Washington to retain around 10,000 Americans (joined by roughly 3,000 Europeans) in the Afghan muddle. President Obama proclaimed a "historic day" when the Kabul authorities signed the accords, which would "strengthen sovereignty, stability, unity and prosperity, and contribute to our shared goal of defeating al-Qaeda and its extremist affiliates."

Alas, virtually none of these are true. The good economic times were fleeting: Departing Westerners are taking their hard currencies with them. Opium helps keep the economy afloat. Afghanistan's restored sovereignty will survive only so long as the Ghani government keeps the Taliban at bay. Domestic political comity is largely a mirage. Alas, growing pressure from a reenergized insurgency is as likely to divide as unify.

Washington has much at stake in claiming success in Afghanistan. In fact, the U.S. defeated al-Qaeda. The few operatives who remain in Afghanistan are of little account. Affiliate organizations active in Pakistan, Syria and Yemen are far more significant. Little likely would change if the Taliban again dominated the country: Pashtuns interested only in governing themselves learned that misbehaving foreign guests bring down the wrath of a superpower. It's not an experience they likely would repeat.

The U.S. still has an interest in preserving an intelligence presence in Afghanistan. Embassy security will remain a challenge. Small training missions could prove useful. However, these functions do not require thousands of military personnel authorized to engage in combat if "mutually agreed."

Some policymakers hope to leave a liberal, democratic outpost in Central Asia. Afghanistan today is a much more advanced, enlightened, and engaged nation than under the Taliban. But the gains are fragile and failures are significant. The central government has proved unable to serve and protect its people or hold their loyalty. The fraud and waste in international aid programs are epic. Kabul acts as a recruiter for the Taliban when it tortures detainees and fails to deliver justice. So long as the Afghan government remains corrupt and incompetent, the Afghan people remain divided and tribal, the Taliban remains determined and violent, and Pakistan remains hostile and unhelpful, the vision of a stable, peaceful and Westernized Afghanistan will remain a chimera. Maintaining a U.S. military presence is unlikely to change that. Tens of thousands of troops, thousands of lives, hundreds of billions of dollars, and thousands of aid projects from America failed to fix the country. A much smaller U.S. troop presence won't remedy the system's deep deficiencies. The diminished garrison will be too small to defend the government but too large to remain uninvolved, especially if engaged in broadly defined "antiterrorism" activities.

Nation-building in Central Asia never was going to be easy. Afghanistan is not a slightly less developed version of America or Europe. The deep differences were highlighted by deadly riots after Koran burnings by U.S. troops and in America. The *Charlie Hebdo* murders in Paris triggered Afghan protests in favor of the killers; thousands more people protested cartoons published in the next issue.

Afghanistan still could eventually end up with a reasonably liberal society, but only on its own terms. Many Afghans desire liberty and equality. However, the U.S. cannot turn Afghanistan into a modern nation state, at least at reasonable cost in reasonable time. And no one should expect a strong central government along Western principles.

Thankfully, what emerges won't be matter much to America so long as Afghanistan does not host terrorists bent on striking the U.S. The conflict has regional impacts, but not of significant consequence to America. Conflict in Afghanistan destabilizes Pakistan. However, that was the case before Washington intervened. Indeed, America's involvement has resulted in frequent confrontations between Washington and Islamabad.

India, Iran, China and Russia might intervene absent a robust American presence. The surrounding Central Asian states also are interested in Afghanistan; Saudi Arabia and Turkey pay attention at a greater distance. The Great Game inevitably will be played as Washington's force levels drop. But better they do so without America than the U.S. try to block them through a permanent occupation.

American security is not dependent on Central Asian stability. Washington should engage surrounding powers as it leaves to encourage them to cooperate over broadly shared objectives: that no hostile power, whether internal or external, dominates Afghanistan and uses the territory against other states. The best solution would be Afghan nonalignment and foreign noninterference.

There is much more Washington should do as it accelerates its troop withdrawal. The U.S. should offer sanctuary to Afghans who have helped the allies, such as interpreters and liberal-minded Afghans who would be at risk in the new order. The administration also should press discussions with the Taliban warning of America's red lines (primarily al-Qaeda's return) should the movement regain power.

America's most important task may be to use its remaining time to encourage resumption of talks between the Afghan government and Taliban. There should be no illusions about the prospect of success. Attempts to reach peaceful agreement go back more than 40 years, to the 1973 coup which destabilized the country, triggering endless fighting and multiple foreign interventions.

Of course, Washington hopes to forestall a Taliban victory. And one is not preordained. Even the Soviets' much-hated client, Mohammed Najibullah, survived more than three years against the Mujahedeen after Moscow's withdrawal.

Nevertheless, the warning signs are clear: last year was the costliest for the Afghan National Security Forces since the conflict began in 2001. (Civilian casualties also jumped by a fifth, to the highest level since 2009.) The Diplomat's Franz-Stefan Gady reported: "The ANSF still cannot move freely in the country. There are areas that are a no-go for the ANSF, others where they will only go with U.S. air support, and others where they will go on their own," mostly major urban areas.

The costly Afghan National Army faces a high and rising attrition rate and badly missed its end strength goal last year. Last August's level of 169,000 was "the lowest assigned ANA force strength since August 2011," warned the Special Inspector General for Afghanistan Reconstruction. The former deputy U.S. commander in Afghanistan, Lt. Gen. Joseph Anderson, called these attrition rates unsustainable. Are enough young Afghan men prepared to die for the Ghani government without direct U.S. support? The Independent Institute's Ivan Eland worried that the ongoing tendency of the Afghan security forces to give way "will undoubtedly accelerate — that is, if the Afghan security forces don't collapse altogether, as did similarly U.S. trained Iraqi forces in that country."

Kabul's main hope is Taliban weakness. The movement's brutality and misrule have cost support. The United Nations noted "divisions driven primarily by differences over political strategy" as well as factions behaving "with increasing autonomy." In some regions local Taliban act more like criminal gangs. In others, such as northern Badakhshan province, the movement's leaders proved to be surprisingly liberal. The Taliban also faces violent competition from groups claiming allegiance to the Islamic State.

Moreover, the end of active allied combat involvement undercuts the group's mission to oust foreign troops and restore self-rule. Militarily the Taliban also appears to have weakened. As foreign forces have withdrawn the movement has staged spectacular suicide attacks in Kabul, instigated insider shootings, including one which killed an American general last August, and gained ground in Helmand, Kunar and Kunduz provinces, but has captured no city of note. Much of the country remains safer than a few years ago.

Afghanistan is more likely to end up with multiple "governments" than under whoever happens to dominate Kabul. Which gives everyone an incentive to reach a modus vivendi to end the fighting. Polls indicate that a large majority of Afghans favor a negotiated agreement with inclusion of the Taliban in the political system. Reaching an agreement should be easier once the issues are primarily about Afghanistan, not the objectives of America and others.

In fact, the Ghani government appears more diplomatically adept than its predecessor. President Ghani has worked to improve relations with Pakistan. After long backing the Taliban, Islamabad may be ready to encourage negotiations. The murderous December attack on the school for children of military parents in Peshawar may help explain Islamabad's apparent change of heart. Most of

Pakistan's objectives could be achieved without a new Taliban government in Kabul. Even China, with an eye to Afghanistan's mineral wealth, is encouraging a diplomatic settlement.

The administration should live up to its promise to leave Afghanistan. Before the last presidential election Vice President Joe Biden stated: "We are leaving. We are leaving in 2014. Period." Now, said Secretary Carter, the president is considering "possible changes to the timeline for our drawdown of U.S. troops." But thirteen years of combat is more than enough.

Equally important, Washington should abandon its attempts at global social engineering. As the U.S. discovered in Iraq, the Balkans, Yemen, Somalia and Libya, as well as Afghanistan, droning, bombing, invading, and occupying other nations rarely delivers peace or stability. Indeed, Afghanistan forever has been characterized by local control punctuated by persistent violence. Washington's overriding objective should be to prevent creation of a new terrorist sanctuary. Beyond that America's interests fall off sharply in importance. None are worth or likely achievable via military means.

Afghanistan is a tragedy. Unfortunately, that isn't about to change. It is time for America to leave. Some day Afghanistan must stand on its own. That day should be today. Only Afghans can decide Afghanistan's destiny.

SECURITY, DEVELOPMENT AND THE BRITISH EXPERIENCE OF COUNTER-INSURGENCY WARFARE IN AFGHANISTAN

The aim of this essay is to assess the relationship between security and development with regard to the British experience of counter-insurgency in Afghanistan by employing the concept of the security-development nexus, as well as peacebuilding and statebuilding paradigms due to their interconnectedness with counter-insurgency in Afghanistan. Firstly, this essay analyzes the concepts of 'security', 'development' and the security-development nexus and their implications for peacebuilding and statebuilding paradigms since the end of the Cold War. Secondly, this essay demonstrates that peacebuilding and statebuilding aims regarding 'security' and 'development' and the British counter-insurgency considerably merged at the doctrinal level in Afghanistan. Thirdly, this essay discusses the actual British experience of counter-insurgency on the ground in Afghanistan by demonstrating profound gaps between initial aims and achievable objectives regarding security and development. Overall, this essay argues that rather than pursuing holistic doctrinal 'development' of the 'West' linked with democracy, liberal market economy, human security and security in the long run, the primary goal of the British (and their coalition partners) should have been to achieve security in the narrow sense by overcoming the Taliban-led insurgency in Afghanistan and employing limited physical reconstruction. Only after this is achieved, specifically tailored development strategy should be pursued and should complement the Afghan-style long-term security and human security.

THE SECURITY-DEVELOPMENT NEXUS

In order to assess the British experience of counter-insurgency warfare in Afghanistan, it is vital to present the relationship between security and development. Following the end of the Cold War, there has been an increased consensus among governments, non-governmental organizations, academic works and international institutions that "development requires security, and without security you cannot have development", that "development and security are inextricably linked" , or "no security without development, no development without security" . This intimate relationship between security and development, or 'the security-development nexus' "has been hailed as...a holistic, coherent or comprehensive approach [to intervention] in non-Western [failing or failed] states", especially after 9/11 . Despite Afghanistan being a somewhat distinct case from peacebuilding and statebuilding missions in the 1990s due to direct external military involvement on the ground and ongoing insurgency, it is crucial to understand the broader dynamics of these missions. They involve external interventionist mechanisms, employing multidimensional techniques in order to contain and consequently reverse insecurity and underdevelopment in societies devastated by an armed conflict. However, these 'missions' largely reflect liberal ideas, the consensus of international institutions and liberal states that insecurity and underdevelopment are interconnected and cause armed conflicts that threaten stable and lasting peace. Consequently, in order to overcome these threats of failing or failed states, they have to be transformed according to the 'Western' liberal consensus into "liberal market democracies as quickly as possible" by pursuing political and economic liberalization . However, in most of the cases this approach "produced destabilizing side effects that worked against the consolidation of peace" . By abstracting these cases from their specific historical, cultural and political context and employing "an ahistorical and static view of the challenges posed" , the liberal consensus with regard to development and security is deemed to be overly self-celebratory and lacking realism and pragmatism.

'Development' and 'security'

Before proceeding to the discussion of the British approach to counter-insurgency in Afghanistan that merged with peacebuilding and statebuilding practices, terms 'development' and 'security' require further analysis. To provide a single precise uncontested meaning of these terms is virtually impossible, because it would require a certain degree of politicization and reductionism that simplify the multidimensionality and complexity of security and development. Instead, there are multiple 'developments' and 'securities' that constitute the web of 'nexuses', for example, Stern and Öjendal (2010:21) identify six development-security nexuses. For the purpose of this essay, four of those are used: development-security as modern narrative, humanizing development-security, development-security as a technique of governmentality and globalized development-security.

The first and the last dimensions were presented in the previous paragraph with regard to the liberal 'modern' consensus and global diffused norms regarding security and development. The key dimension to be discussed here is the humanization of security and development linked to the liberal modern narrative and global norms. Both security and development have been redefined from their initial sense, such as security of state or development as an indicator of GDP and trade to encompass the 'human security' and human well-being. The Voices of the Poor study of the World Bank indicated that "the number one priority for the poor was security" (Chandler, 2007:367). Duffield (2007:111) notes with regard to human security that "international security is menaced by the modalities of underdevelopment ... [and] demands that states play a central role in protecting and securing people". The implication of 'Western' liberal humanization of development and security is the export and implementation of norms, such as good governance, human rights, democracy, sustainability, access to education, eradication of poverty, economic growth and conflict-prevention to 'non-Western', 'underdeveloped' and 'insecure' failing or failed states. Moreover, this relationship has been increasingly 'securitized' following the 9/11, with the preventive character of development "subordinated to security-relevant goals" (Trachsler, 2008:2). By having assessed 'development' and 'security' and their relationship, this essay proceeds to link peacebuilding and statebuilding practices with the British experience of counter-insurgency in Afghanistan.

PEACEBUILDING, STATEBUILDING AND COUNTER-INSURGENCY

With regard to peacebuilding and statebuilding in the 1990s, strategies of security and development have been pursued after the formal termination of a given conflict, where some kind of political settlement was reached between competing forces. Consequently, the role of the peacekeeping military operating with an international mandate has been to maintain stability and act as a guardian of peace. This is in contrast to counter-insurgency, which involves an ongoing armed struggle between insurgents and counter-insurgents in the absence of political settlement between the two. Thus, strategies of development and security are pursued by counter-insurgency in a process of war-fighting in order to overcome the insurgency. However, peacebuilding, statebuilding and the British counter-insurgency approach, especially with regard to Afghanistan, overlap in certain strategies and mechanisms. They involve joint external civilian-military missions importing and employing 'Western' liberal conceptions of humanized development and security as preconditions to stability and sustainable absence of armed conflict. Arguably, the role of military involvement is much greater in counter-insurgency than in peacebuilding or statebuilding. However, political dimension is crucial across the whole spectrum. Galula (1964:88) described counter-insurgency as "80% political, 20% military", while Kilcullen (2006:123) notes that "modern counter-insurgency may be 100% political". Moreover, the open and frequent use of armed force by the external interveners is highly discouraged not only in post-conflict missions, but also in the Afghan counter-insurgency mission with "the people-centred human security-like discourse" supporting it (Gilmore, 2011:22). Additionally, the intimate relationship between security and development, or the security-development nexus, manifested itself at the doctrinal level as a comprehensive approach with regard to Afghanistan. Rather than providing security by military means alone, "it requires good governance, justice, and the rule of law, reinforced by reconstruction and development" (Williams, 2011:64).

Development, security and the British COIN in Afghanistan

There have been numerous gaps between the doctrinal ambitions outlined in the previous paragraph and the realization of these objectives in Afghanistan. These gaps are based on a somewhat flawed approach to counter-insurgency with regard to development and security, as well as lack of commitment, financial and non-financial resources, complexity and incoherence among actors. With regard to the British experience of counter-insurgency in the Helmand province since 2006, as well as numerous other provinces that are not under the exclusive Afghan central government or coalition control, they experience an ongoing Taliban-led insurgency. Therefore, counter-insurgency does not possess monopoly on armed violence and these areas lack security even in the narrow sense. Consequently, the civilian organizations are constrained to carry out humanized development strategies, when the military is unable to deal with the short-term and traditional conception of security. The British task force commander, Jerry Thomas, emphasized security as the "pre-eminent line of activity [and that] once security is in place, development will gather momentum and provide the best tool with which to counter this insurgency" (quoted in Egnell, 2011:304). However, there seems to be a contradiction between the doctrinal pursuit of the minimum force in the counter-insurgency campaign and the actual situation on the ground that would require a more intense and frequent use of armed forces in order to achieve security in the narrow sense. NATO, the US and even the UK – with their alleged 'softer' approach, have been extensively criticized by using too much force with regard to air strikes and ground fire resulting in the civilian deaths (Roberts, 2009:41).

Another relevant aspect to be discussed is the impact of the relationship between Taliban-led insurgency, counter-insurgency and Afghan population on security and development. The classical British approach to counter-insurgency since the campaign in Malaya has been to win the 'hearts and minds' of the people, in the case of this essay the Afghan populace. Generally, this approach involves using carrots in the form of development projects, assurances of security and the minimum use of force in order to win over the local population, consequently defeating insurgent subversion and support (Crawshaw, 2012:1). However, the 'hearts and minds' approach "may be useful in public relations terms, but it undermines the theory as a guide to operations, because it can be interpreted in such divergent ways" (Dixon, 2009:353). Additionally, as the previous paragraph demonstrated, the application of the minimum use of force is highly difficult to pursue consistently in Afghanistan. Thus, by using force openly too much and its association with the civilian deaths, the local population feels increasingly alienated with the counter-insurgency and its false promise of security. This is jointly applicable to the internal and external dimension of counter-insurgency through the politicization and activation of local grievances by Taliban, pointing to the historical continuity and portraying the Afghan National Security Forces and the Afghan central government as puppets of the infidel external occupants.

Afghanistan has been shaped by the armed conflict for decades dating back to the Cold War activating and strengthening its contested tribal, ethnic or religious identities. Historically, central state institutions in Afghanistan "have been notoriously weak" contributing to the local attachment rather than the state attachment among the diverse Afghan population (Roberts, 2009:38). In the current situation, the strong central presidency of Karzai, penetrated by insurgent groups and discredited by the rampant corruption reflects the unrealistic ambitions of the external Western powers to provide functioning democracy with the recognized central authority.

Furthermore, the Western coalition forces including the UK have "focused heavily on economic factors, structural incentives, and individual preferences [emphasizing] rationalist and materialist approaches" to address the counter-insurgency and development in Afghanistan (Fitzsimmons, 2008:356). This holistic doctrinal approach of the West by pursuing its own standards of democracy and liberal market economy neglects the distinctive Afghan internal and historical complexities that are incompatible with the Western vision. Rather, a more narrow approach of reconstruction should have been initially pursued, understood as "the restoration of the condition of the assets and infrastructure ... to the same or similar state in which they were found before the outbreak of hostilities" (Etzioni, 2009:101).

Regarding the economic factors, the issue of illegal opium production in Afghanistan linking transnational criminal networks, insurgents and local farmers is both crucial and extremely difficult to address. There have been tensions among the US and the UK in destroying the opium poppy fields, with the UK being reluctant to destroy those "in Helmand province until alternative forms of income can be provided to the farmers" (Dixon, 2009:375). This has two contradictory implications. The first one is the aim to win the 'hearts and minds' of the local population by not destroying their source of income, thus contributing to overcoming the insurgent subversion, the second being a financial income to the insurgents from illegal drug trafficking and opium production sustaining and strengthening the insurgency. The fact is that the opium poppy cultivation is on the rise since 2001 (Jones, 2008:81). This discredits plans of the Western coalition to provide an alternative agricultural cultivation on a large impactful scale that would limit the influence of the insurgents on the local population.

Aside from the top tier core of the Taliban-led insurgency driven by radical Islamism, the low tier insurgents recruited from the local population and supported by it are motivated by unemployment, disenchantment or anger (Jones, 2008:60-61), further strengthened by the fear of personal insecurity.

Despite some success stories of the British experience of counter-insurgency in Helmand province, for example, limited strategic territorial gains in 2010 with the support of US marines, or the 2008 Afghan development zones strategy (Egnell, 2011:297), overall strategic objectives of the counter-insurgency have not been achieved by the British, possibly resulting in the "operational failure [or] strategic defeat" (Betz and Cormack, 2009:320). This has been largely due to the rapid and inappropriate application of the Western liberal consensus on the security-development nexus with their wrongly perceived long-term positive impact on Afghanistan. These have proved counterproductive, by further fuelling the insurgency, thus maintaining, or even strengthening insecurity in the narrow sense. Employing modest, short-term and achievable objectives firstly and then introducing gradual changes specifically tailored to Afghan complexity with the local consensus over several decades might have been a better approach for achieving security and development in the long-run. However, also the British (and coalition) domestic factors have been deficient to pursue a successful counter-insurgency campaign, with the British Government's "lukewarm commitment to Afghanistan ... in part as a reflection of public opinion" (Betz and Cormack, 2009:321).

Conclusion

To conclude, this essay demonstrated that the intimate relationship between security and development manifested in the security-development nexus is essentially a Western liberal construct seeking to diffuse the application of humanized character of these concepts to non-Western underdeveloped and insecure societies in conflict or post-conflict situations. As has been the case in numerous post-Cold War external interventionist missions, the pursuit of doctrinal holistic approach has had largely negative outcomes in Afghanistan. This has proved consistent with regard to the British experience of counter-insurgency in Afghanistan. Realities on the ground in Afghanistan indicate that there has been insecurity in the narrow sense, while pursuing wrongly designed development and security strategies. The Taliban-led insurgency is far from being overcome and 'hearts and minds' of the population are not won over. The primary initial objective should have been to decouple security from development in their Western liberal understanding in order to achieve security and stability in the narrow sense as the absence of regular armed violence, while pursuing limited physical reconstruction and empowering the local decentralized, even undemocratic governance.

AFGHANISTAN, ISLAMIC MILITANCY, AND THE NEXUS WITH KASHMIR

One was that Islamic extremists could destabilize Pakistan domestically, making it hard to govern. The other was that Pakistan's influence with India over the Kashmir question (Pakistan's leaders believed this had been revived by the insurgency that began in Kashmir in 1988–89) would now be neutralized. Pakistan's fifty-year-old claims to that disputed territory might be lost irretrievably. It remains a fundamental tenet of Pakistani politics that no government that makes deep concessions on the future of Kashmir, let alone surrenders it to India altogether, can survive.

These two threats were closely intertwined in the aftermath of 9/11. Musharraf had to face the dilemma that Islamic militancy would be aroused at home by the assault on the Taliban, and extremism could overturn the moderate core and national goals of Pakistan itself. Yet Islamic militancy operating within Kashmir itself, led in part by Kashmiri Muslims, was also viewed as a crucial source of pressure on India to negotiate Kashmir's future. Moreover, Islamic militancy was increasingly being seen abroad as the core of "international terrorism," and this could stigmatize all efforts to free Kashmiris, including native Kashmiri insurgents, as forms of terrorism.

Fundamentalist Islamic political parties and groups emerged in British India long before India and Pakistan became independent and have always been a troublesome undercurrent in Pakistan's modern politics, much as Hindu extremist groups have been in

India. Islamic extremist tendencies during Pakistan's early years were restrained or diffused by the conduct of elections and the moderate outlook on Islam that was prevalent in the subcontinent, as well as by the usual bread-and-butter issues of all politics. Islamic fundamentalist parties collectively have won relatively few seats in Pakistan's past national and provincial elections.

Nonetheless, the potency of Islamic fundamentalist parties and the violent propensities of their armed militia formations have increased over time in Pakistan. Contributing factors or stimuli came from the armed seizure of power from Zulfiqar Ali Bhutto by General Zia ul-Haq in 1977, the shock effects on the wider region of the Islamic revolution in Iran in 1979, and the mobilization of mujahideen groups to carry the Afghan war against the Soviets in the 1980s. In the period since the Soviet withdrawal, the smoldering civil war in Afghanistan, a secular slowdown in the Pakistani economy, stagnation of the public school system, and the initially spontaneous emergence of a liberation struggle in Indian-held Kashmir have given the Pakistani Islamicist organizations—and not just Islamic extremist groups— additional footholds.

A common theme that has emerged among analysts in the wake of these developments is that a nexus has emerged between extremist Islamic groups and their allegedly terrorist operations in Afghanistan, Pakistan, and Kashmir—creating a so-called Kalashnikov culture.

While there may be a kernel of truth here, it is also a gross oversimplification to ascribe the aims of these groups and the political linkages that may exist among some of them to the singular design, common inspiration, and coherent direction of Pakistani armed and security organizations, notably the ISI. Where official ties with these groups may exist to use them externally, the internal objectives are to play them off against each other and prevent their uniting against the state.

Islamic religious fundamentalism, Islamic political radicalism, and Islamic armed militancy are distinct conceptually, and their organized forms seldom if ever exist under a single roof. There is no homogeneous Islamic fundamentalism, but rather a variety of schools of thought, many cultural variants of each, and even more varieties of styles of Islamic life and behaviour—readily visible when moving from one Muslim society or community to the next. "Terrorism" as a generic phenomenon—targeted killing of innocents—is as antithetical to Islamic tenets as it is to the mainstream of any world religion, or to the norms of modern civilization. Political violence frequently has a political context without which it is not properly understood. By understanding political violence in any particular instance, one need not condone it or justify it, or hesitate to pursue means to stop or eradicate it. But neither is it productive automatically to equate "terrorism" with freedom struggles against invaders and occupiers, revolutionary actions against perceived tyranny or oppression, or the use of force in response to force over a historical dispute—whether differences of religion are involved or not.

That said, several Pakistani fundamentalist following groups have not only willingly joined the Afghan wars and the Kashmir insur-gency—against "foreign occupiers" as they see it—but have, like the *ayatollah* and *pasdaran* movements against the secular regime of the Shah of Iran—developed revolutionary aspirations vis-à-vis the liberal constitution and representative governing institutions of Pakistan. Their goals are to replace the existing political order with their own concepts of Islamic society.

Naturally, the real content of their visions of Islamic society varies from group to group, by school of thought and by organizational proclivity. In most cases the vision of an Islamic order is traditional and based on the *shari'a,* but their styles of interpretation of Islamic law and tradition vary. One of Pakistan's three most prominent Islamicist parties, the Jamaat-i-Islami (JI), actually has a modernist idea of Islamic revival that accommodates genuine learning and even natural science, and thus has strong appeal in certain intellectual, professional, and middle class circles. But the JI counterparts in Afghanistan and Kashmir do not necessarily subscribe to the same program or ideas, or draw from the same social base, as does the JI in Pakistan. While the government of Pakistan actively supported the role of these groups in Afghanistan, their efforts in Kashmir are best understood as an extension of their efforts to build platforms for the takeover of political power within Pakistan itself.

Moreover, one should understand the revolutionary aspirations of these Islamic parties not in terms of how many votes or seats they can win in national elections but rather in terms of how they build bastions of local influence, incrementally. This is achieved by the largest and arguably most aggressive of these Pakistani Islamist organizations, the Jamiat Ulema Islam (JUI)—which split many years ago into two branches led by Maulana Fazlur Rahman and Maulana Sami-ul-Haq, respectively. The two JUI organizations use intimidation and infiltration of authority, the building of mosques, development of welfare institutions, publication of local language newspapers and magazines, recruitment of supporters, targeting and acquisition of disputed land and property, and accumulation of other resources, at the local levels to aggrandize power and influence in society. JUI leaders pursue these goals in a decentralized way—in districts, towns, and major cities. The armed militias not only provide protection to the leaders and their political activities but also serve as agents in putting the squeeze on vulnerable local property owners and influentials.

Some of these organizations also ruthlessly exploit the sectarian divisions of Islamic society, especially Sunni versus Shia, confusing their ultimate objectives with near-term and situational objectives. The leaders of these organizations are often quite entrepreneurial, and some of the most successful also receive funds from Islamic groups in Saudi Arabia or other Gulf states. In their defensive and essentially introspective response within Pakistan, Shia leaders and organizations have also received financial help from Iran. The Pakistan-based extremist groups that have been most active in the fighting in Afghanistan, as well as those that have joined the insurgency in Kashmir, are generally Sunni by sectarian affiliation.

Views differ on whether the activities in Kashmir of the Pakistani militants were also actively sponsored by the Pakistan government, or provided official assistance by some cabal of bureaucratic and armed officials behind the scenes. But there seems little doubt that successive political and armed governments turned a blind eye to the infiltration of these groups into Kashmir to join the insurgency in the early 1990s. It is also possible that even if the militant formations were privately recruited and trained, they found tacit encouragement in Islamabad's official political and armed circles. Mujahideen training of Pakistani recruits, and perhaps some combat experiences with groups in Afghanistan, were readily transferable to Kashmir. The influx of light arms and ammunition to support the guerrilla war against the Soviets left stockpiles that could be put to other uses.

The insurgency in Kashmir began spontaneously in late 1989, led by native Kashmiri militant groups that recruited fighters from a younger generation of Muslim Kashmiris who were frustrated with Indian political interference in state elections and government. It was some time, therefore, before groups in Pakistan began to react in an organized way, with the infiltration and support of militants from Pakistani sources broadly welcomed by most politically active Kashmiris in the Vale of Kashmir, especially in the initial years.

In the development of resistance objectives and tactics, several of the Pakistani militant groups developed reputations for taking greater risk and using more aggressive tactics against Indian security forces than did their Kashmiri counterparts, but a majority of these groups shunned wanton terrorism—avoiding direct attacks on civilians and ordinary Kashmiri property. The Jammu and Kashmir Liberation Front (JKLF), based essentially in Kashmiris in both Pakistan- and Indian-held parts of Kashmir, for instance, began with a militant approach to Indian security installations (avoiding violence on civilians, and never deliberately terrorist) but changed course later to adopt exclusively political methods.

A handful of Pakistan-origin extremist groups, however, did cross the line during the 1990s to terrorist actions, pure and simple, including capture and execution of foreign tourists, as well as other attacks on civilians and civilian infrastructure. Pakistani-origin groups reportedly associated with such activities in the early 1990s included al-Badr (sponsored by the Pakistani JI) and Harkat-ul-Ansar, later renamed Harkat-ul-Mujahideen. The Harkat-ul-Ansar was the earliest of these militant Pakistani or Kashmiri organizations to be put on the list of terrorist organizations by the U.S. Department of State. The sponsor of the Harkats was the Sami-ul-Haq branch of the JUI in Pakistan; this branch of the

JUI is believed to have had closer Afghanistan ties than any of the other Pakistani Islamic parties and is suspected of having early contacts with Osama bin Laden, dating back to the late 1980s during the Afghan war against the Soviets.

In the late 1990s, the Lashkar-e-Toiba (sometimes written Lashkar-i-Tayyaba), sponsored by the politically invisible but Wahabi-dedicated Ahl-e-Hadith, and the Jaish-e-Muhammed, a more recent extremist offshoot of the Sami-ul-Haq branch of the JUI, became active in Kashmir.

India pointed to the Jaish-e-Muhammed and the Lashkar-e-Toiba as the source of the attack on parliament in New Delhi on December 13, 2001, claimed that the attackers were Pakistanis, and accused Pakistan of sponsoring their attack. The State Department also added these organizations to its official list of terrorist organizations in December 2001.

India began a full-scale armed mobilization of seven hundred thousand troops opposite Pakistan—along the entire border and in the Arabian Sea—and made a series of demands, including total cessation of Pakistani-origin infiltration and "terrorism" in Kashmir.

AFGHANISTAN–PAKISTAN RELATIONS

Afghanistan–Pakistan relations began in 1949 after British India was partitioned into the Republic of India and the Islamic Republic of Pakistan.

Afghanistan and Pakistan are usually described as inseparable states due to their historical, religious, cultural, linguistic, and ethnic ties, as well as their multiple trade and economic ties. Both neighbouring states are Islamic republics and part of the South Asian Association for Regional Cooperation. However, the relationship between the two has been affected by the Durand Line, the issues of Pashtunistan and Balochistan, the 1980s Soviet war, the rise of the Taliban, the 2001-present war in Afghanistan, and Afghanistan's relations with India and Shia Iran.

Southern and eastern Afghanistan is predominately a Pashto-speaking region, like the adjacent Khyber-Pakhtunkhwa, Federally Administered Tribal Areas, and northern Balochistan in Pakistan. This entire area is inhabited by the indigenous Pashtuns who belong to different Pashtun tribes. The Pashtuns have lived in this region for thousands of years, since at least the 1st millennium BC.

The Durand Line

The Afghan government does not recognize the Durand Line as the official border between the two states, claiming that the Durand Line Agreement has been void in the past due to violations by Pakistan as well as other reasons. Pakistan, on the other side, issued a warning to Afghanistan that it would not "tolerate any violations of its borders".

Relations have continued to be strained, as several top Afghan officials stated that they are weary of Pakistan's negative influence in the country. The Afghan government usually accuses Pakistan of using its intelligence agency, the Inter-Services Intelligence (ISI), in aiding the Taliban militants.

Pakistan has denied the allegations but has said it does not have full control of the actions of the ISI. Relations became even more strained as the United States supports an Afghan invasion of rogue tribal regions.

Other Contemporary Issues

Following the Soviet invasion of Afghanistan in 1979, the Pakistani government played a vital role in supporting the Mujahideen and assisting Afghan refugees. Pakistan absorbed an estimated 3 million refugees and provided shelter, education, and places to work.

After the Soviet withdrawal in February 1989, Pakistan, with cooperation from the world community, continued to provide extensive support for displaced Afghans. In 1999, the United States provided approximately $70 million in humanitarian assistance to Afghanistan and Afghan refugees in Pakistan, mainly through multilateral organizations and Non-governmental organizations (NGOs).

Pakistani strategists view Afghanistan as providing "strategic depth" in the event of a war with neighbouring India. In the event that the Indian Army crosses into Pakistan, the Pakistan Army would temporary locate supplies in Afghanistan and prepare for a counter-offensive. Furthermore, many Pakistanis see in

Afghanistan and Afghans a common bond based on religion, history, culture, language and ethnic ties. At various times, Pakistan backed the mujahideen against the Soviets, mujahideen against each other and the Taliban against the Iranian-backed Northern Alliance.

The overthrow of the Taliban regime in November 2001 has seen somewhat strained relations between Afghanistan and Pakistan. The present Karzai administration in Kabul feels that the remnants of the former Taliban government are being supported by factions within Pakistan for the same above reasons.

However, Pakistan has said the government cannot control all elements of its intelligence agency, the ISI, which several countries accuse of contributing to instability in Afghanistan. In 2006 Afghan President Hamid Karzai warned that "Iran and Pakistan and others are not fooling anyone" when it come to interfering in his country.

"If they don't stop, the consequences will be ... that the region will suffer with us equally. In the past we have suffered alone; this time everybody will suffer with us.... Any effort to divide Afghanistan ethnically or weaken it will create the same thing in the neighbouring countries. All the countries in the neighborhood have the same ethnic groups that we have, so they should know that it is a different ball game this time." —Hamid Karzai, *February 17, 2006*

Afghan-Pak Transit Trade Agreement

In October 2010, Afghanistan and Pakistan finally inked together the long-awaited Afghan-Pak Transit Trade Agreement (APTTA) between the two states. The landmark agreement was signed by Pakistani Commerce Minister Makhdoom Amin Fahim and Anwar ul-Haq Ahady, Afghan Ministry of Commerce. The ceremony was attended by Richard Holbrooke, U.S. Special Representative for Afghanistan and Pakistan, and a number of foreign ambassadors, Afghan parliamentarians and senior officials. In July 2010, a Memorandum of understanding (MoU) was reached between the two states, which was observed by U.S. Secretary of State Hillary Clinton.

It would allow each nation's shipping trucks into the others; Afghan container trucks will be allowed to drive through Pakistan to the Wagah border with India, including to the port cities of Karachi and Gwadar. Also in July 2010, the two states signed a Memorandum of Understanding agreeing the construction of rail tracks in Afghanistan to connect with Pakistan Railways (PR). Work on the proposed project is set to start in the next four months, which has been in the making since at least 2005. In November 2010, the two states formed a joint chamber of commerce to expande trade relations and solve the problems traders face. The APTTA agreement is to take affect in February 2011.

Relationship between Pakistan and Afghanistan

A poll showed that Afghans rated India as the most favourable country, while Pakistan was the least favoured country with only 2% popularity.

9

The Afghan National Army

The Afghan National Army has been built "from scratch" since 2002—it is not a direct continuation of the national army that existed from the 1880s until the Taliban era. That national army all but disintegrated during the 1992-1996 *mujahedin* civil war and the 1996-2001 Taliban period. However, some Afghan officers who served prior to the Taliban have joined the ANA.

U.S. and allied officers say that the ANA is becoming a major force in stabilizing the country and a national symbol. It now has at least some presence in most of Afghanistan's 34 provinces, working with the PRTs, and it deployed outside Afghanistan to assist relief efforts for victims of the October 2005 Pakistan earthquake. ANA battalions, or "Kandaks," are the main unit of the Afghan force.

The ANA is able to lead a growing percentage of all combat operations, but there is substantial skepticism within the U.S. defence establishment that it can assume full security responsibility by 2014, which is the target time frame announced by Karzai. U.S. military assessments say the force remains poorly led. It still suffers from at least a 20% desertion rate. Some accounts say that a typical ANA unit is only at about 50% of its authorized strength at any given time, and there are significant shortages in about 40% of equipment items. The high desertion rate complicates U.S.-led efforts to steadily grow the force. Some recruits take long trips to their home towns to remit funds to their families, and often then return to the ANA after a long absence. Others, according to U.S. observers, often refuse to serve far from their home towns. The

FY2005 foreign aid appropriation (P.L. 108-447) required that ANA recruits be vetted for terrorism, human rights violations, and drug trafficking.

On the other hand, the ANA is assuming more responsibility without faltering outright. In August 2008, the ANA took over security of Kabul city from Italy, and it took formal control of Kabul Province in early 2009. The commando forces of the ANA, trained by U.S. Special Operations Forces, and numbering about 5,300, are considered well-trained and are taking the lead in some operations against high-value targets.

To assist its performance, the United States is attempting to better equip the ANA. Approximately $2.7 billion worth of vehicles, weapons, equipment, and aircraft are being provided during August 2011-March 2012. General Caldwell stated in June 2011 that the United States is also helping the ANSF build up an indigenous weapons production capability. However, in line with U.S. efforts to cut costs for the ANSF, the Defence Department reportedly plans to shift in FY2013 from providing new equipment to maintaining existing equipment, including Russian-supplied helicopters.

The United States has built five ANA bases: Herat (Corps 207), Gardez (Corps 203), Qandahar (Corps 205), Mazar-e-Sharif (Corps 209), and Kabul (Division HQ, Corps 201, Air Corps). Coalition officers conduct heavy weapons training for a heavy brigade as part of the "Kabul Corps," based in Pol-e-Charki, east of Kabul.

ANA Racial and Factional Considerations

At the time the United States first began establishing the ANA, Northern Alliance figures who were then in key security positions weighted recruitment for the national army toward its Tajik ethnic base. Many Pashtuns, in reaction, refused recruitment or left the ANA program. The naming of a Pashtun, Abdul Rahim Wardak, as Defence Minister in December 2004 reduced desertions among Pashtuns (he remains in that position). U.S. officials in Afghanistan say this problem was further alleviated with better pay and more close involvement by U.S. forces, and that the force is ethnically integrated in each unit and representative. With about 41% Pashtuns, 34% Tajiks, 12% Hazaras, and 8% Uzbeks, the force is roughly in line with the broad demographics of the country, according to the April 2010 DOD report. However, U.S. commanders say that those Pashtuns who are in the force are disproportionately eastern Pashtuns (from the Ghilzai tribal confederations) rather than southern Pashtuns (mostly Durrani tribal confederations). Defence Minister Wardak said in February 2011 that a greater proportion of southern Pashtuns are being recruited to redress that imbalance somewhat, and the October 2011 DOD report says a re-evaluation in 2011 shows that there are more southern Pashtuns in the force than previously thought. The chief of staff was General Bismillah Khan, a Tajik who was a Northern Alliance commander, although as of June 2010 he is Interior Minister.

Afghan Air Force

Equipment, maintenance, and logistical difficulties continue to plague the Afghan Air Force, and it remains mostly a support force for ground operations rather than a combat-oriented force. However, the Afghan Air Force has been able to make ANA units nearly self-sufficient in airlift. The force is a carryover from the Afghan Air Force that existed prior to the Soviet invasion, and is expanding gradually after its equipment was virtually eliminated in the 2001-2002 U.S. combat against the Taliban regime. It now has about over 5,240 personnel, including 400 pilots, of a target size of about 8,000 by 2016. It has about 86 aircraft including gunship, attack, and transport helicopters—of a planned fleet of 145 aircraft. Afghan pilots are based at Bagram air base. There are five female Afghan Air Force personnel; four arrived in the United States in July 2011 for training as military helicopter pilots.

Afghanistan also is seeking the return of 26 aircraft, including some MiG-2s that were flown to safety in Pakistan and Uzbekistan during the past conflicts in Afghanistan. U.S. plans do not include supply of fixed-wing combat aircraft such as F-16s, which Afghanistan wants, according to U.S. military officials. There is a concern that Afghanistan will not soon have the capability to sustain operations of an aircraft as sophisticated as the F-16. In 2010, Russia and Germany supplied MI-8 helicopters to the Afghan Air Force.

Afghan National Police (ANP)

U.S. and Afghan officials believe that building up a credible and capable national police force is at least as important to combating the insurgency as building the ANA. The DOD reports on Afghanistan, cited earlier, contains substantial detail on U.S.-led efforts to continue what it says are "significant strides [that] have been made in professionalizing the ANP." Outside assessments are widely disparaging, asserting that there is rampant corruption to the point where citizens mistrust and fear the ANP. Among other criticisms are a desertion rate far higher than that of the ANA; substantial illiteracy; involvement in local factional or ethnic disputes because the ANP works in the communities its personnel come from; and widespread use of drugs. It is this view that has led to consideration of stepped up efforts to promote local security solutions such as those discussed above.

Bismillah Khan, the Interior Minister, was highly respected as ANA chief of staff and has taken steps to try to improve the ANP, including through unannounced visits to stations around the country. He has also instituted salary increases and objective standards for promotions and assignments. Still, some Pashtuns might resent his Tajik ethnicity, and some criticized him for direct involvement in combating the September 13, 2011, attack on the U.S. Embassy in Kabul and confusing the lines of authority and reducing the effect of the Afghan counterattack. His reform efforts build on those taken in March 2010, by then-Interior Minister Atmar when he signed a "strategic guidance" document for the ANP, which prioritizes eliminating corruption within the ANP and winning public confidence. About 1,300 ANP are women, demonstrating some commitment to gender integration of the force.

Other U.S. commanders credit a November 2009 raise in police salaries (nearly doubled to about $240 per month for service in high combat areas)—and the streamlining and improvement of the payments system for the ANP—with reducing the solicitation of bribes by the ANP. The raise also stimulated an eightfold increase in the number of Afghans seeking to be recruited. Others note the success, thus far, of efforts to pay police directly (and avoid skimming by commanders) through cell phone-based banking relationships (E-Paisa, run by Roshan cell network).

The United States has worked to correct longstanding equipment deficiencies. According to General Caldwell in June 2011, the ANP is increasingly being provided with heavy weapons and now have about 5,000 armored vehicles countrywide. Still, most police units lack adequate ammunition and vehicles. In some cases, equipment requisitioned by their commanders is being sold and the funds pocketed by the police officers. These activities contributed to the failure of a 2006 "auxiliary police" effort that attempted to rapidly field large numbers of new ANP officers.

The U.S. police training effort was first led by State Department/ INL, but DOD took over the lead in police training in April 2005. Some U.S. officials believe that the United States and its partners still have not centered on a clearly effective police training strategy. A number of programs, such as the auxiliary police program attempted during 2005 was discarded as ineffective, and replaced during 2007-2011 with a program called *"focused district development."* In that program, a district police force was taken out and retrained, its duties temporarily performed by more highly trained police (Afghan National Civil Order Police, or ANCOP, which number about 9,400 nationwide), and then reinserted after the training is complete. However, the ANCOP officers are currently being used mostly to staff new checkpoints that are better securing the most restive districts.

Police training includes instruction in human rights principles and democratic policing concepts, and the State Department human rights report on Afghanistan, referenced above, says the government and outside observers are increasingly monitoring the police force to prevent abuses.

Supplements to the National law enforcement: Afghan Local Police (ALP) and Other Local Forces: The failure of several police training efforts led to efforts, beginning in 2008, to develop local forces to protect their communities. Until mid-2008, U.S. military commanders opposed assisting local militias anywhere in Afghanistan for fear of creating rivals to the central government and of re-creating militias that commit abuses and administer arbitrary justice. However, the urgent security needs in Afghanistan caused reconsideration and, during his command, General Petraeus expanded local security experiments, based on successful experiences in Iraq and after designing mechanisms to reassure Karzai that any local security organs would be firmly under Afghan government (mainly Ministry of Interior) control. Among these initiatives are:

Afghan Local Police. This is a program in which local security organs are formed from local recruits who want to defend their communities. The local units are under the control of district police chiefs and each fighter is vetted by a local shura as well as Afghan intelligence (Petraeus testimony, March 15 and 16, 2011). The initiative has recruited a total of about 11,000 ALP which now operate in 57 different districts in several different provinces, according to U.S. commanders on March 7, 2011. There are three ALP centers in Helmand province.

A total of 100 districts have been approved for the program, each with about 300 fighters, which would bring the target size of the program to about 30,000. However, the ALP program, and associated and preceding such programs discussed below, were heavily criticized in a September 12, 2011, Human Rights Watch report citing wide-scale human rights abuses (killings, rapes, arbitrary detentions, and land grabs) committed by the recruits. The report triggered a U.S. military investigation which substantiated many of the report's findings, although not the most serious of the allegations.

Local Defence Initiative/Village Stability Operations. A separate program, the Local Defence Initiative, began in February 2010 in Arghandab district of Qandahar Province. U.S. Special Forces organized about 25 villagers into a neighborhood watch group, which is armed. The program has been credited by U.S. commanders as bringing normal life back to the district. A different militia was allowed to operate in Konduz to help secure the northern approaches to that city. Problems arose when the militia began arbitrarily administering justice, fueling the concerns discussed above these local security approaches. This program apparently has evolved into a joint Afghan-U.S. Special Operations program called "Village Stability Operations," in which 12 person teams from these forces live in communities to help improve governance, security and development. The program is discussed in the October 2011 DOD "1230 report."

Afghan Provincial Protection Program. The ALP initiative built on another program begun in 2008, termed the "Afghan Provincial Protection Program" (APPP, commonly called "AP3"), funded with DOD (CERP) funds.

The APPP got under way in Wardak Province (Jalrez district) in early 2009 and 100 local security personnel "graduated" in May 2009. It was subsequently expanded to 1,200 personnel. U.S. commanders said no U.S. weapons were supplied to the militias, but the Afghan government provided weapons (Kalashnikov rifles) to the recruits, possibly using U.S. funds. Participants in the program are given $200 per month. General Petraeus showcased Wardak in August 2010 as an example of the success of the APPP and similar efforts. The National Defence Authorization Act (P.L. 111-84) called for a report on the program within 120 days of the October 28, 2009, enactment.

Afghan Public Protection Force. A new force is being developed by the Ministry of Interior, in partnership with ISAF and U.S. Embassy Kabul. The Afghan Public Protection Force is intended to be a guard force of about 14,000 personnel which will help guard diplomatic and development sites. The force was developed to implement Karzai's demands in 2010 that private security

Ernesto Londono. "U.S. Cites Local Afghan Police Abuses." *Washington Post*, December 16, 2011. The Human Rights Watch report is entitled "Just Don't Call It a Militia."September 12, 2011. contractor forces be disbanded and their functions performed by official Afghan government forces by March 20, 2012. That deadline was extended because of the slow pace of standing up the new protection force, and some development organizations continue to use locally hired guard forces.

The local security experiments to date resemble but technically are not *arbokai*, which are private tribal militias. Some believe that the *arbokai* concept should be revived as a means of securing Afghanistan, as the *arbokai* did during the reign of Zahir Shah and in prior pre-Communist eras. Reports persist that some tribal groupings have formed *arbokai* without specific authorization. The local security programs discussed above appear to reverse the 2002-2007 efforts to disarm local sources of armed force.

DDR. The main program, run by UNAMA, was called the "DDR" program—Disarmament, Demobilization, and Reintegration—and it formally concluded on June 30, 2006. The program got off to a slow start because the Afghan Defence Ministry did not reduce the percentage of Tajiks in senior positions by a July 1, 2003, target date, dampening Pashtun recruitment. In September 2003, Karzai replaced 22 senior Tajiks in the Defence Ministry officials with Pashtuns, Uzbeks, and Hazaras, enabling DDR to proceed. The major donor for the program was Japan, which contributed about $140 million. Figures for collected weapons are in and U.S. spending on the programs are in the U.S. aid tables later in the report.

The DDR program was initially expected to demobilize 100,000 fighters, although that figure was later reduced. Of those demobilized, 55,800 former fighters have exercised reintegration options provided by the program: starting small businesses, farming, and other options.

U.N. officials say at least 25% of these found long-term, sustainable jobs. Some studies criticized the DDR program for failing to prevent a certain amount of rearmament of militiamen or stockpiling of weapons and for the rehiring of some militiamen. Part of the DDR program was the collection and cantonment of militia weapons, but generally only poor-quality weapons were collected.

As one example, Fahim, still the main military leader of the Northern Alliance faction, continues to turn heavy weapons over to U.N. and Afghan forces (including four Scud missiles), although the U.N. Assistance Mission in Afghanistan (UNAMA) says that large quantities of weapons remain in the Panjshir Valley.

Despite the earlier demobilization, which affected many of the northern minorities, there are indications that some faction leaders may be seeking to revive disbanded militias. The minorities may fear increased Taliban influence as a result of the Karzai reconciliation efforts, and the minorities want to be sure they could combat any Taliban abuses that might result if the Taliban achieves a share of power.

DIAG. Since June 11, 2005, the disarmament effort has emphasized another program called "DIAG"—Disbandment of Illegal Armed Groups. It is run by the Afghan Disarmament and Reintegration Commission, headed by Vice President Khalili. Under the DIAG, no payments are available to fighters, and the program depends on persuasion rather than use of force against the illegal groups. DIAG has not been as well funded as was DDR: it has received $11 million in operating funds. As an incentive for compliance, Japan and other donors have made available

$35 million for development projects where illegal groups have disbanded. These incentives were intended to accomplish the disarmament of a pool of as many as 150,000 members of 1,800 different "illegal armed groups": militiamen that were not part of recognized local forces (Afghan Military Forces, AMF) and were never on the rolls of the Defence Ministry. These goals were not met by the December 2007 target date in part because armed groups in the south say they need to remain armed against the Taliban, but UNAMA reports that 100 out of 140 districts planned for DIAG are now considered "DIAG compliant." (U.N. Secretary General Report, March 9, 2011).

Regulation of Law/Criminal Justice Sector

Many experts believe that an effective justice sector is vital to Afghan governance. Some of the criticisms and allegations of corruption at all levels of the Afghan bureaucracy have been discussed throughout this report. U.S. justice sector programs generally focus on promoting rule of law and building capacity of the judicial system, including police training and court construction. The rule of law issue is covered in detail in CRS Report R41484, *Afghanistan: U.S. Rule of Law and Justice Sector Assistance*, by Liana Sun Wyler and Kenneth Katzman.

ANSF Funding

Because the Afghan government has so few resources, the Afghan security sector is funded almost entirely through international donations. In 2011, NTM-A had a budget of $10 billion, almost all of which is U.S. funded, including $3 billion for infrastructure; $3 billion for equipment; $1 billion for training; and $3 billion for "sustainment" (food and salaries for the Afghan forces, and related costs).

The United States, as noted in tables later in this paper, will spend about $11.2 billion on the ANSF in FY2012. A reduction to $5.75 billion is requested for FY2013. In March 2012, the United States reportedly discussed with allies a post-2014 ANSF budget of about $4.1 billion, of which $1.3 billion would come from non-U.S. donors, about $500 million would be provided by the Afghan government, and about $2.3 billion would be provided by the United States. The options under discussion to reduce the post-2014 size of the ANSF represent an effort to bring the costs of the force in line with this budgeting effort.

The time frame for Afghan financial self-sufficiency for its security is far in the future. As noted elsewhere, the Afghan government will take in less than $2 billion in total revenue in 2011. In December 2009, Karzai asserted that the Afghan government could not likely fund its own security forces until 2024, and no Afghan or other official has shortened that time frame since.

Recent appropriations for the ANA and ANP are contained in the tables at the end of this report, which also contain breakdowns for Commanders Emergency Response Program funds, or CERP, which is used for projects that build goodwill and presumably reduce the threat to use forces. CERP has also been used for what could be considered development projects, a point of contention among some observers. As noted in the tables, as of FY2005, the security forces funding has been DOD funds, not State Department funds (Foreign Military Financing, FMF).

NATO Trust finance for the ANA: In 2007 ISAF set up a trust fund for donor contributions to fund the transportation of equipment donated to and the training of the ANA; the mandate was expanded in 2009 to include sustainment costs. In November 2010 a further expansion was agreed on to support literacy training for the ANA. As of January 2012, national contributions and pledges to the ANA Trust Fund total about $600 million. U.S. funding for the ANA is provided separately, not through this fund.

Law and Order Trust Fund for the ANP: There is also a separate "Law and Order Trust Fund" (LOTF) for Afghanistan, run by the U.N. Development Program, which is used to pay the salaries of the ANP and other police-related functions. From 2002-2010, donors contributed $1.74 billion to the Fund, of which the United States contributed about $620 million, according to the April 2011 DOD report (p. 41). Japan's 2009 pledge to pay the expenses of the Afghan police for at least six months (about $125 million for each six month period) is implemented through the LOTF.

Other Bilateral Donations: The October 2011 DOD report discusses other bilateral donations to the ANSF, both in funds and in arms and equipment donations. There is a "NATO Equipment Donation Program," through which donor countries supply the ANSF with equipment. Since 2002, about $2.9 billion in assistance to the ANSF has come from these sources. As an example, in October 2011, Croatia and Slovenia donated a total of over 20,000 AK-47 assault rifles to the ANP. Australia contributed $40 million to relocate the ANA's 205th Corps, and South Korea contributed $30 million for medical and communications equipment.

There is also a NATO-Russia Council Helicopter Maintenance Trust Fund. Launched in March 2011, this fund provides maintenance and repair capacity to the Afghan Air Force helicopter fleet, much of which is Russian-made.

NARCO-TERRORISM IN AFGHANISTAN: COUNTERNARCOTICS AND COUNTERINSURGENCY

Since the 2001 invasion and the lifting of the Taliban opium ban, opium production in Afghanistan has increased from 70 percent of the overall global illicit opium production to 92 percent today. This increase has occurred in tandem with the declining security situation precipitated by the 2001 coalition invasion of the country. The loose relationship between terrorist organizations, violence, decentralized governance, and poverty that existed prior to the Global War on Terrorism (GWOT) in Afghanistan, has coalesced into a truly narco-terrorism-driven system. The implications of this are severe to both Afghanistan's and America's long-term goals. Corruption, lawlessness, instability, violence, and human suffering all contribute to, and result from, the precipitous increase in opium cultivation and narcotics production and trafficking. Thus, in attempting to subdue the Taliban- and al-Qaeda-led insurgencies, and to forge a stable and effective government in Afghanistan, there must also be effective and socially conscious measures undertaken to eliminate the pervasive narco-economy. As President Karzai has stated, "The question of drugs . . . is one that will determine Afghanistan's future. . . . [I]f we fail, we will fail as a state eventually, and we will fall back in the hands of terrorism."

BACKGROUND

The relationship between Afghanistan and the opium poppy has existed for thousands of years. However, it is only in the last three decades that the country has become responsible for cultivating an overwhelming majority of the world's opium. The catalysts behind this marked increase in both Afghanistan's overall production, and in the country's percentage of total world production are three-fold: (1) ongoing warfare and civil strife; (2) the historical absence of a legitimate centralized government; and (3) effective contemporary interdiction campaigns elsewhere in the world. Furthermore, in the wake of the coalition invasion in 2001, the first two elements have worsened, and a fourth element, a "marriage of convenience" between insurgency forces and the opium industry, has come to exist.

The advent of war in Afghanistan predates Western civilization. Having historically served as a strategic entry point into India, and more recently as an arena for the ideological wars against both communism and terrorism, Afghanistan is a country with a culture and society that have been significantly shaped by war. It was only in recent times, however, with the Soviet invasion of Afghanistan in 1979, that warfare and opium began to form a symbiotic relationship. The need for capital to purchase weaponry that would be effective against Soviet gunships and troops prompted the mujahidin insurgency to resort to opium cultivation and trafficking. Many of the mujahidin leaders and warlords, the future political actors of a post-Soviet Afghanistan, thus became narco-leaders. With the fall of the Soviet Union in 1992, civil war between the various mujahidin groups erupted, causing widespread destabilization. In 1998, the "hard-line, Islamic-based, Pakistani sponsored" Taliban gained control of the country. Despite having an ideological abhorrence towards drug use, the Taliban allowed, and even encouraged, continued opium cultivation as a means of financially propping up their regime until imposing an opium ban in 2000 using a strict religious rhetoric. As a result, opium cultivation steadily increased from 1995 to 2000.

Afghanistan: A Failed State?

Throughout its history, Afghanistan has struggled to establish stable and centralized governance. Afghanistan, founded in 1847, was placed under the rule of the British Empire from 1826 until the end of World War I. Following this period of foreign control, Afghanistan was ruled by various autocrats with power frequently changing hands, generally through military coups, the last of which installed a communist regime under the Soviet Union. Unfortunately, the enduring state of violence brought on by the Soviet invasion dashed any chances of a strong Afghan state coming to fruition. Over two decades, domination by insurgency, civil strife, and draconian autocracy, has had a severe and deleterious effect upon the nation's ability to provide for security, infrastructure, and general economic well-being. During this period of time, Afghanistan's overall status has alternated between collapsed and failed statehood. Warlords, militias, drug lords and corrupt provincial administrators were able to lay claim to huge swaths of Afghanistan's periphery. Consequently, Afghanistan became the perfect environment for the establishment and maintenance of a robust illicit economy based on the cultivation of opium.

Violence and the lack of a stable self governance has led to virtual anarchy in Afghanistan, making opium cultivation, production and trafficking a way of life for many people. Even though poppy has existed in Afghanistan, since the time of Alexander the great, Afghanistan's narco-economy is a modern day phenomenon. The success of the war on drugs in the golden triangle has been a major contributing factor in this phenomenon.

According to the United Nations Office of Drugs and Crime (UNODC), the rise of opium cultivation in Afghanistan has occurred parallel to an 87 percent decline in poppy cultivation in Southeast Asia's "golden triangle" (Myanmar, Laos, Vietnam, and Thailand) over the last decade. Similar successes in eliminating cultivation also occurred within neighboring Iran and Pakistan beginning in the 1970s. The result follows a basic market principle: a decline in overall supply relative to a stable or increasing demand leads to either price increases or the market finding a new means of supply. Thus, given the preexisting conditions of widespread violence and the lack of a stable, centralized government, Afghanistan was the perfect candidate to fill the void in the global opium production market.

EFFECTS AND IMPLICATIONS OF THE DRUG TRADE SINCE 2001

Since the 2001 coalition invasion of Afghanistan, opium cultivation has increased precipitously, reaching record levels (193,000 hectacres) in 2007. According to the UNODC 2007 Afghanistan Opium Winter Rapid Assessment Survey, this trend is expected to continue through 2008. The deteriorating security situation brought on by NATO and the United States deposing the Taliban regime and thus placing them at the vanguard of the insurgency has served to reinvigorate the opium economy in the wake of the 2000 Taliban opium ban. Furthermore, the creation of a common enemy the Karzai government and Western military forces has led to a marriage of convenience between the drug lords and the insurgency leaders. Nevertheless, in working with the Afghani government, NATO and the United States are continuing to fight two separate wars: the war on drugs, and the war on terror. While NATO fights the insurgency (but lacks any mandate to directly aid in interdiction), and the Afghan, British, and U.S. governments work to implement a multifaceted counternarcotics policy, the insurgents and drug lords are working together to undermine the Karzai government and fund their respective operations through the opium trade.

The current strategic conceptualization of two wars in Afghanistan belies the fact that the country is steadily becoming a "narco-terrorist" state. The linkage between the insurgency and the opium industry is widely evidenced. Over 62 percent of coalition fatalities have occurred in the southern Helmand province, which is also the primary opium producing province in Afghanistan. Further, the Taliban receives nearly 70 percent of its income from protection money and the sale of opium (much of this income comes from "taxes imposed upon opium farmers). Additionally, the Taliban is receiving arms and money from traffickers and drug lords in return for protection. Also contributing to the insurgency is a disproportionate reliance upon crop eradication policies, which has created an increasingly large recruitment pool of disaffected farmers and other peasants. For example, the Taliban have begun to offer men $200 a month to join their ranks, a staggering amount when compared to the $70 a month earned by the average Afghan police officer.

In the same way that the failings of the state economically have served to legitimize the drug industry, the failings of the state politically and in terms of providing security (exacerbated by the drug industry), have served to legitimize the insurgency. Both in the political and security realms the drug lords and insurgents are entirely reliant upon a steady supply of able Afghanis. As noted earlier, the drug interdiction and eradication policies that have ignored the elements political, economic, historical, and societal that drive farmers to produce opium, are serving to drive them towards the insurgency for support and protection. Further, many farmers have little choice regarding what to grow, as groups such as the Taliban directly coerce farmers to plant, saying "You start growing it, or we will kill you and your family." Therefore, it is apparent that, given the striking degree to which the insurgency and the drug industry have come to benefit from each other, any policy which aims to combat one element must also consider the other.

AFGHANISTAN'S NARCO-ECONOMY

Afghanis are primarily responsible for opium within Afghanistan, cultivating and processing it into low-grade heroin, and trafficking it to the borders of Afghanistan's neighboring countries (Iran, Uzbekistan, Tajikistan, etc) Given the lack of global contacts and the overall lack of organization of the Afghanistan narco-industry, the opium is then handed off to the respective ethnic nationals of each country (Tajiks, Uzbeks, etc.) for further trafficking into Russia, Iran, Europe, and Asia. The most common route, according to the UNODC, is through Tajikistan, with over 96 percent of all seizures taking place within the country. The effects of Afghanistan's narco-economy are far-reaching: it is the producer of over 90 percent of Europe's heroin; it perpetuates addiction and HIV/AIDS endemics in Pakistan and Iran. Iran by itself has over 4 million drug users.

The World Bank reports that the estimated opium GDP of Afghanistan is between $2.6 and $2.7 billion, which amounts to 27 percent of the country's total GDP (both licit and illicit). Despite these staggering statistics, opium is a minor crop in terms of relative cultivation levels, with only 3 percent of natural agricultural land used towards its cultivation. Nearly half of the 364 districts in Afghanistan report no opium poppy cultivation. Nevertheless, the districts that do report high levels of opium production are responsible for an increase overall in both Afghan and global production levels (100 percent and 50 percent over the last decade, respectively).

Poverty is widespread in Afghanistan, and many farmers are driven to the illicit economy in order to survive. With an 80 percent poverty rate, and a per capita income of only $800, Afghanistan was ranked 173rd out of 177 countries by the UN Development Project in terms of its effectiveness in meeting Millennium goals. While only 12 percent of Afghanistan's land is arable, agriculture is the primary means of existence for over 70 percent of the citizenry. Thus, given that opium is valued at over $4,500 per hectare, as opposed to only $266 for wheat; many farmers have little choice when it comes to being able to feed their families. Furthermore, given the potential profits that organizations, warlords, and landowners can gain from opium cultivation, many farmers are pressured or forced into the illicit economy.

Although opium is a high value cash crop, which can be grown and transported easily, and used in lieu of actual currency, there are still many farmers who choose not to grow opium.

Perhaps the most surprisingly effective reasons are the social and religious norms that stigmatize those who produce the drug. Drug use, and by extension its production, is prohibited in the Quran, and this prohibition serves as one of the most common reasons given by those who choose to not cultivate opium. In addition, the widespread exploitation of opium farmers, the labor-intensiveness of, and expertise required in cultivation, and the fear of eradication are other effective deterrents. However, as noted previously, despite the desire to abstain from cultivating opium, many farmers are coerced, either through exploitative sharecropping agreements, or by insurgent organizations under threat of violence.

The economic situation is much better for those higher up on the criminal food chain. Despite the fact that the bulk of the 2.9 million Afghanis who are involved in the drug trade are farmers, they receive less than 20 percent of the revenue. The rest of the proceeds go to land owners, warlords, traffickers, public officials, and terrorist organizations such as the Taliban. Furthermore, these actors commonly levy harsh taxes and impose exploitative sharecropping and land tenure agreements upon the impoverished opium farmers. Further inequities are created through the credit system that has formed around opium cultivation, which allows farmers to borrow money from landholders using their expected crop yields as collateral; farmers become trapped in an endless cycle of debt and repayment in the wake of a drought or a lower-than-expected crop yield.

POLICY OPTIONS IN AFGHANISTAN

Current Counternarcotics Strategy

Counternarcotics operations are currently being conducted in Afghanistan through a cooperative effort between Afghan, U.K., and U.S. agencies. President Karzai, upon taking office, declared a "jihad against poppy," citing that growing poppy was both illegal under Islam and harmful to the very future of the state. This sentiment was then underlined by the establishment of a strict "zero-tolerance" counternarcotics law, "making it illegal to traffic in any quantity of opium and by introducing the Afghan National

Drug Control Strategy (NDCS)." Within the Afghan strategy are four key elements: (1) disrupting the drug trade; (2) strengthening and diversifying legal rural livelihoods; (3) reducing demand and providing treatment to problem drug users; and (4) developing state institutions at the central and provincial level to combat drug trafficking. The Ministry of Counternarcotics, which works under the guidance of the U.K., and the Ministry of Interior are in charge of the counternarcotics effort. Within the Ministry of Interior, the Counternarcotics Police of Afghanistan (CNPA) and the Afghan Special Narcotics Force (ASNF) have been created to implement counternarcotics policies, but are nevertheless strongly reliant upon U.S. and U.K. training and funding to function.

Developed in parallel to the Afghan government's NDCS, the U.S. counternarcotics strategy in Afghanistan is outlined by five pillars: (1) alternative livelihoods; (2) elimination/eradication; (3) interdiction; (4) law enforcement/justice reform; and (5) public information. The agencies assisting Afghanistan in pursuit of these goals are: the U.S. Department of State, the U.S. Agency for International Development (USAID), the Department of Defense (DoD), and the Department of Justice (DoJ). The DEA and USAID provide direct enforcement, public diplomacy, and education efforts, while State, DoD, and DoJ provide support to U.S. agents and Afghan agencies. In 2005, the United States spent a total of $782 million to support U.S. counternarcotics programs and projects in Afghanistan. According to the U.S. General Accountability Office, the largest portion of those funds, $258 million, went towards eradication policies, which were administered through the DoD and the DEA. However, despite UNODC reported eradication of 15,300 hectares, or nearly 10 percent of the opium poppy crop, and heroin seizures of over 100 metric tons, overall levels of opium poppy cultivation, opium production, and heroin processing still markedly increased in 2006.

Counterterrorism and Counternarcotics

As a result of the rapidly declining security situation in Afghanistan following the 2001 invasion, approximately 55,000 foreign troops still occupy the war-torn and fragmented nation. Of these troops, 43,250 belong to the NATO-led International

Security Assistance Force (ISAF), while the remaining 12,000 are U.S. troops, primarily special operations and Marines, who operate independently. NATO and the U.S. military have both resisted taking an active role in counternarcotics operations within Afghanistan. Reasons that have been cited in defense of this sentiment mirror the comments of former NATO Commander U.S. General James Jones that counternarcotics enforcement is "not a military mission," stating that "having NATO troops out there burning crops, for example, is not going to significantly contribute to the war on drugs." Further, many military and government officials fear that, were NATO to take direct action in the drug war, its ability to acquire reliable human intelligence would become compromised. Nevertheless, NATO intervention is necessary to help defeat the drug trade in Afghanistan through offering security, law and order, and, when necessary, a powerful offensive capability against traffickers.

Currently, the ISAF acts only in a support capacity to the foreign and domestic organizations directly involved in counternarcotics efforts in Afghanistan. In this respect, its primary role in the war on drugs is to engage in active intelligence sharing. While direct military action in counternarcotics enforcement operations is precluded under the NATO agreement creating the ISAF, the ISAF can, if necessary, provide defensive support to eradication and interdiction actions undertaken by agencies such as the DEA. At present, the dual campaigns to assuage the endemic narco-industry and the insurgencies are suffering from insufficient resources and inefficient mandates.

Problems with Current Counternarcotics Strategy

With violence and lawlessness associated with the narco-industry threatening to destroy the country, it is clear that current policies with respect to counternarcotics and counterterrorism are failing. In contrast to the strategy governing current NATO and U.S. military involvement in Afghanistan, UNODC Director Antonio Maria Costa, following the announcement of record poppy cultivation and opium production in 2005-2006, has called for direct NATO military involvement in counternarcotics enforcement operations in Afghanistan. To date, coun-ternarcotics policies in

Afghanistan have failed for three main reasons: (1) a fundamental lack of security (2) pervasive and crippling corruption; and (3) the pursuit of unbalanced and mis-directed "five-pillar" strategy which is overly focused on eradi-cation. These three elements serve to emphasize both the synergy between politically motivated warfare and economic logic, as well as to point out the need for a reassessment and integration of counternarcotics and counter-insurgency strategies.

Security and Counternarcotics Strategy. Widespread insecurity throughout many of Afghanistan's provinces seriously impedes agents as they attempt to engage in effective counternarcotics operations. The UNODC reports that, "there is a strong link between security conditions and opium poppy cultivation in the southern and western provinces." As of early 2007, over 60 percent of villages existing within provinces described as experiencing "very poor" security were observed to have cultivated opium. In contrast only 26 percent of provinces experiencing "good security," and 10 percent of provinces experiencing "very good" security, were found to be cultivating opium. Moreover, the security situation has been steadily deteriorating, with the total number of direct attacks by insurgents on NATO and U.S. troops nearly tripling from 2005 to 2006. Coalition military responses have only served to escalate the violence, with over 2,000 air strikes conducted over the last six months of 2006 by U.S forces alone.

The significant increase in violence following the 2001 invasion of Afghanistan, coupled with the meteoric rise of the narco-economy, has sent the state spiraling towards failure and eventual collapse. The U.S. Congressional Research Service (CRS) argues that the illicit drug economy has served to undermine "efforts to stabilize Afghanistan, establish the rule of law, and restore a functioning and licit economy." John A. Glaze, a lieu-tenant colonel in the U.S. Air Force, states that, "the Taliban have helped fill the security void left by the weak central government by providing Afghan citizens an alternative source of security." Further, eradication initiatives and kinetic attacks conducted by counternarcotics agents and ISAF forces, respectively, have exacerbated the security problem by forcing Afghans to rely upon the Taliban to provide for their security needs.

Corruption and Lawlessness. Exacerbating the rapid degradation of the Afghan state is the endemic corruption evident throughout the country. The World Bank states that,

The opium economy by all accounts is a massive source of corruption and undermines public institutions especially in (but not limited to) the security and justice sectors. There are worrying signs of infiltration by the drug industry into higher levels of government and into the emergent politics of the country. Thus the opium trade is widely considered to be one of the greatest threats to state-building, reconstruction, and development in Afghanistan.

Transparency International ranks Afghanistan at 172 out of 179 countries on its Corruption Perception Index. It is estimated that, of 249 new parliamentarians, 17 are believed to be drug smugglers and another 64 are believed to have links to "mafia-type" armed groups. The Strategic Studies Institute reports that, overall, "Afghan government officials are now believed to be involved in at least 70 percent of opium trafficking."

The implications of such persistent corruption throughout the country are severe with respect to conducting successful counternarcotics operations. Corruption in the "implementation of enforcement," on the part of Afghan agencies greatly detracts from the moral legitimacy of the fight against drugs. Also, eradication serves to exacerbate corruption where provincial administrators or enforcement agents receive payment in return for overlooking a particular opium production operation. The result is an eradication policy that is class-discriminating in its implementation, as those hurt the most are the impoverished farmers.

Problems with the "Five-Pillar" Strategy. As discussed previously, the primary problem with the current counternarcotics strategy, exemplified by the U.S. "five-pillar" plan, is the over-emphasis on eradication. Eradication has thus far proved ineffective at deterring cultivation, but instead contributes to insecurity, corruption, and poverty in Afghanistan.

The UNODC Opium Winter Rapid Assessment Survey reported that, "the experience of eradication in 2007 was not a strong factor in influencing the decision at the village level whether or not to grow opium poppy in 2008." Therefore, the other four pillars need to be adequately funded and brought to the forefront of counternarcotics strategy. Currently, Afghanistan lacks the infrastructure, resources, and market mechanisms it needs to support a licit economy. Eradication and other methods of deterrence presuppose the existence of these elements, and without them, they serve only to cause more harm than good.

POLICY RECOMMENDATIONS: COMBATING NARCO-TERRORISM

The dire security situation in Afghanistan, which has destabilized the nation and hindered U.S. and NATO initiatives to establish a legitimate state, is funded and exacerbated by the narco-economy. Combating terrorism and narcotics as individual and isolated problems has only served to strengthen the resolves and legitimacy of the insurgents and drug producers. Therefore, I would offer three policy recommendations. Instead of fighting two "wars" in Afghanistan, counternarcotics and counterterrorism strategies should be fused in such a way as to simultaneously (1) provide a sense of security and law; (2) delegitimize both the opium trade and insurgency; and (3) provide the foundations for a viable licit economy to be created.

In order to provide for the securitization that is necessary for successful counterinsurgency and counternarcotics operations, NATO member nations must increase their troop contributions, eliminate operational limitations, and widen the ISAF mandate to include some counternarcotics capabilities. NATO should exceed or, at the very least, match the proposed U.S. troop deployment of over 3,000 Marines to Afghanistan. At the root of the failure to establish centralized governance, eliminate the drug trade, and to improve the economy in Afghanistan is the ruinous insecurity that plagues the country. In order to provide the security needed in order to stabilize the nation, both troop levels and mandates need to be adjusted, as suggested by the following comment from the International Crisis Group.

NATO-led ISAF has about 90 percent of its stated needs, but many of the missing pieces are vital, such as mobile and re-serve components. . . . [S]ince the needs assessment has always been done with an eye more on availability than true requirements, it would be a "minimalist force" even fully resourced, with limited capacity to intervene effectively.

Furthermore, member nations should be pushed to eliminate individual operational limitations on how and where their troops can be deployed.

The United States should press upon NATO the direness of the situation in Afghanistan, and, if need be, threaten military-aid and other economic consequences for nations who refuse to carry their weight. Such limitations hinder the ability of the ISAF to properly deal with the current security situation.

A unified and adequately manned effort is necessary in order to unseat the Taliban and insurgent forces from their bases of power in the southern, opium-rich regions such as Helmand Province.

Further, such apprehensive mentalities as those exhibited by certain member nations, "feed perceptions of weakening international resolve, and thus influence the dynamics of the insurgency." Correspondingly, failure in Afghanistan as the result of disproportionate involvement on behalf of individual member nations could have drastic, long-term effects endangering the continuance of NATO.

Finally, ISAF's overall mandate should be widened to include involvement in counternarcotics operations. NATO forces should engage in collaborative and coordinated efforts with both domestic and foreign counternarcotics agencies beyond that of mere intelligence sharing. As the looting in Baghdad following the Iraqi invasion evidenced, law and order is vital to successful counterinsurgency. While crop eradication poses potential threats to sources of human intelligence, other elements of counter-narcotics can work to serve military goals. ISAF forces can work with drug enforcement agencies to deter and interdict the traffickers, drug lords, and warlords who perpetuate the drug trade. They can also serve to pressure and apprehend those government officials who tacitly or explicitly perpetuate the drug trade in Afghanistan. This will serve to reduce the environmental pressures that impede farmers and peasants from engaging in licit enterprises.

Attacking Centers of Legitimacy

Counternarcotics and counterinsurgency forces should take ad-vantage of the fact that ostensibly ultra-religious groups such as the Taliban are "treading a fine theological line" in using the drug industry to finance the insurgency. Historically, opium cultivation has been rationalized as being a useful tool for waging jihad against the west. The idea being that heroin poisons the populations of the west and thus it is acceptable to cultivate and profit from the drug. However, this line of reasoning fails when appropriately scrutinized, given that 30 percent of Afghanistan's heroin enters into Iran, a fellow Islamic state. Furthermore, heroin addiction has taken hold in Afghanistan to a startling degree, where 3 percent of the crop is retained and used domestically and over 200,000 Afghans have turned to opium-derived drugs in order to escape from the war-torn environment around them. The millions addicted to heroin and the pervasive spread of HIV/AIDS in Muslim countries exists in stark contrast to insurgent propaganda. Consequently, many farmers who do abstain from cultivation site social and religious stigmas as a primary reason for their decision. Thus, public diplomacy should be employed to reinforce these stigmas and to point out the blatant hypocrisies of insurgent groups such as the Islamist Taliban.

In order to be most effective, the anti-opium public diplomacy campaign needs and Afghan face. The Afghan government, along with Islamic leaders within the country, should be given the resources necessary to make such a campaign successful and pervasive. As the Terrorism Monitor suggests, "for every leaflet and exhortation from the insurgents justifying opium, the Afghan government should be there to highlight the Taliban's hypocrisy and advertise the damage done to other Muslims." Demonizing opium cultivation will serve both counternarcotics and counterterrorist ends: farmers will be even less inclined to grow than they are currently and the Taliban's overall legitimacy and support base will be diminished.

Less Eradication, More Securitization and Education. Eradication has so far proved to be resource intensive, yet ineffective as a deterrent. Further, it has served as a means by which insurgent groups have been able to increase their legitimacy at the expense of the state and bolster their ranks by absorbing poor and disaffected farmers. Therefore, the emphasis that current counternarcotics strategy places upon eradication should be shifted towards the other four pillars of the U.S. plan. The 2007 UNODC Opium Winter Rapid Assessment Survey suggests that in provinces where security is perceived to be "good" or "very good" there exists significantly less opium cultivation. Given this fact, providing a clear sense of security to the average citizen should be a primary objective within both counternarcotics and counterinsurgency strategy.

Additionally, the UNODC reports that narcotics awareness programs have proved successful in certain cases, but they are limited in effectiveness relative to perceived levels of security. Specifically, "[R]egional results indicate that the awareness campaign has had some impact in the central and northern regions and mixed success in the western region. . . . [I]n the south, the campaign has had little impact: 80 percent of villages cultivated poppy in spite of the campaign." This suggests that farmers, when faced with the existential pressures and economic limitations of insecurity, have had little choice but to plant opium. However, public diplomacy campaigns combined with visible securitization efforts have the potential to significantly deter opium cultivation.

Provide a Viable, Long-Term Plan for Sustainable Development

Providing deterrents for opium cultivation, such as increased police presence and public diplomacy, do little good unless they are implemented in parallel with effective alternative livelihood programs. With respect to such programs there exist no short-term solutions or easy fixes. A number of policy groups including the Senlis Council have proposed the option of legalizing opium cultivation for sale in the licit market. Unfortunately, the lack of a suitable Afghan administrative infrastructure, the wide price disparity between licit and illicit opium, and the ongoing demand for illicit opium would most likely render such schemes impotent to counter the multibillion dollar narco-industry. Accordingly, policy think-tanks need to invest their resources towards the formation of long-term sustainable development campaigns, and world governments need to shift fund allocations towards providing increased financial aid to bolster alternate livelihood policies.

A viable alternative livelihood plan should take a form similar to that proposed by the Center for Technology and National Security Policy at the National Defense University. This report suggested that sustainable development can only be achieved through the simultaneous establishment of the resources and facilities required for the cultivation, processing, storage, and international market exportation of alternative licit crops. This includes improving irrigation and access to water, educating farmers on how to plant licit crops, developing large-scale processing and warehouse facilities, and establishing a network linking farmers and producers to buyers throughout the international market. Furthermore, this should take place parallel to international and public works campaigns designed to improve Afghanistan's infrastructure. A lopsided program risks condemning farmers back to illegal subsistence, which is also why any such program well-funded, well planned, and implemented with the long term in mind.

FRONT ROW SEAT: WATCHING COIN FAIL IN AFGHANISTAN

With President Karzai as unlikely as ever to sign a Bilateral Security Agreement with the United States, an early withdrawal of coalition forces from Afghanistan seems increasingly probable. Although the focus will soon turn to determining how to safely extract coalition forces, the United States also needs to think about how to preserve the strategic gains it has won at so great a cost over the past dozen years. Unfortunately, America's own institutional inertia will probably lead Washington to continue pushing a failed national counterinsurgency strategy on the Afghan military. The United States has taught its Afghan allies—albeit not always successfully—to fight and govern as Americans fight and govern, rather than teaching them to do so in a way consistent with their culture and in line with their own strategic beliefs. The current strategy, which requires a unified national policy directed by a strong, legitimate government, is unrealistic in its expectations and inappropriate against violence that is dispersed and motivated by local concerns. Unless the United States begins pushing the Afghan National Security Forces to adopt policies more suited to their current needs and their military culture, the blood and treasure we have poured into Afghanistan over the past twelve years will have been for nothing.

Current counterinsurgency doctrine presumes a national solution to local problems: that a national army, usually with the aid of local police or militias, can come into a fractious area and convince unfriendly locals to ally themselves with the state by bringing security and certain amenities like electricity or economic programs. This strategy requires a functioning and legitimate government and a skilled and disciplined military that can effectively target insurgents who hide amongst the civilian population without causing collateral damage. It assumes that all enemy strongholds must be retaken and that unless the insurgency is defeated in all its parts, the nation cannot survive.

Rather than allowing the Afghans to find their own solutions to the insurgency, the United States bequeathed its ally a reductionist approach. Thus, "the insurgents" were identified with the "Taliban" and the "Taliban" with those who most closely resemble the Taliban of Mullah Omar's failed state. Although the insurgency is strengthened, fueled and spread partly through religious networks, it is fundamentally a localist and anti-government movement.

Conservative rather than radical and tribal rather than religious, the insurgency is less a religious or political organization and more a classic peasant revolt of isolated, anti-modernist and largely landless individuals. These individuals' only familiarity with the central government comes from being taxed and subjected to its military force. The dispersed and decentralized nature of the insurgency is not, as is sometimes argued, evidence of what is fashionably termed "chaoplexy" or otherwise indicative of an advanced cell-based structure. Rather, the insurgency is dispersed and decentralized because there are too many actors with too many different personal agendas dispersed over too large an area with too few communication tools for it to be a unified or coherent political opponent—and it is precisely this that makes it so durable and so difficult to defeat using our current policies.

The success of these local insurgents, as well as the likely reemergence of competing political, economic and social power structures after coalition forces leave Afghanistan, will make it impossible to implement anything resembling a national policy. The Afghan government will only function in a very basic sense outside of Kabul and some northern cities once American military forces leave and foreign aid dries up. After our departure, Afghan society will realign itself on the basis of tribal, religious, and regional ties or coalesce around strongmen funded by the opium trade or government corruption. Attempts at exercising any sort of centralized authority or national planning along democratic lines will falter in the face of these obstacles.

Thus, regardless of how much time and money we spend on training our allies in the ANSF before we depart, the weakness and incoherence of the Afghan state will doom this approach. Kabul does not have the reach or power to employ regional forces coherently, and local commanders will always resist those efforts. For the most part, neither Afghan soldiers nor their commanders believe the Taliban strongholds in the south are worth fighting for—I've had many tell me they don't consider the people who live in Helmand to be entitled to the benefits of Afghan citizenship. ANSF commanders will not expose their units—their most significant source of power, prestige, and income—to danger unless they believe it will directly benefit them, and fighting the Taliban in Helmand or Kandahar doesn't fit that bill. And although many Afghan soldiers are brave to the point of carelessness, they are not fools and will not risk their lives for policies that are not aligned with their own interests or beliefs. Thus, they are willing to accept high levels of civilian casualties in order to protect themselves.

These reasons all suggest that our application of a broad, national counterinsurgency strategy was flawed and that current ANSF policies based on these assumptions will ultimately lead to failure as we transition to an Afghanistan almost—or completely—absent of coalition forces. And although negotiating with the Taliban is often touted as a "local" solution to Afghanistan's counterinsurgency problems, this is a solution that is really only palatable to Pashtuns. It would most likely serve as a means for Karzai to consolidate his own personal power while sparking an even wider conflict by forcing ethnic minorities threatened by the Taliban to seek other avenues to self-preservation.

A more sensible policy would be to broker limited deals with local insurgents (which already happens informally through bribes or threats) rather than with the Taliban's leadership in Pakistan. Alternatively, the US could simply make official practice that which is already accomplished in the breach and encourage the Afghan government to pull the ANSF away from the areas in the south and east that it has shown itself unable and unwilling to hold. This would shorten the lines of defense, conserve manpower, at least partly negate the influence of the opium trade, and significantly reduce casualties within the ANSF. Although a bitter pill for revanchists, a "Pashtunistan" would serve as an outlet for both Pashtun nationalism and political Islamism, while also providing a buffer zone between Pakistan and Afghanistan. Draining reactionary and radical elements would decrease internal violence in both countries and allow for progress in areas such as women's rights and education. In the long term, it is likely that nationalism, historical distrust of foreigners and immediate, earthly needs will prove stronger than the attractions of millenarian terrorist organizations and the area will be stable, albeit unfriendly and anti-modern. This would also allow the development of a strong Afghan government free of Pashtun tribal interests and able to implement cohesive national policies not dependent on the support of local power brokers—policies that would have a chance of being both local and popular and thus more likely to succeed.

The most likely outcome, though, is that we will follow historical precedent and belatedly begin picking regional strongmen within Afghanistan to support once the government crumbles, but this will be done only in a halting and very delayed fashion that will prevent us from maintaining any presence in the country as it descends once more into chaos. In all cases, we should stop insisting on—and funding—the purchase of industrial or high-tech military equipment by the Afghan government. The

ANSF does not need a military based on the American model, it does not know how to effectively employ most of the assets we provide them, and it certainly cannot sustain the logistics system we burdened them with. Their current problems will only get worse as Congress grows tired of funding a failed experiment and slowly ends its financial support for the Afghan military.

In any event, as the US military withdraws from Afghanistan and begins restructuring its forces for future wars, it is important that we not swallow whole the still-fashionable COIN doctrine. A monolith that might have been appropriate against a centralized guerrilla movement—as embodied in our reification of the "Taliban" as a coherent organization—this doctrine was inappropriate against violence that is dispersed and motivated by local concerns. In continuing to support and advise an Afghan military policy guided by these beliefs, we are trying to prove a theory which remains stronger than any observed fact and flies in the face of historical and practical experience to the contrary.

Once we leave, the Afghans will find their own local solutions to the problems that a national counterinsurgency policy cannot answer, but in doing so will doubtless leave minorities and females disenfranchised and oppressed and the country once more exposed to the dangers of radicalism. There may be some cold comfort for those of us who have advised the Afghan military in knowing that our failure comes at the hands of historical forces which extended far beyond our reach and which we could not have hoped to overcome given the tools provided us, but it does leave us the duty to improve those tools for future generations. Or, to paraphrase Gracchus Babeuf, "this is not the real COIN doctrine. COIN is something we have not yet tried."

THE FAILURE OF COUNTERINSURGENCY: AFGHANISTAN

The current power-sharing government among factions in Afghanistan will likely be as successful as the one in Iraq during the Nouri al-Maliki period: not very. A viable democracy is only possible if fair elections produce an acknowledged winner and a losing loyal opposition exists — at least one loyal enough not to fatally undermine the group or groups in power. The political culture of Afghanistan has none of those prerequisites. The last Afghan election was clearly corrupt and therefore perceived as illegitimate, thus rendering it unlikely that any opposition would be loyal. Because of that failed outcome, the United States then arranged that the two electoral antagonists — Ashraf Ghani, representing the Pashuns, and Abdullah Abdullah, representing other ethnic groups — would share power, with Ghani becoming president and Abdullah becoming chief executive.

Yet, democratic elections are supposed to have a winner and a loser, and the winner is supposed promulgate policies and endure their critique by the loyal opposition. But as in Iraq during the Maliki period, the various factions trying to govern together in the power sharing agreement cannot agree on a new cabinet, even despite the unforgiving reality that the wheels are coming off the country's security bus. It is yet another case of politicians fiddling g while Rome burns in a faux democracy that has no genuine culture of political compromise.

A rash of Taliban suicide bombings has rattled the confidence of the Afghan capital, Kabul, while stepped up Taliban attacks in the countryside have lasted longer in the fall than usual and have disadvantaged Afghan army and police forces. Because of this emboldened rebel activity, the United States will continue to provide Afghan security forces with support from air power even after its ground combat mission allegedly ends at the end of this month. Thus, the United States, after already spending tens of billions of dollars fighting with and training the Afghan security forces, as well as spending oodles on what will become wasted development efforts, will continue to pour money down a rat hole in a lost cause.

In my book, *The Failure of Counterinsurgency: Why Hearts and Minds Are Seldom Won,* I explore why such counterinsurgency wars are so hard for great powers to win. And it's not like no prior track record in Afghanistan existed to warn the U.S. government of the perils of such armed social work. No foreign power has subdued Afghanistan since before Christ, including three failed attempts by the British in the 19th and early 20th centuries and one more recent debacle by the Soviets in the 1980s.

Historically, sustained democracy has to bubble up from below, with the proper culture of political compromise existing before institutions can govern in a democratic way, not the other way around. Furthermore, democracy has even less of a chance of lasting if a foreign power imposes it by force, especially in countries that have never before had much of a democratic tradition. Also, a distinction exists between mere majority rule — which can result in a tyranny of the majority, as has happened in Iraq — and a liberal democracy in which all-important minority rights and the rule of law are guaranteed. Often, for a genuine liberal democracy to sustain itself and flourish over the long-term, a certain societal income level has to be achieved, which fosters the rise of a politically powerful middle class that challenges the entrenched elite. In neither Iraq nor Afghanistan has this level been reached. In Iraq, prosperity was sapped by years of war and international economic sanctions; Afghanistan remains a very poor country.

Thus, keeping about 10,000 U.S. ground troops in Afghanistan, plus the use of U.S. air power, merely makes it more likely that the United States will be drawn back into the conflict to save the non-viable power sharing government from the again rising Taliban. The United States has become enmeshed again in Iraq even without leaving sizeable numbers of troops there after the withdrawal date. Brushfire conflicts in such artificial countries with deep societal cleavages will likely continue to rage, whether or not the United States is entangled in them.

If the Taliban didn't learn their lesson by being thrown out of power because of their reluctant sheltering of anti-American terrorists and continue to do so in any future territory they rule, the United States should limit its involvement to occasionally bombing terrorist training camps and infrastructure from the air. Therefore, the United States should withdrawal all remaining ground forces and terminate combat air support for Afghan security forces to avoid getting sucked back into this pointless and endless quagmire that was lost long ago.

A FAR CRY FROM FAILURE IN AFGHANISTAN

Stephen Biddle and Karl Eikenberry are outstanding public servants and scholars, but their respective articles on Afghanistan

("Ending the War in Afghanistan" and "The Limits of Counter-insurgency Doctrine in Afghanistan," September/October 2013) convey excessively negative assessments of how the war is going and of Afghanistan's prospects. Their arguments could reinforce the current American malaise about the ongoing effort and thereby reduce the odds that the United States will continue to play a role in Afghanistan after the current NATO-led security mission there ends in December 2014. That would be regrettable; the United States should lock in and solidify its gains in Afghanistan, not cut its losses.

Biddle argues that the U.S. Congress and other donors are unlikely to keep funding the Afghan government after 2014. Based on this conclusion, he states that the only other viable options for Washington are to broker a power-sharing deal between the Afghan government and the Taliban or to end its mission immediately.

This argument hinges on Biddle's assessment of U.S. politics more than any military or strategic analysis. His reference to U.S. policy in Vietnam in 1973–75 is overdone. A more relevant historical precedent for Afghanistan is the fact that Washington has maintained long-standing security and economic commitments to partners such as Egypt, Greece, Israel, South Korea, Taiwan, and Turkey. These cases belie the contention that the United States has too short an attention span to sustain aid to important allies over a protracted period. Future U.S. commitments to Afghanistan would probably incur only ten percent of the cost and casualties of the war to date. If the mission succeeds, moreover, Congress is likely to continue to provide funding. It is a curious and circular argument to say that because the mission might fail in the future — due to Washington's undependable staying power — the United States should throw in the towel and concede defeat now.

Eikenberry makes some reasonable points about the excessive hopes placed in comprehensive counterinsurgency doctrine over the past decade or so, including in Afghanistan. Many of his specific critiques ring true. But Eikenberry underrates how far Afghanistan has come — in part due to his own efforts as U.S. military commander in Afghanistan and then U.S. ambassador to Kabul. The Afghan security forces have many good leaders and dedicated troops; they now lead 99 percent of all combat operations and sustain 200 or more fatalities a month without cracking. That represents a partial success of the counterinsurgency policy that Eikenberry criticizes. So does the community of Afghan reformers that Eikenberry and others personally helped nurture in recent years. It is true that counterinsurgency strategy may have fallen short of its proponents' aspirations and may require an overhaul before being applied to future conflicts. But that fact does not make the overall concept or its application in Afghanistan a failure.

Even if political reforms and counterinsurgency have not achieved the loftier goals that U.S. policymakers once imagined for Afghanistan, the United States can still achieve its core strategic goals there by building up a state that is at least resilient enough to fend off the Taliban in most population and economic centers. The situation in Afghanistan today is a far cry from failure, and the case for pulling up stakes and coming home now is strategically unpersuasive.

Bibliography

Ahmad, Ilyas : *Sovereignty, Islamic and Modern,* Allies Book Corporation, Karachi, 1965.

Alastair Lamb, Kashmir: *A Disputed Legacy 1846–1990,* Hertingfordbury, Herts: Roxford Books, 1991.

Alperovitz, Gar. *The Decision to Use the Atomic Bomb.* New York: Vintage Books, 1996.

Anderson, J.: *Transnational Democracy: Political Spaces and Border Crossings,* Routledge: London and New York, 2002.

Anil, K.C.: *Military and Democracy in South Asia : Challenges, Politics and Power,* Sumit Enterprises, Delhi, 2009.

Ayesha Siddiqa-Agha: *Military Inc.: Inside Pakistan's Military Economy,* London: Pluto, 2007.

Aziz, Mazhar: *Military Control: The Parallel State,* London: Routledge, 2008.

Bahedur, Kalim : *The Jamaat-i-Islami of Pakistan,* Progressive Books, Lahore, 1978.

Benjamin, Joseph : *China-Pak Relations : Prospect and Retrospect,* Reference Press, Delhi, 2004.

Brian Cloughley: *War, Coups, and Terror: Pakistan's Army in Years of Turmoil,* New York: Skyhorse, 2008.

Choudhury, Golam W: *Pakistan: Transition from Military to Civilian Rule,* Scorpion, 1988.

Cohen, Stephen P., *The Pakistan Army,* University of California Press, 1989.

Donnan, H. and Wilson, T. M.: *Borders: Frontiers of Identity, Nation and State,* Oxford: Berg, 1999.

Duscha, Julius. *Arms, Money and Politics.* New York, 1965.

Evelyn Goh, *Meeting the Afghanistan Challenge: The U.S. in Southeast Asian Regional Security Strategies*, DC: East-West Center, 2005.

Fletcher, Arnold: *Afghanistan, Highway of Conquest*, Ithaca, New York, Cornell University, 1965.

Hoffman, Bruce, *Inside Terrorism in Afghanistan*, New York: Columbia University Press, 1998.

Janowitz, M.: *The Professional Soldier: A Social and Political Portrait*, N.Y., The Free Press, 1960.

Juvale, R.P. : *Military Strategy and Diplomacy*, Cyber Tech Publications, Delhi, 2010.

Keane J.: *Democracy and Civil Liberty in Afghanistan*, London, Verso, 1988.

Kunju, N. : *Indo-Pak : Nuclear Cold War*, Reliance, Delhi, 2002.

Nayyar, K K : *National Security : Military Aspects*, Rupa, Delhi, 2003.

Norris, James A.: *The First Afghan War 1838-1842*, Cambridge, University Press, 1967.

Posen, B.R.: *The Sources of Indian Military Doctrine*, Ithaca, 1984, Cornell Univ. Press.

Rosen, P.: *Societies and Military Power: India and its Armies*, Ithaca, Cornell University Press, 1996.

Saxena, V. K. : *Muslims and the Indian National Congress*, Discovery Publishing House, New Delhi, 1985.

Shaun Narine, *Explaining ASEAN: Regionalism in Southeast Asia*, Boulder, CO: Lynne Rienner Publishers, 2002.

Worster, Donald : *Dust Bowl: The Southern Plains in the 1930s*, New York, Oxford University Press, 1979.

Index

R

S

W

❑❑❑